Baron Burkard von Müllenheim-Rechberg is a former naval officer, lawyer, and ambassador. Born in Spandau into a family where the profession of arms was an established tradition, he entered the navy of the Weimar Republic in 1929. During his naval career he served as an instructor at the Mürwik Naval School, as an assistant naval attaché at the German Embassy in London, and in cruisers and destroyers. He was assigned to the *Bismarck* in May 1940 and was the senior survivor at the time of her sinking on 27 May 1941.

In 1952 the Baron joined the diplomatic service of the Federal Republic of Germany and served in a variety of posts. At one time, he was Consul General in Toronto. He was also Ambassador to the West Indies, as well as to Zaire and Tanzania. He is still involved in study and research into the political and economic problems of African countries.

The author spent countless hours on research for *Battleship Bismarck* and his valuable recollections have helped film producers and other writers who have dealt with the subject of the Second World War. In 1971 he was interviewed by the BBC for a documentary film on the *Bismarck* that attracted a record British audience of twelve million viewers.

Baron von Müllenheim-Rechberg and his wife make their home near Munich, Bavaria.

Baron Burkard
von Müllenheim-Rechberg

Battleship Bismarck

A Survivor's Story

Translated by Jack Sweetman

**TRIAD
GRANADA**

Published by Triad/Granada in 1982

ISBN 0 583 13560 9

Triad Paperbacks Ltd is an imprint of
Chatto, Bodley Head & Jonathan Cape Ltd and
Granada Publishing Ltd

First published in Great Britain by
The Bodley Head Ltd 1981
Copyright © 1980 by the United States Naval
Institute, Annapolis, Maryland

Printed and bound in Great Britain by
Cox and Wyman Ltd, Reading
Set in Times

To the memory
of my fallen comrades
of the battleship *Bismarck*
and
to those on the British side who lost their lives
during Exercise Rhine

Contents

Preface

It is somewhat unusual to write a personal account of something that happened nearly forty years after the event. However, the idea of writing this book was born while I was still standing on the upper deck of the sinking *Bismarck* on 27 May 1941: since there is no vantage point from which the whole of this giant ship is visible, I thought, will it ever be possible for anyone, even an eyewitness, to assemble the countless details of the battle now ending into a complete and coherent account? If so, who would do it and when? Given the uncertainty of my own fate and against the background of the war, it was an absurd thought and it left my mind as quickly as it had entered it. But it did not die.

I had to resist the temptation to spend the endless time I had on my hands as a prisoner of war in England and Canada in making notes about the ship's operations while they were still fresh in my mind, because, in that status, I had no way of safeguarding secret, or even confidential, papers. The only thing I could do was keep my recollections as intact as possible and rely on written records to fill in at least some of the gaps later.

In May 1949 I received a letter from Dr Kurt Hesse, a writer on military affairs. He wrote to me at the suggestion of Admiral Walter Gladisch, one of our former Fleet Commanders, urging me to publish my unique story. He thereby encouraged me to do what I had first thought about doing eight years earlier. But at that time there were several reasons why I had to push it into the back of my mind again: so much of Germany was still lying in ruins that it did not seem an appropriate time to write on a military subject; not enough time had elapsed for me to be able to write about something that touched me so deeply; I was studying law at Johann Wolfgang Goethe University; I had to finance not only my schooling but my subsistence, no easy task in the immediate postwar years, and at the same time engage in the urgent and time-consuming business of seeking a new profession.

During my years of service overseas as consul general and ambassador of the Federal Republic of Germany, many people, particularly foreigners, told me, 'you *must* write about the *Bismarck* some day.' But not until 1975, when I retired, did I have the time and other prerequisites to deal responsibly with the subject; by that time the British had returned the official records of the German Navy to the Federal German Archives.

Much had already been written, both at home and abroad, on the operations and sinking of the *Bismarck*. Naturally, none of the writers was able to provide the reasoning behind the crucial tactical decisions that the Fleet Commander, Admiral Günther Lütjens, made during the ship's Atlantic sortie. Nor, of course, can I, but in the pages that follow I have tried to put myself in Lütjens's place and frame of mind and I believe that, having been an officer in the ship, I can make a contribution to the history of the *Bismarck* and Exercise Rhine.

This book is dedicated to the memory of all who died as a result of the sinking of the *Bismarck* but especially to the memory of her commanding officer, Kapitän zur See Ernst Lindemann. As captain of a flagship, he served in the shadow of his Fleet Commander, and did not have the opportunity to demonstrate the outstanding leadership of which he was capable.

Burkard von Müllenheim-Rechberg
Herrsching am Ammersee
November 1979

Acknowledgements

I would like to thank Dr Jürgen Rohwer and Vice Admiral B. B. Schofield for permission to use their track charts of Exercise Rhine; Fregattenkapitän Paul Schmalenbach, second gunnery officer in the *Prinz Eugen* during Exercise Rhine, for photographs of the battle off Iceland; Kapitänleutnant Herbert Wohlfarth, captain of the *U-556* in May 1941, for permission to use the certificate proclaiming the *U-556* the guardian of the *Bismarck*; and Herr Rolf Schindler, for preparing the track charts for publication.

I would also like to thank the following people and institutions for their advice and deeds: Captain Robert L. Bridges, USN (Ret.), Castle Creek, New York, USA; Herr Joachim Fensch, Weingarten, Federal Republic of Germany; Mr Daniel Gibson Harris, Ottawa, Canada, who was assistant to the British naval attaché in Stockholm in May 1941; Herr Franz Hahn of the Military Historical Training Centre, Mürwik Naval School, Federal Republic of Germany; Dr Mathias Haupt of the Bundesarchiv, Koblenz, Federal Republic of Germany; Herr Bodo Herzog, Oberhausen, Federal Republic of Germany; Herr Hans H. Hildebrand, Hamburg, Federal Republic of Germany; Konteradmiral Günther Horstmann, German Navy (Ret.), Basel, Switzerland; the Department of Photographs of the Imperial War Museum, London, England; Mr Esmond Knight, London, England, who was a lieutenant in the Royal Naval Volunteer Reserve aboard the *Prince of Wales* in May 1941; Dr Hansjoseph Maierhöfer of the Bundesarchiv-Militärarchiv-Freiburg, Federal Republic of Germany; Mr

Philip Mathias, Toronto, Canada; Mrs Mary Z. Pain, London, England; Fregattenkapitän Dr Werner Rahn, Mürwik, Federal Republic of Germany; Dr Hans Ulrich Sareyko, Aüswärtigen Amt, Bonn, Federal Republic of Germany; Kapitän zur See Hans-Henning von Schultz, German Navy (Ret.), Ramsau, Federal Republic of Germany, who was the intelligence officer aboard the *Prinz Eugen* during Exercise Rhine; Herr Torsten Spiller of the *Deutsche Dienststelle (WASt)*, Berlin, Federal Republic of Germany; and Mr Tom Wharam, Cardiff, Wales.

I want to convey my special thanks to those who have prepared this English-language edition. I am grateful to my translator, Dr Jack Sweetman, who has succeeded admirably in retaining the flavour and spirit of my story; to my technical adviser, Dr Karl Lautenschlager, whose expertise in naval matters, especially those pertaining to the German Navy, earned my great admiration; and to my editor, Mrs Mary Veronica Amoss, Senior Manuscript Editor of the Naval Institute Press, who demonstrated rare skill in making my story appear as if it were written originally in English. Others at the Naval Institute Press to whom I would like to express my gratitude are Mr Thomas F. Epley, Editorial Director, for many invaluable suggestions and for his careful management of my book from start to finish; Miss Beverly S. Baum, Design Manager, for the painstaking care with which she designed the book; Mrs Marjorie B. Whittington, Administrative and Editorial Assistant, for her many typings of the English-language manuscript and her conscientious handling of all matters relating to photographs and drawings; and Miss Rita Connolly, Production Manager, who, in face of great odds, successfully maintained a tight production schedule.

B.v.M-R.

Translator's Note

For assistance in the preparation of this translation, it is a pleasure to record my thanks to: Lieutenant Commander George L. Breeden III, USN, Lieutenant Fred H. Rainbow, USNR, and Lieutenant Commander Paul Stillwell, USNR, whose expert advice was invaluable in dealing with technical matters; the author, Baron Burkard von Müllenheim-Rechberg, who kindly read and commented on the translation of his book; Mary Veronica Amoss, Senior Manuscript Editor of the Naval Institute Press, who eliminated many infelicities of expression; and, last but never least, my wife, Gisela, who helped in countless ways.

J.S.

Table of Equivalent Ranks

Kriegsmarine	United States Navy	Royal Navy
Grossadmiral	—	—
Generaladmiral	Fleet Admiral	Admiral of the Fleet
Admiral	Admiral	Admiral
Vizeadmiral	Vice Admiral	Vice-Admiral
Konteradmiral	Rear Admiral	Rear-Admiral
Kommodore	Commodore	Commodore
Kapitän zur See	Captain	Captain
Fregattenkapitän	Commander	Commander
Korvettenkapitän	Lieutenant Commander	Lieutenant Commander
Kapitänleutnant	Lieutenant	Lieutenant
Oberleutnant zur See	Lieutenant, Junior Grade	—
Leutnant zur See	Ensign	Sub-Lieutenant
Oberfähnrich zur See	—	—
Fähnrich zur See	Midshipman	Midshipman
—	—	Cadet
Stabsoberbootsmann*	Chief Warrant Officer	—
Oberbootsmann*	Warrant Officer (W-3)	Warrant Officer
Stabsbootsmann*	Warrant Officer (W-2)	—
Bootsmann*	Warrant Officer (W-1)	—
—	Master Chief Petty Officer	—
—	Senior Chief Petty Officer	—
Oberbootsmannsmaat*	Chief Petty Officer	Chief Petty Officer
Bootsmannsmaat*	Petty Officer 1st Class	Petty Officer
Matrosenstabsobergefreiter	Petty Officer 2nd Class	—

Matrosenstabsgefreiter	Petty Officer 3rd Class	Leading Seaman
Matrosenhauptgefreiter	Seaman	Able Seaman
Matrosenobergefreiter	—	—
Matrosengefreiter	Seaman Apprentice	Ordinary Seaman
Matrose	Seaman Recruit	—

* *Bootsmann* designates the rating or speciality of petty officers and warrant officers. The suffix *maat* designates a senior petty officer. A title without a suffix designates a warrant officer. Other ratings are substituted as appropriate. For example: Maschinenmaat, Obersignalmaat, Oberartilleriemechaniker, Stabsoberbootsmann.

1

The Bismarck *and Her Captain*

Sea Battle Between the English and French! Churchill Bombards the French Fleet! So read the giant headlines in the daily newspapers on Hamburg kiosks. This sensational display told the German public of the bloody attack by a British naval force on French warships lying in the harbour at Oran, Algeria, at the beginning of July 1940. The attack was part of a determined British attempt to prevent the Germans from seizing the French Navy, a threat raised by the French surrender late in June. Nominally, the fleet was under the control of the Pétain government, but most of it had taken refuge in ports outside of France. On the morning of 3 July, a British naval force, consisting of two battleships, a battle cruiser, an aircraft carrier, two cruisers, and eleven destroyers, appeared off the coast of Algeria. Its commander immediately presented the French admiral with an ultimatum to surrender his ships. When the allotted time had expired and the French had taken no action, the British opened fire. Thirteen hundred French seamen were killed that afternoon, and three French battleships were destroyed or damaged. Only the battleship *Strasbourg* and five destroyers managed to escape to Toulon.

As I read the news accounts of this amazing event, I was reminded of the British seizure of the Danish fleet at Copenhagen in the midst of peace in the year 1807. But this attack, taking place in my day and between two states that had been allies until then, impressed me so deeply that I made note of the Commander of the task force and ships involved: Vice Admiral Sir James Somerville, the battle cruiser *Hood*, and the aircraft carrier *Ark Royal*. Still, I had no inkling of the role that within a year this Admiral and these ships would play in the fate of the battleship *Bismarck*, to which I, a thirty-year-old Kapitän-leutnant,[1] had just been assigned.

In June 1940, when I first saw the *Bismarck*, she was in the Hamburg yard of her builders, Blohm & Voss, awaiting completion and acceptance by the German Navy. Therefore, what I saw was a dusty steel giant, made fast to a wharf and littered with tools, welding equipment, and cables. An army of workmen was hustling to complete the job, while the crew already on board were familiarizing themselves with the ship and conducting whatever training was possible under the circumstances.

But under this disguise, the distinctive features, both traditional and novel, of the future battleship were already apparent. There it was again – that elegant curve of the ship's silhouette fore and aft from the tip of the tower mast – then a characteristic of German warship design that sometimes led the enemy to confuse our ship types at long range. Other things about her were familiar to me because I had served in the battleship *Scharnhorst*, but everything about the *Bismarck* was bigger and more powerful: her dimensions, especially her enormous beam, her high superstructure, her 38 centimetre main-battery guns (first of that calibre installed in the Kriegs-marine), the great number of guns she had in her secondary and antiaircraft batteries, and the heavy armour-plating of her hull, gun turrets, and forward command- and fire-control station. She had a double-ended aircraft catapult athwartships, another first for the Kriegsmarine, and, as did the *Scharnhorst* and her sister

[1] Lieutenant

the *Gneisenau*, the new, spherical splinter shields on her antiaircraft stations on both sides of her tower mast.

At first sight of this gigantic ship, so heavily armed and armoured, I felt sure that she would be able to rise to any challenge, and that it would be a long time before she met her match. A long life was very obviously in store for her. Still, I thought, the British fleet had numerical superiority, and the outcome of any action would depend on the combination of forces engaged. But questions like that seemed to lie far in the future, as I began my service in the *Bismarck*. I had supreme confidence in this ship. How could it be otherwise?

When my assignment to the battleship *Bismarck* reached me in May 1940, eleven years of naval service lay behind me. I was born in Spandau in 1910, into a family that originated in Baden but some of whom migrated to the east. The profession of arms was a family tradition. My father was killed in action as a major in command of the 5th Jäger Battalion in the Argonne in April 1916; my only brother, who was younger than I and a captain in the Luftwaffe, was killed on 2 September 1939 while serving as a squadron commander in the Richthofen Wing during the Polish campaign.

In April 1929, I graduated 'with excellence' from a classical high school and entered the Weimar Republic's 15,000-man Reichsmarine. By the time the several thousand applicants had been subjected to rigorous examination, the class of 1929, to which I belonged, numbered about eighty men. A year-long cruise in a light cruiser to Africa, the West Indies, and the United States in 1930 got us accustomed to life aboard ship, and at the same time assuaged our yearning to see the big, wide world, which naturally had played a role in our choice of profession. We then went through the Naval School and took the standard courses on weapons before, towards the end of 1932, we were dispersed among the various ships of the Reichsmarine as Fähnriche zur See.[2]

A year later, together with my classmates, I became a Leutnant sur See[3] and then served as a junior officer in a deck division and as range-finder officer in the light cruisers *Königsberg* and *Karlsruhe*. Following my promotion to Oberleutnant zur See[4] in 1935, I spent a year as a group officer at the Mürwik Naval School, training midshipmen. Early in 1936, I took a course at the Naval Gunnery School in Kiel in fire control, which began my specialization in naval ordnance. There followed two years in our then-very-modern destroyers, first as adjutant to the commander of the 1st Destroyer Division, then as a division and gunnery officer. At the end of these tours, I was promoted to Kapitänleutnant.

In the autumn of 1938 the Oberkommando der Kriegsmarine[5] first sent assistants to the naval attachés in the most important countries. There were very few of these posts and when I was offered one of them, and moreover the important one in London, not only did I feel honoured but I felt that an inner longing was being satisfied. I accepted it and took up my post with great pleasure.

The outbreak of the Second World War brought this assignment to an abrupt end and, in October 1939, I began two months' service as fourth gunnery officer of the battleship *Scharnhorst*. The following month, I took part in the sweep into the Faeroes-Shetland passage, which was led by the Fleet Commander, Admiral Wilhelm Marschall, in his flagship *Gneisenau*, and which culminated in the sinking of the British auxiliary cruiser *Rawalpindi*. Afterwards, the *Scharnhorst* had to go into the yard

[2] Midshipmen
[3] Ensign
[4] Lieutenant, Junior Grade
[5] Naval High Command

for an extensive overhaul and I was appointed first officer of the destroyer *Erich Giese*. As such, I participated in mine-laying operations off the east coast of Britain in the winter of 1939–40 and in the occupation of Narvik during the Norwegian campaign of April 1940. All ten of the German destroyers engaged in this operation were lost, half of Germany's destroyer force. I had to be given a new assignment and, because of my weapons training, I was appointed fourth gunnery officer, my action station being the after fire-control station, in the *Bismarck*, which was soon to be commissioned. I looked forward with keen anticipation to serving in this wonderful, new ship.

Before going to my new duty, however, I took a short leave. In the quiet of an Upper Bavarian health resort, where visitors were few in wartime, my thoughts continually wandered back, whether I wanted them to or not, to the moving months I had spent in London, only a year earlier. What changes had taken place in Anglo-German relations since then, so completely at variance with my hopes and wishes! Very early in life, actually during my school days, I acquired a special interest in Great Britain, her people, language, history, and political system. My own family history influenced me in this direction. In the eighteenth century, Sir George Browne, son of John, Count of Altamont, of the house of Neale O'Connor, an Anglo-Norman family that settled in Ireland and later spread to England, entered French service. Subsequently, he transferred to the Prussian Army, in which he fought in the Seven Years' War. Made a privy councillor after the war, he became a chamberlain and treasurer in Lower Silesia. His daughter, Franziska, married one of my direct forebears. Visits to Britain over the years had deepened my interest in that country. In 1936 I accepted an invitation to the home of English friends in Colchester, and now I could not forget the long discussions we held over the burning necessity to preserve peace between our two peoples.

Unfortunately, the time I had spent as assistant naval attaché in London, personally very enjoyable, was tragically overshadowed from the outset by the continued deterioration of Anglo-German relations. A relentless succession of international events was responsible. I remembered it with a heavy heart.

By the time I arrived in London in November 1938, the British public had all but given up hope that the ceding of the German-populated Sudetenland to the Reich, which had been forced upon the Czech government with British and French consent at Munich the previous September, would produce the hoped-for relaxation of international tensions. An aggressive speech by Hitler at Saarbrücken barely two weeks after the conference in Munich had contributed to Britain's anxiety: disillusionment grew and it became ever clearer that a policy of appeasement would be disastrous for Europe.

The attack launched by German state authorities on 9 November against Jewish life and property within the territory of the Reich came as another shock and created a worldwide sensation. The evening before my departure from Berlin for London, I myself had witnessed the sudden appearance on the Kurfürstendamm of organized squads armed with tyre rods and crowbars, the destruction and plundering of Jewish stores, flames enveloping the synagogue on the Fasanenstrasse. An invisible speaker constantly admonished the subdued crowd that witnessed this spectacle, in silence or whispering under its breath, 'Go on!', 'Don't stand around!', 'No picture-taking!' In the ugly face of this naked force and brutal suppression, I had recognized the unmistakable harbinger of still worse things to come.

Early on the morning of 11 November, I reached London in a spotlessly clean British railway car. The lead article in *The Times*, 'A Black Day for Germany', unreservedly condemned the violence. It voiced my opinion exactly; I could have signed every sentence. It was terribly depressing to be starting out on my first mission abroad under these circumstances, and I was grateful to my British friends for being so tactful as not to mention to me the events in the Reich that must have shamed all decent German patriots.

Germany took another politically significant step in December 1938, this time concerning the German naval construction programme, which then conformed to the terms of the Anglo-German Naval Treaty of June 1935. In this agreement, Germany pledged not to increase the strength of its fleet to more than 35 per cent of the strength of the British fleet. This percentage applied not only to the total strength of the fleet, but to individual ship categories, as well. Although the treaty granted Germany the right to parity in submarine strength, the Reich professed its willingness not to go beyond 45 per cent of British submarine strength. Should it ever appear necessary to exceed these limitations, the matter was to be discussed. At the time it was signed, the treaty was accepted with satisfaction in Germany, because it overturned the limitations set by the Treaty of Versailles and made possible the building of a bigger and a balanced fleet.

Now, in December 1938, the Reich called the attention of the British government to the clause in the treaty that allowed Germany to exceed the 45 per cent limit on its submarine strength if 'a situation arose' which, in the opinion of Germany, made it necessary to do so. Such a situation, Berlin informed London, now existed. The government of the Reich, therefore, intended to build up its submarine tonnage to parity with the British. Simultaneously, it announced its intention to arm two cruisers under construction more heavily than had been originally provided.

Technically, the German claims were perfectly in order. But were they being made at a politically propitious moment? The British, aware of the capacity of Germany's shipyards, were bound to know that the Reich would not have its increased submarine tonnage available for several years. And political opinion in Great Britain, already disturbed by the Munich agreement, was such that the presentation of Germany's claims at this moment could only work to the political disadvantage of the Reich: this view was frequently expressed in conversations in London at the time and widely voiced by the British press. Therefore, why not patiently await the tactically correct moment? It was actions such as this that made it possible to read aggressive intent into everything Germany did, even when it was not there.

The next crisis came in the spring of 1939, and it was a serious one. In mid-March, Hitler forced the Czech government to conclude a treaty making the province of Bohemia and Moravia a German protectorate. In violation of the Munich Agreement, he then occupied that area and incorporated it into the Reich. Czechoslovakia, as such, disappeared from the map. This action shook Europe like an earthquake. The British government and public were the hardest hit; the policy of appeasement towards Germany appeared to be shattered once and for all. Thereafter, many circles of British society avoided all contact with official representatives of the Reich. The German embassy tried desperately to find a way of interpreting the event to its host country. I realized that a political turning point had been reached.

At the end of March, I attended a social gathering in

HMS *Calliope*. This venerable sailing ship was used for training the Tyne Division of the Royal Naval Volunteer Reserve. Her home port was Newcastle. The affair was to commemorate the fiftieth anniversary of the Samoan hurricane of 1889, which the *Calliope* had been fortunate enough to survive. Because some German and American fighting ships were also caught in the storm, the naval attachés of both countries were invited to the ceremony. The American attaché was represented by his assistant, Lieutenant Robert Lord Campbell, with whom I travelled to Newcastle. On the way, I wondered what effect events in Czechoslovakia would have on the gathering in HMS *Calliope*. I need not have worried. I had a pleasant evening of good comradeship, only slightly dampened by Germany's treatment of its new protectorate. In his welcoming address, the British host spoke of 'troublesome times' but did not go into particulars, and the evening's planners saw to it that no one else spoke. 'It's a shame,' Campbell said to me afterwards, 'I had thought of a few things to say and would have been more than happy to do so.' I could not exactly share his regret.

Only a month after the events in Prague, more alarming diplomatic signals came from Berlin. In his speech to the Reichstag on 28 April Hitler gave notice that he was cancelling two treaties: the German-Polish Nonaggression Pact of 1934 and the Anglo-German Naval Treaty of 1935. In Great Britain, the cancellation of the naval treaty was seen as the prelude to an unrestrained expansion of the German fleet; while that of the pact with Poland appeared to augur another dangerous political adventure. Hitler had switched the course of European affairs onto another track. Whether the tremendous international risks he was taking would lead to the preservation of peace or to war was a question on which observers in London became increasingly contradictory.

During the days when I was trying to find the answer to this question, I often thought of an unforgettable meeting I had in London not long before. In the British Admiralty, the Director of Naval Intelligence, Rear-Admiral Troup, a rather taciturn Scot, was responsible for liaison with the accredited naval attachés. His assistant in this duty was the cosmopolitan, suave Commander Casper S. B. Swinley, who handled the day-to-day business of liaison. At a routine official gathering soon after my arrival in London, Troup said to me, 'Baron, one day soon you and I will dress in our cutaways, put on our top hats, climb into a taxi and visit Lady Jellicoe.' I replied, 'Admiral, it would be a great honour.' At that time no German naval officer had to be told who Lady Jellicoe was. But that was long ago, so I should explain that she was the widow of Admiral of the Fleet Lord Jellicoe, who died in 1935. Lord Jellicoe commanded the British Grand Fleet at the Battle of Jutland in May 1916 and was later First Sea Lord. He enjoyed great esteem in German naval circles as well as in his own country.

Troup's first invitation to visit Lady Jellicoe was, however, not followed up, and I almost forgot about it. Then, at another meeting, Troup again said, 'Baron, soon you and I will dress in our cutaways, put on our top hats and go in a taxi to visit Lady Jellicoe.' I said, 'Admiral, I would be delighted.' But once again it seemed that nothing was going to happen. Then one day Troup called me up: 'Be at my house in the designated dress tomorrow afternoon. We'll drive to Lady Jellicoe from here.' And so we did.

Lady Jellicoe received us in her tastefully furnished London flat. The drawing room was decorated with many souvenirs of her husband's long and distinguished naval career, notably a silver model of his flagship *Iron Duke*.

'I am delighted that Admiral Troup was so kind as to

bring you to me,' Lady Jellicoe told me, 'and I bid you a cordial welcome.' Then we discussed the two navies, the events of the world war at sea, the promising start towards an Anglo-German understanding around the turn of the century, its breakdown, and the subsequent, unhappy course of events. We parted with the mutual hope that peace between our two countries would be preserved – and that was more than an empty wish. I thought about this visit for a long time afterwards. Why had Lady Jellicoe wanted to see me? Ever since the end of the world war, her husband had been convinced that a political settlement with Germany would be in Britain's best interest. He had worked for it with all his strength to the last, and this was the spirit in which Lady Jellicoe talked to me.

On a daily basis, most of my duties as assistant to the German naval attaché were performed in the office. My dealings with the Royal Navy were limited to liaison with the Admiralty; I did not visit any British ships. I evaluated the daily and monthly press, professional periodicals, and literature on naval topics, and I cultivated my contacts with the assistant naval attachés of other countries. I assisted my chief in his reporting activities, one of which was to observe the effects of Franco's declaration of a blockade of the Republican coastal areas during the Spanish Civil War. Implementation of the 1935 naval treaty was naturally a very important facet of Anglo-German relations. Although the main business connected with that was not conducted in the office of the German naval attaché in London, correspondence on the subject came to our attention. In it, the two governments informed one another of the most important data regarding the warships they had under construction and had completed. This is how we learned the names of new British ships; for example, the battleships *King George V* and

Prince of Wales and the aircraft carriers *Ark Royal* and *Victorious*. A report from our consulate in Glasgow in the summer of 1939 stated that the twenty-two shipyards on the Clyde would be working to capacity on new naval construction into the winter, and some of them for more than two years. When the *Prince of Wales* was launched at Birkenhead on 3 May 1939, the London agency of the German News Bureau reported: 'This morning in Birkenhead the battleship *Prince of Wales* left the stocks, christened by the sister of the king. She is one of the fastest and most powerful ships in the British fleet. She has a displacement of 35,000 tons and is armed with ten 14-inch guns in three turrets, sixteen 5.25-inch guns in eight turrets, and numerous smaller guns. Her speed is said to be greater than that of the battleship *Nelson*, which makes 23 knots. The *Prince of Wales* is the second ship of its class to leave the stocks. The first was the *King George V*, which left the stocks in the presence of the king in February. Three more ships of the same class will follow.'

That is where my reminiscences ended. Now, these 'ships on paper' were about to take on tangible form, and my ship, the *Bismarck*, would certainly meet one or another of them at sea. But the veil of the future still lay over the when and the where.

My leave flew past, and at the beginning of June I arrived in Hamburg in typical 'Hamburg weather' – rain. I registered at a hotel and awaited the morrow, when I was to report for duty to the commanding officer of the *Bismarck*, Kapitän zur See[6] Ernst Lindemann. Lindemann's reputation as a naval officer was distinguished; he was known as an outstanding gunnery expert, but also as a strict superior, and so it was with some nervousness that I anticipated my first encounter with him.

[6] Captain

Ernst Lindemann was born in Altenkirchen/Wester-wald in 1894 and entered the Imperial German Navy on 1 April 1913. Because he was not very strong physically, he was accepted only 'on probation'. With the tenacity and energy that already characterized him, however, he weathered the hardships of a year of cadet training under a particularly strict officer in the heavy cruiser *Hertha* as well as did any of his comrades. Later, one of his classmates who served side by side with him as a naval cadet, wrote me: 'His zeal and his concept of duty were exemplary; I cannot recall that he ever fell into disfavour or aroused the anger of our cadet officer.' When one thinks what trifling misdemeanours could expose the cadets of that period to censure, it becomes obvious that Lindemann had unusual concentration and strength of will. 'Yet he was definitely not a careerist in the negative sense; he was an unselfish, helpful, and popular human being,' wrote the same classmate, who also praised his strict and uncompromising concept of the personal and professional obligations of a naval officer. Nevertheless, he was not lacking in ambition. When in later years, Linde-mann, who had in the meanwhile become an acknow-ledged gunnery expert, was told by his classmate that he, Lindemann, would certainly become Inspector of Naval Gunnery some day, he replied: 'I still hope at least to become commander of the first battleship squadron in the Kriegsmarine.' But there was not such a squadron again in his lifetime.

Lindemann went to the Mürwik Naval School in April 1914. Owing to the outbreak of the world war, this assignment had to be broken off and the examination usually given at the end of training was not held. Like his classmates, he was given sea duty and in 1915 was promoted to Leutnant zur See. In the rank list for 1918 he stood fifth among his approximately 210 classmates, and later in the Reichsmarine and Kriegsmarine he ranked second in his class.

Most of Lindemann's service was in large combatants, on staffs, and at the Naval Gunnery School in Kiel. Early in his career, he made gunnery his speciality and he studied every aspect of it. In 1920, as an Oberleutnant zur See, he was posted to the fleet section of the Naval Staff in Berlin, and thereafter to the predreadnought *Hannover*. By 1925, he had been promoted to Kapitänleutnant and was on the admiral's staff at the Baltic Sea Naval Station in Kiel. When that tour ended, he went as second gunnery officer in the predreadnoughts *Elsass* and, later, *Schleswig-Holstein*. 'Lindemann always performed his duties with the same industry and the same conscientiousness,' said the classmate quoted above, 'for example, as second gunnery officer of the *Elsass* he took paperwork home with him, even though that billet in a predreadnought was generally considered a relatively soft job.' After a tour as an instructor at the Naval Gunnery School in Kiel and after being promoted to Korvettenkapitän[7] in 1932, Lindemann became first gunnery officer in the pocket battleship *Admiral Scheer*. It was at about this time, when more than twenty years of very successful service lay behind him, that he once told some friends that, actually, he was still 'on probation', because he had never been advised of his final acceptance into the navy! In 1936, he was assigned as a Fregattenkapitän[8] to the operations section of the Naval Staff, and, in 1938, as Kapitän zur See, he became Chief of the Naval Training Section in the Naval High Command. This post was followed by one that was a high point in his long and successful career as a gunner, command of the Naval Gunnery School. Without doubt, given his specialization in ordnance and his other professional and

[7] Lieutenant Commander
[8] Commander

personal qualities, he was destined to have command of the newest, biggest, and most heavily armed German battleship: the *Bismarck*. The appointment reached him in the spring of 1940.

The morning after my arrival in Hamburg Lindemann awaited me in the captain's cabin aboard ship. I appeared, as was usual in such cases, in 'small service dress', that is, a blue jacket with rank stripes around the cuff, and blue trousers. Lindemann, of medium height and build, with sharply chiselled features, stood, similarly dressed, before his desk and looked at me intently with his blue eyes as I announced, 'Kapitänleutnant von Müllenheim reporting aboard for duty, as ordered.'

'I thank you for your report and bid you welcome aboard,' he replied with a friendly smile and gave me his hand. 'My objective,' he continued, 'is to make this beautiful, powerful ship ready for action as rapidly as possible, and I expect your full cooperation. Because of your training in the fire control of heavy guns, your action station will be the after fire-control station, as you already know. But that won't be enough to keep you busy before the ship is commissioned and for a while after that, so I've decided to make you my personal adjutant; you've been an adjutant before and also had an interesting tour in London.' I was surprised – and very pleased – to hear that I was to be adjutant. He went on to explain what he expected of me. 'This duty won't occupy more than your mornings, and in the afternoons you'll be at the disposal of the first gunnery officer, who'll tell you just what he wants you to do. This will be your schedule until the maintenance of the combat readiness of the ship requires you to work all day in gunnery. As adjutant, your main job will be to prepare records and reports, supervise correspondence, and carry out whatever orders I might issue.' After a short pause, Lindemann added: 'One more thing. In the future, I would prefer to hear people on board use the masculine form when speaking of the *Bismarck*. So powerful a ship as this could only be a *he*, not a *she*.' I resolved to accede to his wish and, although I have had a few slips of the tongue, have done so ever since.[9]

Then Lindemann gave me his hand again, wished me well in my new assignment, and the interview was at an end. As I closed the door of the cabin behind me, I was certain I had just met a very impressive personality, a man who would carry out his new assignment intelligently and conscientiously. Lindemann's manner was in all respects professional.

Being an adjutant was good duty under any circumstances, but in this particular case it would also lead me into a close working relationship with an obviously ideal commanding officer.

[9] Out of respect for the one and only commanding officer of the *Bismarck*, this rule has also been followed in the German edition of this book.

2

The Bismarck *Joins the Kriegsmarine*

24 August 1940: commissioning day for the *Bismarck*! Beneath a cloudy sky, a strong, chilly wind from the east bank of the Elbe was raising whitecaps in the river and sweeping over the stern of the ship, whose port side was still made fast to a wharf of the Blohm & Voss building yard. The sun was not shining but, at least, I thought to myself, with the wind coming from that quarter, the ceremony would not be spoiled by rain, and that was something to be thankful for. The crew, in pea jackets and service caps, was lined up three or four deep on either side of the upper deck, from the quarterdeck to the forecastle, the officers and senior petty officers wearing their ceremonial daggers, and the officers their silver-brocade belts, as well. The division officers drew up their men along the joints in the deck's planks and reported to the First Officer, Fregattenkapitän Hans Oels, that their divisions had been formed. The ship's staff officers stood in a body slightly aft of the starboard gangway, opposite which was the honour guard, with a drummer and a bugler. The fleet band was ready on the quarterdeck. Farther forward, under the barrels of the aftermost 38-centimetre turret, representatives of Blohm & Voss added a civilian touch to this otherwise thoroughly military scene.

'Attention! Face to starboard,' barked Oels as a sleek white motorboat bearing the battle ensign and the commission pennant came into view, and the bugler sounded the appropriate signal. All eyes were fixed on the boat, which slowed down and came alongside the gangway. The

honour guard presented arms and the commanding officer
was piped aboard by the bosun. 'Crew formed for commissioning ceremony,' reported Oels. Followed by Oels
and myself as adjutant, Lindemann reviewed the crew,
then mounted a podium on the quarterdeck to deliver an
address. The men, now standing in ranks eleven or twelve
deep, faced their commanding officer and the flagstaff at
the stern. Two signalmen held the halyards taut, ready to
raise the battle ensign.

'Seamen of the *Bismarck*!'[1] Lindemann began, 'Commissioning day for our splendid ship has come at last.' He
called on the crew, on each individual to do his best to
make her a truly effective instrument of war in the
shortest possible time, and thanked Blohm & Voss for
having worked so hard that she had been completed ahead
of schedule. He spoke of the significance of the hour at
hand, which demanded a military solution to the fateful
questions facing the nation, and quoted from one of
Prince Otto von Bismarck's speeches to the Reichstag,
'Policy is not made with speeches, shooting festivals, or
songs, it is made only by blood and iron.' After expressing
certainty that the ship would fulfil any mission assigned to
her, he gave the command, 'Hoist flag and pennant!' The
honour guard again presented arms and, to the strains of
the national anthem, the ensign was hoisted on the
flagstaff at the stern and the pennant on the mainmast.
Both waved smartly in the wind. The battleship *Bismarck*
had joined the Kriegsmarine.

Laid down on 1 July 1936 and launched on 14 February
1939, the *Bismarck* had a net displacement of 45,950
metric tons and a full-load displacement of 50,955.7

---

[1] Lindemann actually said, 'Soldiers of the *Bismarck*.' The Germans
refer to their naval seamen as 'soldiers,' but use 'seamen' when referring
to men in their merchant marine.

metric tons.[2] Her overall length was 251 metres, her beam 36 metres, and her designed draft was 9.33 metres or, at maximum displacement, 10.20 metres.

Of special interest is the fact that, in comparison with most large warships of the period, her beam was relatively wide in proportion to her length. This characteristic ran counter to the prevalent desire for ever more speed, which called for the least beam possible in relation to length. However, the *Bismarck*'s wide beam seemed to work to her overall advantage, because it lessened any tendency to roll in a seaway and, thus, increased her value as a gun platform. It also reduced her draft, which could be important in the shallow waters of the North Sea. Furthermore, it allowed a more efficient use of space, better placement of armour, a greater distance between the armoured outer shell and the longitudinal torpedo bulkheads, which protected the ship against underwater explosions, and simplified the arrangement of the twin turrets of the secondary battery and of the heavy antiaircraft guns.

More than 90 per cent of the *Bismarck*'s steel hull was welded. As added protection against an underwater hit, her double bottom extended over approximately 80 per cent of her length. Her upper deck ran from bow to stern, and beneath it were the battery deck, the armoured deck, and the upper and middle platform decks. A lower platform deck ran parallel with the stowage spaces, which formed the overhead of the double bottom, almost throughout. Longitudinally, the ship divided into twenty-two compartments, numbered in sequence from the stern forward.

---

[2] According to calculations contained in a report of the US Naval Technical Mission in Europe, whose records include the construction specifications of both the *Bismarck* and the *Tirpitz*, when the *Bismarck* was completed, her full-load displacement was 53,546 metric tons.

Armour comprised the highest percentage of the ship's total weight, some 40 per cent, and qualitatively as well as quantitatively it was mounted in proportion to the importance of the position to be protected. The upper deck was reinforced by armour that ran almost its entire length. This armour was only 50 millimetres thick but it provided protection against splinters and would slow down an incoming projectile so that it would explode before striking the armoured deck below, which protected the ship's vital spaces. The armour on this deck was from 80 to 120 millimetres thick and ran longitudinally between two armoured transverse bulkheads, 170 metres apart. At the stern, the armour thickened into an inclined plane to protect the steering gear. Between the transverse bulkheads, the ship's outer shell was covered by an armoured belt, whose thickness varied up to 320 millimetres and which protected such important installations as the turbines, boilers, and magazines. Higher up, the armour was between 120 and 145 millimetres thick and it formed a sort of citadel to protect the decks above the armoured deck. The two-storey forward conning tower, the elevated after section of which served as the forward fire-control station, was also armoured in varying thicknesses.

Since as a weapon system the *Bismarck* was almost exclusively a gun platform, protection of her guns was of the utmost importance. Her main turrets were protected by armour that ranged in thickness from 150 to 360 millimetres. Her secondary armament was less heavily protected; indeed, the relatively light armour in those areas left something to be desired as protection against heavy projectiles.

The arrangement of the superstructure was very similar to that of the *Prinz Eugen* and other German heavy cruisers. There were four decks forward and three aft. The tower mast was on the forward bridge, and atop it were the main fire-control stations for both the antiaircraft guns and the surface batteries.

The propulsion plant, which comprised 9 per cent of the total weight of the ship, consisted of three sets of turbines for which twelve high-pressure boilers supplied steam. The plant was designed to provide a top speed of 29 knots at a total horsepower for the three shafts of 138,000, but subsequent modification increased these maximums to more than 30 knots and 150,000 horsepower. By the time she had been completed, the *Bismarck* was one of the fastest battleships built up to that time.

Her maximum fuel-oil capacity was 8,700 tons, which gave her an operating range of 8,900 nautical miles at a speed of 17 knots, and 9,280 nautical miles at 16 knots. This was a remarkable range for a turbine ship of that day, and it shows that, from the outset, the *Bismarck* was intended for high-seas operations. However, it was some 1,000 nautical miles less than the range of the preceding *Scharnhorst*-class of turbine battleships, and it might be that this relative lack of endurance contributed to the *Bismarck*'s unhappy end.

Electric-drive steering gear controlled two rudders mounted in parallel, each with an area of 24 square metres.

A big-gun ship such as the *Bismarck* needed an enormous amount of electrical energy. To supply it, there were five generating plants comprised of two 500-kilowatt diesel generators and six steam-driven turbo-generators. In total, these generators delivered approximately 7,900 kilowatts at 220 volts.

The battleship's main armament consisted of four double 38-centimetre turrets, two of which, Anton and Bruno, were mounted forward, and two, Caesar and Dora, aft. Their maximum range was 36,200 metres. For these guns, her normal load was 840 rounds, her maximum load 960, each of which consisted of the shell, a primer, and a principal charge. The shells were so heavy that they had to be conveyed from the magazines on the middle platform deck to the turrets by means of a mechanical hoist. Secondary armament consisted of twelve 15-centimetre guns in six double turrets equally divided on either side of the ship. They had a maximum range of 23,000 metres. The normal ammunition supply for these was 1,800 rounds. Antiaircraft defence consisted of heavy, medium, and light guns. As heavy flak, the *Bismarck* carried sixteen 10.5-centimetre quick-firing guns in twin mounts, with a maximum range of 18,000 metres. Sixteen 3.7-centimetre guns in twin mounts provided medium flak, and eighteen 2-centimetre in ten single and two quadruple mounts provided light flak.

Since a battleship is essentially a floating gun platform, a description of the *Bismarck*'s gunnery equipment and procedures may be helpful, especially because these differed from navy to navy. Her surface fire-control system was installed in armoured stations forward, aft, and in the foretop. Inside each station were two or three directors. A rotating cupola above each station housed an optical

Foretop Fire-Control Station
Admiral's Bridge
Forward Fire-Control Station
Charthouse
Armored Conning Tower
Open Bridge
Turret Bruno
Turret Anton
"First" 14-inch Hit from *Prince of Wales*
Battery Deck
Armored Deck
Upper Platform Deck
Middle Platform Deck
BL
XIII — XIV — XV — XVI — XVII — XVIII — XIX — XX — XXI — XXII
Boiler Rooms (Port, Center, Stbd)
Forward Gunnery Computer Room
"Second" 14-inch Hit

range finder and served as a mount for one of three radar antennaes.

The director, which was basically a high-powered telescope, was used to measure bearing for surface targets. In contrast to most other navies, the Kriegsmarine did not mount its directors in the rotating range-finder cupola, but below it, inside the fire-control station. The director was designed like a periscope so that only the upper lens protruded slightly above the armoured roof of the fire-control station.

Not only the optical range finders but also the radar sets were used to measure range to the target. German radar had a shorter range and poorer bearing accuracy than the optical equipment. It gave exact range information in pitch darkness or heavy weather, but it was extremely sensitive to shock caused by the recoil of heavy guns. Range and bearing information from directors, range finders, and radar were received in two fire-control centres, or gunnery-computer rooms, which provided continuous solutions to ballistic problems.

Control of the guns was primarily the task of a gunnery

officer. His personality, as expressed by his choice of words and tone of voice, could influence the morale of his men. Either the main battery or the secondary battery could be controlled from any one of the three stations, whose directors were brought to bear on a target by two petty officers under the direction of a gunnery officer who observed the fall of shot. In each station, there was a 'lock-ready-shoot' indicator whose three-coloured lights showed the readiness of the battery, the salvo, and any possible malfunctions in the guns. When the battery was ready, the petty officer on the right side of the director would fire by pressing a button or blowing into a mouthpiece. It was also possible to actuate the firing system from any of the computer rooms.

The gunnery officer could order a 'test shoot' to find the range, or he could order a series of full or partial salvoes. Rather than waiting to spot each splash between salvoes of a 'test shoot', he could use a 'bracket' to find the target. A 'bracketing group' consisted of three salvoes separated by a uniform range, usually 400 metres, and fired so rapidly that they were all in the air at the same time. On the *Bismarck* it was customary to fire 'bracketing groups' and, with the aid of our high-resolution optical range finders, we usually succeeded in boxing or straddling the target on the first fall of shot. The gunnery officer was aided in spotting the fall of shot by one of the gunnery-computer rooms, which signalled him by buzzer when the calculated time of projectile flight had expired.

Once the range and bearing had been found, the gunnery officer in control would order, 'Good rapid'. He could choose to fire full salvoes of all eight guns or partial, four-gun salvoes fore and aft. In either case, the 'firing for effect' was as rapid as possible.

Firing could also be controlled by the individual turret commanders. This allowed great flexibility in case of battle damage. However, in action it was most important for the senior gunnery officer to retain control of the batteries for as long as possible, because central fire control with the help of computer rooms was far superior to independent firing under the control of the turret commanders.

As defence against magnetic mines and torpedoes, the *Bismarck* was equipped with a Mineneigenschutz.[3] This device consisted of a series of cables that encircled the ship inside the outer hull below the waterline. It was supposed to dissipate the magnetic field generated by the ship so that the enemy's magnetic mines and torpedoes would not detonate.

For reconnaissance, the spotting of shot, and liaison with friendly forces, the *Bismarck* carried four single-engine, low-wing Arado-196 aircraft with twin floats, which also served as light fighters. Two of these machines were stored in a hangar beneath the mainmast, the other two in ready hangars that held one aircraft each on either side of the stack. The planes were launched by means of a catapult located between the stack and the mainmast. This installation ran laterally across the deck as a double catapult, so that launching could be to either starboard or port.

The crew consisted of 103 officers, including the ship's surgeons and midshipmen, and 1,962 petty officers and men. It was divided into twelve divisions, whose numerical strength varied from 180 to 220 men. The battle stations of Division 1 through Division 4 were the main and secondary batteries, Division 5 and Division 6 manned the antiaircraft guns. Division 7 consisted of what we called 'functionaries', that is, such specialists as master carpenters, yeomen, cooks, and cobblers. Division 8 consisted of the ordnancemen, and Division 9 combined

[3] Degaussing gear

signalmen, radiomen, and quartermasters. Division 10 through Division 12 were the engineers. During our operational cruise, Division 1 through Division 6, reinforced by approximately half of Divisions 7 and 8, occupied every other action station, checker-board-style. When 'Clear for action!' was sounded, the free watch occupied the vacant action stations.

The pilots and aviation mechanics we had on board belonged to the Luftwaffe and wore Luftwaffe uniforms. The air observation people were naval officers who were experienced in the recognition and evaluation of events at sea and had been detailed to the Luftwaffe; they served also as radiomen. When we departed on our Atlantic operation, the fleet staff, prize crews, and war correspondents raised the total number embarked to more than 2,200. On 27 May 1941, when the *Bismarck* sank, only 115 of them were saved.

At the time I joined the ship, her entire crew had not yet been ordered aboard. Some sixty-five technical officers, petty officers, and men had been aboard since around the middle of April, and sixty or so members of the gunnery department arrived in June. These men were subjected to what was called a building course, the purpose of which was to familiarize them with the ship's equipment from the keel up. Many of them, when they first saw the *Bismarck*, with her mighty guns and heavy armour-plating, said to themselves, 'Well, nothing can happen to me here, this is really floating life insurance!' The petty officers buried themselves in the intricacies of the engine rooms, the weapons, the trunking and valves, then made drawings and prepared lectures for the instruction of the men. Because of the building work that was still going on, the crew was not, at this time, living aboard. Most of them were housed in two barracks ships, the *Oceana* and the *General Artigas*.

Training began, and the petty officers and their men were assigned their stations. In order to get to know their ship, the men moved through her in small groups, crawling through the hold and ventilation shafts, climbing the bridge and the tower mast, and making themselves familiar with the double bottom, the stowage spaces, the bunkers and the workshops. Instruction was given on general shipboard duties, on individual areas of competence, and on procedures for clearing for action. So-called emergency exercises began early. We were already at war, so first of all, we had aircraft- and fire-alarm exercises, then damage-control and clear-for-action exercises. These were gone over again and again, always at an increased tempo.

Signalmen and radio operators, corpsmen, cooks, and stewards began arriving. It was a very young crew; the average age of its members was around twenty-one years, and very few of them had ever been in combat. For many, the *Bismarck* was their first ship. The daily routine was: reveille at 0600, breakfast at 0630, sweep the decks and clean up at 0715, muster at 0800, then either instruction or practical work at such things as maintenance of the ship and stowing the masses of provisions that were being taken aboard at this time – flags, signal books, binoculars, charts, foul-weather gear, enciphered documents, typewriters, medications, food, drink, everything needed for a ship's company of more than 2,000 men. The noon break was from 1130 to 1330, after which duties similar to those of the morning continued until 1700, when the evening meal was served. At 1830 the deck was cleaned again, then the duty day came to a close. The call to swing hammocks was sounded at around 2200.

During this period, Lindemann lived only to accomplish what he had identified as his primary objective when I reported aboard: to have his ship combat-ready, in terms of both men and material, in the shortest possible time. He had his officers report to him regularly on the progress being made in training the crew and outfitting the various departments, but he did not rely solely on these reports. He was frequently to be seen around the ship, satisfying himself on the spot, attending training, supervising whatever construction remained to be done, asking cogent questions, giving orders, and meting out praise and censure. In addition to these activities, he spent a great deal of time on his paper-work, especially reports on questions concerning the ship's guns, with which he was so familiar. I can still see the clear, steep handwriting in which, in polished terms, he explained his requests and wishes, amended the drafts of other people's correspondence, or put proposals that would lead to the earlier combat-readiness of the ship into a style that made them irresistible.

As a rule, Lindemann gave me his orders when I reported to his cabin in the morning. Shortly after I took up my duties, he told me to prepare a schedule of official visits, on which I would have to accompany him, to Hamburg's civil and military authorities. In due course, we visited the senate of the Free and Hanseatic City in Hamburg's venerable Rathaus, or town hall, called on the admiral of the Hamburg Naval Headquarters, and on various military commanders and headquarters important to the ship. In August and September 1940 Hamburg was already a target of quite frequent but not very heavy British night bombing raids. Whenever possible, the *Bismarck*'s guns joined in the city's antiaircraft defences, and so one of our calls was on the commander of Hamburg's air defences, Brigadier General Theodor Spiess, in his roomy offices on the Aussenalster. During visits such as this, wartime security put something of a constraint on the subjects of our conversation, but nevertheless we gained an insight into the morale of official Hamburg. Optimism and confidence in victory were universal. What else, indeed, would one expect, right after the fall of France?

Most of the visits involved a boat ride across the Elbe from the Blohm & Voss yard. The first time we made this crossing, Lindemann suddenly asked, 'Do you know how big the *Bismarck* really is?' He asked this because the *Bismarck* was officially rated at 35,000 tons, and very few people knew her true tonnage. 'Well,' I answered, '35,000 tons plus fuel and water, I think.' Not without pride, Lindemann said, '53,000 tons, fully equipped.' When he saw how much that impressed me, he added, 'But that is strictly secret information!' Of course, I promised not to divulge it and didn't until the end of the war.

I found Lindemann a thoroughly competent naval officer and gunnery man, one who not only quoted but lived by Prince Otto von Bismarck's motto, *Patriae inserviendo consumor* (I am consumed in the service of the fatherland). He seemed to be always on duty. When his name came up in the wardroom, it invariably evoked high respect and there was a feeling that it would be impossible to equal his almost ascetic-seeming devotion to duty. Nevertheless, the man had a big heart, a characteristic he was more inclined to exhibit to his men than to his officers, and a radiant smile that greatly contributed to the affection he enjoyed among the crew. Maschinengefreiter[4] Hermann Budich said later: 'I completed a year's building course in the *Bismarck* and was then steward to the Rollenoffizier,[5] Korvettenkapitän Max Rollmann, who

[4] Seaman Apprentice (Machinist)
[5] The Detailing Officer, who assisted the First Officer in distributing the seamen of the ship's company among the battle stations, as called for by the battle or clear-for-action drills. The composition of the divisions was determined and drill stations were assigned on this basis. Every member of the crew had to be berthed in a space as near as possible to his action station so that he could reach it without interrupting the ship's traffic patterns.

occupied a cabin in the *General Artigas*. Here I encountered many officers, and began to know and esteem
Kapitän zur See Lindemann. When one bumped into an
officer in the confines of the barracks ship, 90 per cent of
the time a bawling-out resulted. When the 'Old Man'
came aboard, he radiated an aristocratic but not over-
bearing calm. If there was any excitement, he immediately
took charge. In short, the ordinary sailor came to trust this
man, despite his "piston rings".[6]

---

[6] Captain's stripes

3

Sea Trials and Battle Practice

The day came for the *Bismarck* to leave the Hanseatic City for the first time and undergo her trials, which were to be conducted in the eastern Baltic. She had been lying with her stern to the Elbe, but on 14 September 1940 tugs turned her 180 degrees. A day later she slid into the channel and steamed through a mass of ships and launches, past the familiar landscape of the village of Blankenese, to the lower Elbe. How often I had passed this way on ships in peacetime, when the banks were full of people waving friendly greetings. But now it was wartime; the *Bismarck*'s sailing had not been announced, and the banks were empty. Early in the evening we dropped anchor in Brunsbüttel Roads, in order to enter the Kiel Canal the next morning. Naturally, the first time we anchored, I wanted to watch the operation. The anchor chain ran out with what to those who were forward of the navigation bridge sounded like a great roar but, because of the length of the ship, was scarcely audible to those aft. Furthermore, since the hull of the ship remained completely motionless, which is far from the case when a cruiser drops anchor, anchoring must have seemed to the men aft like something that was going on in 'another part of town'. After darkness fell, the air raid alarm sounded; the 'Brits' were back. Aided by the light of a searchlight ashore, the *Bismarck* joined in the antiaircraft fire. But there was no visible result.

On 16 September, we entered the canal with the ship in a state of 'heightened watertight integrity'. In the highest state of readiness, that is, 'cleared for action,' all passageway doors and ventilation fittings, both intake and outlet, were closed, so that the *Bismarck* was divided into eighteen watertight compartments and a number of hermetically sealed spaces. In 'heightened watertight integrity', which was usually ordered when navigation was hazardous, passageway doors and ventilation fittings remained open. There was also an intermediate state, 'wartime steaming condition', which was used when there was a high risk of encountering the enemy.

The transit of the canal took two days and on the evening of 17 September we made fast in Scheerhafen, near Kiel. For the young engineers who had their hands on levers controlling 150,000 horsepower, bringing this giant of a ship through the narrow canal on her maiden voyage was a great achievement. The slightest error on their part could have had disastrous consequences for both the ship and the canal. And so, when we got to Kiel, Lindemann came on the ship's loudspeakers and congratulated the men in the boiler rooms and engine rooms.

The following week was devoted to aligning the ship's batteries. After spending a few more days at a harbour buoy, on 28 September we steamed under the escort of *Sperrbrecher 13*[1] for Arkona, on the island of Rügen, then went on to Gotenhafen (now Gdynia) without escort.

We spent fully two months at the Gotenhafen naval base, trying out the ship and her systems in the Gulf of Danzig. After testing her degaussing gear, we made measured-mile, endurance, and high-speed runs and tested her general manoeuvrability. Not until 23 October were the engines cleared for full speed.

Our ship did very well in all these tests. She was

---

[1] A Sperrbrecher was a converted merchant ship, whose function was to sweep mines that the Kriegsmarine's regular minesweepers might possibly have missed. One such vessel was generally assigned to protect large German warships in waters where there was a high risk of mines. The ship being protected followed in the Sperrbrecher's wake.

extremely steady, and rolled and pitched very little, even in a seaway. Her rudder response was almost immediate, and she did not heel excessively when she made a turn; when backing, even at speeds close to bare steerageway, she turned so easily that she could get out of tight spots without the help of tugs. We also tested to see how manoeuvrable she would be if only her engines were used in case her steering gear and rudders should be put totally out of action during an engagement. It was found that with both rudders locked in an amidships position, the *Bismarck* could be held on course only with great difficulty. The reason for this was that the convergent design of her propeller shafts provided only a weak turning movement, even with the outboard shafts rotating in opposition at full power. No one aboard at the time could have had any idea of the fateful effect this flaw would one day have.

Lastly, with the thought that only the powered steering gear might be disabled while the rudders could still function, turning the rudders by manpower alone was practised. For such manual steering, the crews of both after 15-centimetre turrets, a total of 32 men, would have to proceed as expeditiously as possible to Compartment II of the upper platform deck, where the manual steering gear was located. Of course, full speed could not be maintained with manual steering because of the pressure of the water against the rudders. The upper speed limit under these conditions was about 20 knots.

To us in the ship, high-speed runs were the most exciting of the tests. Then, the giant warship would surge forward with the full power of her engines at play, yet she lay steady in the water, making but a small bow wave. On the upper deck, there seemed to be hardly any vibration, but sometimes the men on the living decks had to hold their plates and utensils on the tables to keep them from bouncing to the floor. This shaking did not occur at the highest speeds; however, but at a slightly lower, so-called critical speed, at which the vibrations of the different parts of the ship were mutually reinforced and created maximum vibration throughout the ship. Earlier, when I was serving in the *Königsberg*, she sometimes vibrated so violently that the optical fire-control instruments could not be used. Ultimately, the problem was remedied by keeping away from the critical speed so as to minimize the reinforcement effect. But I never experienced anything like that in the *Bismarck*.

The speed trials continued into November, a speed of 30.8 knots being recorded on one occasion. That exceeded the designed speed! Not only were there joy and pride on board, but an appreciation of the tactical advantage that such a speed might provide during the coming operation in the Atlantic. The crew's already boundless confidence in their ship was once again justified.

One day, after a series of measured-mile runs, we had an unusual experience. In a fairly rough sea, we were entering the harbour of Gotenhafen when we suddenly suffered a minor malfunction of our steering mechanism, and came to a full stop to repair it. Nearby was a fishing boat, lying low in the water and labouring along. So low, in fact, was she lying that her abundant catch was obviously about to be spilled back into the water. By megaphone, she called to the *Bismarck*: 'Could you give us lee? Our catch was so good that we can't stow it safely.' Briskly, Lindemann ordered the officer of the watch to do as requested, and we escorted the boat into the calm waters of Gotenhafen Roads. Next day the *Bismarck* had fish on the menu!

Along with the mile runs, we carried out intensive training in the safe operation of the ship at sea. The green crew found their sea legs and became thoroughly familiar

with their new surroundings. Emergency drills were followed by more emergency drills, or Rollenschwoof,[2] as
the men called them. The word would be passed to 'Make
fast the passageways!' which meant 'Set the cleared-for-
action state of watertight integrity.' Or, 'Fire!' When that
word was passed, the source of the flames would be sealed
off and hoses made ready to extinguish them. Or, 'Man
overboard!' In this exercise, a life buoy would be thrown
over the side to mark the spot where the man fell. A
lifeboat would be launched with all possible speed, pick
up the buoy, and then be hoisted in. Every man had to
know his station and, at drill, proceed to it at once and
perform his duties as instinctively as a sleepwalker.
Emergency drills often began on the quarterdeck, where
the off-duty section of the crew, some 1,600 men, would
be mustered. Alarm bells would sound an emergency
signal – for example, *tuy-tuy-tuy-tuy-tuy* (make fast the
passageways!) – and these 1,600 men would storm down
assigned companionways to their posts. Step lively! step
lively! but not on the head or fingers of the man below you.
Two steps down, get a good grip, swing down, spring off to
the right, always faster, lively, lively. So well practised did
the crew become that five minutes after the word was
passed, the bridge had a report from every station.

Hermann Budich and two of his comrades, wanting to
be first at their station in Compartment IX of the lower
platform deck and therefore to avoid the choked companionways, sought a different route. They discovered a
little-used companionway aft. Hanging onto the inner
edge of the hatch, they took their usual two steps down,
let go, and flew, rather than ran, for their station – all this
with heavy tools stuck in the belts of their work clothes.
Out of breath, they reached their goal, the first to do so,

[2] Emergency rushes

and reported it 'clear'. But hadn't Budich brushed against something soft at the bottom of the companionway? What could it have been? The men's division officer, Kapitän-leutnant (Ingenieurwesen)[3] Werner Schock, did not attend the critique that followed the drill, but when it was over they were ordered to report to his cabin at once. There, a corpsman was applying cold compresses to a beautiful black eye. 'Gentlemen,' he began what prom-ised to be an unpleasant interview, 'if it weren't that everyone looks so much alike in work clothes, I would have caught you earlier. I know you move fast, but you don't have to ram your tools down my throat! Be more careful! Now, get out!' They did shout 'Warsaw!'[4] before they jumped, but that was to alert anyone who might have been there to move out of the way, not to tell him to stay put.

During emergency drills First Officer Oels had heavy responsibilities. His station at such times was in a secon-dary command centre that had been set up in Compart-ment XIV of the upper platform deck. Since he was primarily responsible for the defence of the ship against fire, gas, and flooding, as well as for the maintenance of buoyancy and trim, the damage-control centre was in the same compartment. There, also, was the ship's security station, in which were kept plans that showed all the ways in which the pumping, flooding, fire-extinguishing, and ventilation systems could be used to combat the above-mentioned dangers. This area was the heart, so to speak, of the ship, where vital information was delivered and equally vital decisions were made.

In mid-October Lindemann made an operational-readiness inspection. He ordered the most important emergency drills, then went around to each station,

---

[3] Lieutenant (Engineering)
[4] Used in the German Navy for 'gangway!'

watched how the men handled their equipment, and asked pertinent questions. What he saw satisfied him. 'Seamen of the battleship *Bismarck*,' he said in closing his critique, 'this day has convinced me that you have made good progress. Thanks to your instructors and to your own enthusiasm, the *Bismarck* is well on her way to becoming operational.' The crew had completed a kind of crash course. In peacetime, it usually took at least a year to bring a warship from commissioning to combat-readiness but, because of urgent missions to come, the *Bismarck* could count on no more than nine months.

My tour of duty as Lindemann's adjutant ended about this time. The change, which I foresaw from the start, was brought about by my assignment to a three-week gunnery course at the Naval Gunnery School in Kiel, in November 1940. At the end of August 1939, the school's course on fire control for large-calibre guns, which I was then taking, was interrupted by the threat of war. Now it was to be revived as the completion of gunnery training. At an 'all men aft' assembly held for some special reason at the beginning of November, Lindemann remarked that on account of my 'valuable' professional training I would henceforth serve in gunnery only. My place as adjutant was taken by Leutnant zur See Wolfgang Reiner. Although I left Lindemann most unwillingly, I realized it was a move that had to be made. As operational deployment approached, all that mattered was the combat-readiness of the ship, and that required that the utmost advantage be taken of everyone's speciality.

The second half of November was spent in more tests of the *Bismarck* and her engines. The only thing new was that gunnery drill was added to the routine. Not only were the brand-new guns tested for steadiness, the smooth working of their mechanisms, ballistic performance, and accuracy, but the resistance of the ship's components to recoil was also tested. Practice firings served to train the gunlayers in the best way of keeping on target. These drills could be carried out satisfactorily at close range with 8.8- or 5-centimetre subcalibre guns inserted into the barrels of the heavy and medium guns. Because the shells and powder charges used were relatively light, this kind of firing was economical. At the same time, it gave the gunnery officers practice in fire control.

Full-calibre firing! Unforgettable was the day the *Bismarck*'s heavy guns fired their first full salvo. How far, how violently would the recoil cause the ship to heel over, how quickly would she right herself? Below, in the engine rooms, where steam pressure was 56 times that of the atmosphere, the seconds passed slowly. A single crack in the main steam line caused by the shock of firing could result in the death of everyone in the engine room. Boom! The ship seemed to be abruptly jarred sideways, a few loose objects came adrift, a few light bulbs shattered, but that was all. Topside and in the control centres, it was quite different. Up there, the sideways movement was scarcely noticeable. Of course, the concussion had already been felt throughout the ship. Her steadiness in the water showed the *Bismarck* to be an ideal gun platform.

At the end of her trials, the ship was scheduled to return to Blohm & Voss in Hamburg so that the yard could give her the 'finishing touches' it had not been able to complete by September. On 5 December, therefore, the *Bismarck* departed Rügen under escort of *Sperrbrecher 6* and steamed for Kiel. Passage of the canal again took two days, and on 9 December we were back in Hamburg.

Over Christmas, we were given leave. For most of us, this was our last chance to be with our families. Those who could not get away were able to spend a few more hours in hospitable Hamburg. I enjoyed two weeks of marvellous skiing in the Bavarian mountains.

On 24 January 1941, the finishing touches to our ship were completed, but we could not immediately return to the Baltic to continue our trials and battle practice, as we had intended to do. A sunken ore ship was blocking the Kiel Canal, and the thick ice that had formed during this exceptionally severe winter was delaying salvage work. The idea of our making the long detour around Jutland was rejected by Berlin. Therefore, while we awaited our sailing date, set for 5 February, we conducted training and battle drills in Hamburg Harbour. When that day came the canal had still not been cleared, but we could not have left, anyway, because some of our pressure gauges and electrical lines to the boiler-room ventilators had been damaged by the extreme cold, and we were not ready for sea. Although this situation was remedied by 16 February, the canal remained blocked and our departure had to be postponed again, this time to 5 March. At the end of February, Lindemann complained in the War Diary: 'The ship has been "detained" in Hamburg since 24 January. Five weeks of training time at sea have been lost!'

On 6 March, we cast off from the wharf at the Blohm & Voss yard, steamed out into the Elbe, and once again headed downstream. As the familiar silhouette of Hamburg slowly sank astern, I had the feeling that this time our absence from the beautiful Hanseatic City would be longer. For part of the way, the admiral commanding the Hamburg Naval Headquarters did us the honour of escorting us in his flagship. Scattered passers-by waved from the banks of the river. At midday we dropped anchor in Brunsbüttel Roads. Three fighters flew air cover for us and an icebreaker and two Sperrbrechers anchored nearby to protect us against possible aerial torpedo attacks. We entered the canal the next day and, on 8 March, reached Kiel, where we spent a few days in Scheerhafen again aligning our batteries. Also, we had to take aboard ammunition, two of our four assigned air-craft, provisions, fuel, and water. Leaving Kiel, we con-tinued our voyage east. Because of the thick ice in the western Baltic, the predreadnought *Schlesien*, a veteran of the Imperial Navy, went ahead of us to act as an ice-breaker. Behind her came *Sperrbrecher 36*, then the *Bismarck*. On the afternoon of 17 March we once again dropped anchor at Gotenhafen, which was to be our principal base until we sailed on our first operational cruise.

The following days saw a great deal of activity. We conducted more high-speed trials and endurance runs and tried out our hydrophone gear. This apparatus emitted a sound impulse, by whose echo the range, bearing, nature, and conduct of its contact could be determined. A well-trained listener could even identify the type of vessel the echo came from. I still remember the report made by an operator in the *Prinz Eugen*, our companion on our Atlantic cruise, before the battle off Iceland on the morning of 24 May 1941, 'Noise of two fast-moving turbine ships at 280° relative bearing.' The ships proved to be the *Hood* and the *Prince of Wales*.

The most important thing now was intensive testing of our batteries. Practice firing for the instruction of the fire-control officers and gun crews alternated with carrying out projects for the Gunnery Research Command for Ships, an organization that ran its own trials on new ships with a view to improving the ordnance of various ship types. For me, as a gunnery officer, these tests were exciting but for the crew they just meant drill and still more drill. Battle practice in the daytime, battle practice at night! The men did not complain, however; they were in the swing of things and were becoming more and more anxious for our first operation at sea to get under way.

On 19 March, Lindemann learned from the captain of

our younger sister ship, the *Tirpitz*, that, according to a directive issued by the Seekriegsleitung,[5] the *Bismarck* was to be ready for her first mission from three to four weeks earlier than originally intended – now she was to be ready at the end of April. This meant that Lindemann had to cut short the programme of the Gunnery Research Command for Ships. He arranged for it to end on 2 April, after which time we conducted our own surface and antiaircraft firing practices. We also spent more time than before in 'clear for action' drills and in training our air crews. Since the *Prinz Eugen*, which was commissioned three weeks earlier than the *Bismarck*, was to be our escort on the upcoming operation in the Atlantic, we conducted tactical exercises with her. We also exercised with the 25th U-Boat Flotilla and, with the help of the tanker *Bromberg*, we practised refuelling at sea. It was at this time that we started doing searchlight drills. We carried seven searchlights; one was on the forward edge of the tower mast, two were atop the main hangar, and the other four were high up on either side of the stack. They were directed to their target through the use of large high-powered binoculars mounted in posts on the sides of the forward battle command station. The purpose of these drills was to provide practice at picking up an indicated object at first try and keeping the light on it.

Besides the frozen lines to the boiler-room ventilators mentioned earlier, we were having a few other problems with the propulsion plant: some hairline cracks in superheaters; a broken ball-bearing ring on the middle main coupling; a loose sleeve in one of the main steam lines; salt in one of the turbines. All these insignificant defects in the plant were repaired in short order, but in the War Diary Lindemann complained that they tended 'to tarnish

[5] Naval War Staff

the good impression previously gained of its reliability.'
When Naval Group Command North, to which the ship
was subordinate, read his comment in the middle of April,
it added: 'Considering that this is new construction, the
engine malfunctions were very minor. In fact, the propulsion plant has been running more smoothly than
expected.' Lindemann must have felt increasingly impa-
tient to be able to report to the Seekriegsleitung that his
ship was ready for operational deployment.

Over Easter, which fell on 13 April that year, the
Bismarck went in to Gotenhafen for four days. There, we
were to take on more ammunition and have some work
done on our engines.

When we were at sea, the routine was still battle
practice, more battle practice, and battle problems. In a
battle problem, a particular tactical situation was
assumed: we were, for example, covering an attack by the
Prinz Eugen on a British convoy that was escorted by a
battleship. We went into action with the battleship, in the
course of which we received two hits. The damage done to
the *Bismarck* would be presented as realistically as possible: electrical breakdowns by removing fuses, fires by
using smoke bombs, gaseous fumes by using tear gas, and
so forth. In the case of damage that could not be por-
trayed, 'damage notices' would be posted in the relevant
parts of the ship; for example, 'To the commander of the
port II 15-centimetre turret: Turret destroyed by a direct
hit. Your gun crew has been wiped out.' That turret
commander and his men would then cease to take part. In
partially destroyed compartments, there was feverish
activity: fire hoses were hooked up, openings were sealed
tight, alternate piping routes established, and all damage
was brought under control. Obermaschinist[6] Oskar Barho,

[6] Warrant Officer (Machinist)

of the main electrical control station, enjoyed the break-downs and kept calm in the face of them. He gave precise instructions and repeatedly told his men: 'If I become a casualty, you must keep everything going exactly the same way, regardless of your grade! If you think one of my orders is incorrect, report it!'

The officers told their men again and again: 'If only two or three are still alive at your station, carry on. That's right, carry on! Execute the required emergency proce-dures at once!' This could be somewhat difficult for a young seaman or stoker who received a damage notice and had to decide how to deal with it himself. He would then have to give orders, which previously had been done by officers – how often they had practised that! Superiors intervened only when lack of experience led the men into making serious mistakes. Not a bad way to accustom a young man to thinking and acting on his own.

After a battle problem, there would be a muster on the quarterdeck. Under the leadership of the captain, the damage done and the countermeasures taken were discus-sed in detail. Lindemann understood how to ask the right questions. Not only was he thoroughly conversant with the duties of naval officers and with his own specialty, naval ordnance, but he had a good understanding of technical matters. When the engines were the subject of discussion, he was quick to expose excuses for mistakes and attempts to gloss them over. Being a competent judge of these things, he would close the muster by distributing praise and censure. But his tone was always objective. The point of it all was that every man should learn and should have his confidence in himself and his ship built up. 'When we made a mistake,' said Maschinengefreiter Budich, 'we did not hear angry words from our superiors.'

From time to time, the ship went in to Gotenhafen Roads to catch her breath. When the sky was clear and a gentle wind blew over the ship, we experienced some truly enchanting nights there. Once, when the full moon drew a broad silver track across the mirror-calm water, Matrose[7] Paul Hillen was on watch on the upper deck. Seeing the captain coming towards him, he prepared to make his report, but Lindemann waved it aside and said: 'Isn't that a wonderful sight? Many people would give a great deal of money to see it, and we have it for free.' Later, Hillen, who had only recently come aboard, said, 'It was the first time I heard, not an order, but a personal remark from a high-ranking officer.' Yes, Lindemann had a winning way, which inspired affection. Many of the ship's survivors have testified eloquently to that. One of them put it this way: 'We admired, indeed we loved, our commanding officer, Kapitän zur See Lindemann. He was like a father to us. He always had an open ear for the cares and needs of his crew.'

One day, after being at sea a long time, we dropped anchor and the signal was piped: 'Work details to the forecastle!' That could mean only that the mailboat was coming out from Gotenhafen. And there it was, already quite close. Suddenly it was too close, and we heard a crash. Commented the chief bosun, 'Shit, no mail!' Sadly he watched over the stern post as the boat, already taking on water dangerously, and its longed-for cargo returned, stern first, to Gotenhafen.

Lindemann's entry in the War Diary for the month of April was: 'In sum, all our time was taken up in training. Heavy emphasis was placed on how the crew would perform in the upcoming operation. The men seem to have come to recognize for the first time the magnitude of our mission, which they still don't know, but easily guess.' He was right. Rumours were rife that we were about to

[7] Seaman Recruit

depart on a mission. Watchwords surfaced, were whispered from man to man, then disappeared to make room for new ones.

The *Tirpitz* appeared in the Gulf of Danzig for her own working-up exercises and that provoked speculation that we were about to form a task force with her.

4

Plans for Commerce-Raiding

At the beginning of the war, for which the navy was not prepared, the inferiority of the German fleet in relation to the British was incredible. The ratio was around one to ten. All we had ready for immediate deployment in the Atlantic were two pocket battleships, the *Deutschland* (soon renamed *Lützow*) and the *Admiral Graf Spee*, and twenty-six U-boats, and that small number of ships could not be expected to have a decisive effect on the war. The commander in chief of the Kriegsmarine, Grossadmiral Erich Raeder, who was taken completely by surprise by the outbreak of war with Great Britain, commented, 'Our surface forces are still so inferior to the British in numbers and strength that, should they become fully committed, the only thing they could show is that they know how to die gallantly.' At least initially, the only naval bases Germany had at her disposal were in the southeast corner of the North Sea, as had been the case in the First World War; whereas, thanks to their geographical position and worldwide bases, the British could control every important sea lane and impede the passage of German warships to and from the Atlantic. However, when Germany occupied Norway and France in 1940, the Seekriegsleitung had advance bases to the north and west, which made it easier to deploy our surface forces and U-boats on the oceans.

'The Kriegsmarine is to carry out commerce warfare, and it will be aimed primarily against England.' Overnight, this statement, contained in Directive No. 1 for the Conduct of the War of 31 August 1939, became the basis of the Seekriegsleitung's strategic objectives. The weakness of her fleet obliged Germany to confine herself to conducting economic warfare and to design an appropriate strategy. The Seekriegsleitung was convinced that, by cutting Britain off from her Atlantic supply lines, Germany could win the war, providing *all* resources were concentrated on this objective. To Raeder, 'all resources' meant all naval resources which, in turn, meant that our long-range, heavy surface units – battleships and pocket battleships – were to conduct commerce warfare on the high seas. This strategy was intended not only to disrupt Britain's trade but to tie down her forces and keep them from concentrating: when German commerce-raiders appeared in a certain ocean, Britain would have to move naval forces there, thus denuding some other area. In this way, it was hoped, other German operations such as a ship's breakout into the Atlantic or its return to port would be facilitated.

This offensive reached its high point in the first quarter of 1941. Between January and March, the battleships *Scharnhorst* and *Gneisenau*, under Fleet Commander, Admiral Günther Lütjens, spent eight weeks operating against British commerce in the Atlantic. The total of shipping sunk was relatively low, 122,000 gross register tons, but the mere presence of German battleships in the Atlantic had forced the British Admiralty to take inconvenient countermeasures. It had to deploy significant forces in the ocean areas menaced by the *Scharnhorst* and *Gneisenau* and in the northern passages into the Atlantic, and the whole convoy system was thrown into disarray because, now, every convoy had to be escorted by at least one battleship. The Seekriegsleitung responded with a plan to form a four-battleship task force – the *Bismarck*, *Tirpitz*, *Scharnhorst*, and *Gneisenau* – and send it into the Atlantic to prey on convoys. Although the intention was to send this force out as soon as possible, it turned out that the *Tirpitz*, commissioned on 25 February, could not be operational until the late fall, and in the meantime the Seekriegsleitung would have to be content with the *Bismarck*, *Scharnhorst*, and *Gneisenau*. No wonder it was anxious for the powerful *Bismarck* to be operationally ready.

The expectation with which the *Bismarck* was awaited was matched by a corresponding anxiety on the British side. To the Admiralty, it was clear that, when the German commerce-raiders in the Atlantic were joined by the *Bismarck*, the situation could only get worse. Therefore, it watched the *Bismarck*'s progress towards operational readiness very closely and apprehensively. It was reported at one point that the *Bismarck* in company with light forces had passed Skagen on a northwesterly course on 18 April 1941. That day the *Bismarck* was still training in the Gulf of Danzig.

British interest in the *Bismarck* went further back than that, however. Since the beginning of the war, Winston Churchill, first as First Lord of the Admiralty and, after May 1940, as Prime Minister, had repeatedly pointed out the danger inherent in the German fleet being reinforced by the addition of the *Bismarck* and had taken part in discussions as to how this danger could best be countered. In February 1941, the *Bismarck* still not being operational, he tried to foresee what the Seekriegsleitung would do. He reasoned that it would not make a move until the *Bismarck* and the *Tirpitz* had been completed – and up to that point, he guessed Berlin's intentions correctly. It seemed to him that Germany could not make better use of these great ships than to keep them in the Baltic and, every now and again, start a rumour that they were about to depart for the Atlantic. This would compel Great Britain to keep a powerful force at Scapa Flow, the Home

Fleet's main base, to the detriment of other missions. It would also give Germany the advantage of being able to select her own timing for any operation; she would not have to keep her ships in constant readiness. And since the British ships would naturally have to go into the yard from time to time, it would be very difficult for the Admiralty to maintain superiority over the German commerce-raiders at all times.

Two months later, Churchill coupled a reference to the serious damage that the *Scharnhorst* and *Gneisenau* had done to British trade at the beginning of the year with the remark that the situation would shortly be made worse by the appearance of the *Bismarck*. Several times since the war began, he had pointed out the necessity of mounting air attacks to delay the construction of the *Bismarck* by at least three of four months, and said that success in such a mission would be helpful to British fleet dispositions worldwide. In August 1940, he wrote to the British Air Minister, 'Even a few months' delay in *Bismarck* will affect the whole balance of sea-power to a serious degree.'[1] And in October, he wrote to the Combined Chiefs of Staff, 'The greatest prize open to Bomber Command is the disabling of *Bismarck* and *Tirpitz*.'[2]

However, these hopes about the fate of the *Bismarck* were not to be fulfilled before she put to sea on her first operational cruise.

[1] Winston Churchill, *The Second World War*, Vol. II, p. 578
[2] Winston Churchill, *op. cit.*, p. 445

5

Operation Orders for Exercise Rhine

The success of the *Gneisenau* and *Scharnhorst* as commerce-raiders naturally led the Seekriegsleitung to intensify its conduct of this form of warfare with heavy ships. On 2 April 1941, as the *Bismarck* approached combat-readiness, it issued an operational directive that read in part:

During the past winter the conduct of the war was fundamentally in accord with the directives of the Seekriegsleitung . . . and closed with the first extended battleship operation in the open Atlantic. Besides achieving important tactical results, this operation showed what important strategic effects a similar sortie could have. They would reach beyond the immediate area of operations to other theatres of war (the Mediterranean and the South Atlantic). The goal of the naval high command must be to maintain and increase these effects by repeating such operations as often as possible.

We must not lose sight of the fact that the decisive objective in our struggle with England is to destroy her trade. This can be most effectively accomplished in the North Atlantic, where all her supply lines come together and where, even in case of interruption in more distant seas, supplies can still get through on the direct route from North America.

Gaining command of the sea in the North Atlantic is the best solution to this problem, but this is not possible with the forces that at this moment we can commit to this purpose, and given the constraint that we must preserve our numerically inferior forces. Nevertheless, we must strive for local and temporary command of the sea in this area and gradually, methodically, and systematically extend it.

During the first battleship operation in the Atlantic the enemy was able always to deploy one battleship against our two on both of the main supply lines. However, it became clear that providing this defence of his convoys brought him to the limit of the possibilities open to him, and the only way he can significantly strengthen his escort forces is by weakening positions important to him (Mediterranean, home waters) or by reducing convoy traffic.

As soon as the two battleships of the *Bismarck* class are ready for deployment, we will be able to seek engagement with the forces escorting enemy convoys and, when they have been eliminated, destroy the convoy itself. As of now, we cannot follow that course, but it will soon be possible, as an intermediate step, for us to use the battleship *Bismarck* to distract the hostile escorting forces, in order to enable the other units engaged to operate against the convoy itself. In the beginning, we will have the advantage of surprise because some of the ships involved[1] will be making their first appearance and, based on his experience in the previous battleship operations, the enemy will assume that *one* battleship will be enough to defend a convoy.

At the earliest possible date, which it is hoped will be during the new-moon period of April, the *Bismarck* and the *Prinz Eugen,* led by the Fleet Commander, are to be deployed as commerce-raiders in the Atlantic. The *Gneisenau* will also be sent into the Atlantic, but that will depend on when her repairs have been completed.[2]

The lessons learned in the last battleship operation indicate that the *Gneisenau* should join up with the *Bismarck* group, but a diversionary sweep by the *Gneisenau* in the area between Cape Verde and the Azores may be planned before that happens.

The heavy cruiser *Prinz Eugen* is to spend most of her time operating tactically with the *Bismarck* or with the *Bismarck* and the *Gneisenau.*

In contrast to previous directives to the *Gneisenau–Scharnhorst* task force, it is the mission of this task force to also attack escorted convoys. However, the objective of the battleship *Bismarck* should not be to defeat enemies of equal strength, but to tie them down in a delaying action, while preserving her own combat capability as much as possible, so as to allow the other ships to get at the merchant vessels in the convoy. The primary target in this operation is the enemy's

---

[1] The *Bismarck* and the *Prinz Eugen.*
[2] The *Scharnhorst* was undergoing a lengthy overhaul of her engines.

merchant shipping; enemy warships will be engaged only when that objective makes it necessary and it can be done without excessive risk.

The operational area will be defined as the entire North Atlantic north of the equator, with the exception of the territorial waters of neutral states.

The Group Commands have operational control in their zones. The Fleet Commander has control at sea.[3]

The Group Commands mentioned in the above directive were Naval Group Command North in Wilhelmshaven and Naval Group Command West in Paris. Both commands, each of which was then headed by a Generaladmiral,[4] were responsible for the conduct of operations in their geographically defined areas of authority. They were immediately subordinate to the Seekriegsleitung in Berlin, and the senior officers afloat were subordinate to them. This form of organization was adopted for several reasons: a headquarters ashore would have the best intelligence available; it would have much better communications than the senior officer afloat; and its communications system was less vulnerable. The Fleet Commander had control over all tactical matters and, obviously, in action.

The directive had no sooner reached the Fleet Commander, Admiral Lütjens, than it was out of date. On 6 April, the *Gneisenau*, then undergoing repairs in Brest, was hit by a British aerial torpedo and a few days later by four bombs. She would not be available for a long time. The task force was now reduced to the *Bismarck* and the *Prinz Eugen*. Nevertheless, Lütjens proceeded to issue orders for the overall operation, and Group North and

---

[3] 'Weisung für weitere Unternehmungen von Überwasserstreitkräften.' Skl.1 Op 410/41 Gkdos Chefsache, 2. IV. 1941. For the full text, *see* Appendix A.
[4] Admiral of the Fleet.

Group West did the same for their respective areas of authority. Group North was responsible until the task force entered the Atlantic, at which point Group West took over.

In his order of 22 April, Lütjens gave the forthcoming operation the code name Rheinübung (Exercise Rhine),[5] and set forth his strategy; taking every precaution not to be detected, the task force was to steam through the Great Belt, the North Sea, and the Denmark Strait to the North Atlantic, where it would attack convoys on the Halifax–England route. Subsequent missions would depend on what the situation was, but munitions and stores would be replenished at a port in western France.

Under Lütjens's command were to be the *Bismarck* and *Prinz Eugen*; the U-boats operating along the north–south Atlantic routes; after the end of May, the four U-boats on the Halifax–England convoy route; the scouts *Gonzenheim* and *Kota Penang*; two fleet supply ships; and five tankers. For protection, *Sperrbrecher 13* and *Sperrbrecher 31* would precede the force on its way from Arkona to the Great Belt, and the 5th Minesweeping Flotilla would escort it through the Skagerrak minefield. Thereafter, it would have a destroyer escort consisting of the *Z-23*, *Z-24*, *Hans Lody*, and *Friedrich Eckoldt*. Independently operating forces such as reconnaissance planes and fighters were to provide cover as prescribed by Group North and Group West.

Group North timed the task force's passage through the Great Belt so that it would transit the channel in the outer Kristiansand-South minefield around 2030 on the third

[5] 'Operationsbefehl des Flottenchefs für die Atlantikoperation mit "Bismarck" und "Prinz Eugen" (Deckbezeichnung "Rheinübung"),' Flottenkommando B. Nr. Gkdos 100/41 Al Chefsache of 22. IV. 1941, Annex 1: 'Allgemeiner Befehl für die Atlantikunternehmung,' is reproduced in Appendix B.

day of the operation and enter Korsfjord (now Kross-fjord), near Bergen, the following morning. After spend-ing that day in the fjord, which would allow the *Prinz Eugen* and the destroyers to refuel from a tanker, at nightfall the formation would depart through the northern exit of Hjeltefjord and steam at high speed for a point thirty nautical miles west of Sognefjord. Thereafter, it would continue at its own discretion.

Group North recommended that, weather permitting, the force should straightaway enter the Atlantic through the narrow Iceland–Faeroes passage, keeping far away from the coast of Iceland. Should that not be possible, it should wait in the Norwegian Sea for more favourable weather and make use of the opportunity to fuel from the tanker *Weissenburg*, which would be in the area.

Group West allowed the Fleet Commander a free hand in carrying out the mission in the area of operations, but stipulated that, although the *Prinz Eugen* was to spend most of her time operating in tactical combination with the *Bismarck*, she would be subject to being sent on special missions at the direction of Group West or at the discretion of the Fleet Commander. It stated that if the breakout into the Atlantic should be detected, the mission would remain the same, being shortened or broken off, as necessary. Group West emphasized that the important thing was to preserve the combat-readiness of the ships; combat with enemy forces of equal strength should there-fore be avoided. Contact with a single battleship covering a convoy was permissible only if it could be done without fully engaging her and if it gave the cruiser a chance to engage successfully the remaining escort or the convoy. If combat was unavoidable, it was to be conducted as forcefully as possible.

Two points in the above directives require comment. One point is that the Seekriegsleitung's admonition that our forces strive 'gradually, methodically, and systematically' to establish command of the sea in the North Atlantic, even 'local and temporary' command, was, in view of our limited surface strength, unrealistic. Apparently, it was born of a certain euphoria in Berlin.

The other point is that the brevity with which the directives treated the matter of a sortie being undetected might give the reader the impression that this aspect of an operation, though desirable, was almost incidental. Such was far from the truth, but the few lines devoted to it sufficed because it was axiomatic with German naval officers at that time that if they could get out into the Atlantic without being detected the chances of their operations being successful were enormously improved. Indeed, concealment was their highest priority, at least until the first attack had been made on a convoy. For our side, the weaker side, surprise was half, if not more, of the battle. And it must be said that surprise in later phases of an operation was equally important. Once the position of a German commerce-raider had been disclosed by a contact with the enemy, the raider might just as well make for remote areas of the high seas, from which it could later emerge with renewed surprise. An undetected sortie was the first link in this hoped-for chain of surprise, and was recognized as a prerequisite to the success of our surface ships in the Atlantic.

On the other hand, and this also should be noted, the Seekriegsleitung did not go so far as to make concealment a *sine qua non* of a sortie. If it had done this, every time a force was detected its commander would have had to immediately break off or at least delay his operation. And this in turn would have meant aborting any serious threat to Great Britain from the very form of warfare upon which the Seekriegsleitung had just decided. There was no getting away from the fact that Germany had to live with the risk of her intentions being prematurely disclosed because Great Britain was strategically situated on the routes to the Atlantic. It was left to the force commanders to decide whether to proceed immediately or to turn back and try again later.

On the morning of 25 April the *Bismarck* received orders to depart Gotenhafen in company with the *Prinz Eugen* on the evening of the twenty-eighth. The 6th Destroyer Flotilla was to escort the task force. This order had hardly arrived on board when we were informed that our departure on Exercise Rhine would be postponed by from seven to twelve days because, as the *Prinz Eugen* was making her way to Kiel, a mine exploded near her and did her considerable damage.

Lütjens spent 26 April in Berlin, conferring with Raeder on Exercise Rhine. The mishap to the *Prinz Eugen* gave the two admirals an opportunity to go over once more the composition of our surface task forces in the Atlantic. Lütjens declared that if there was to be no change in the plan to send the *Bismarck* and *Prinz Eugen* out as a pair, either it should be done as soon as the latter was repaired, or they should wait for the next new moon after the one just waning. But there were also valid reasons for awaiting the availability of the *Scharnhorst*, which was still in the midst of an engine overhaul, if not for the *Tirpitz*, which was nearing completion, as well. The appearance of all four would make the operation much more effective than it would be with 'teaspoon' deployment now. Lastly, if one of our new and powerful battleships were to appear now as a commerce-raider, the enemy would have time to take countermeasures that would reduce the prospect for success when joint operations became possible. Nevertheless, it was deemed wiser to resume the Battle of the Atlantic as soon as possible: in plain language, the *Bismarck* and *Prinz Eugen* should not await reinforcement, they should go into action right away.

And with this return to the original operation order, Lütjens came to agree fully and completely with the basic thinking of Raeder. In Raeder's opinion, any interruption in the battle against Great Britain's Atlantic commerce could only strengthen the enemy. Furthermore, in the northern latitudes the passing season was bringing ever shorter nights and every delay increased the difficulty of reaching the Atlantic under cover of darkness. But, he told Lütjens: 'Deliberate, careful operations are indicated. It would be a mistake to risk a heavy engagement for limited and perhaps uncertain results. Our objective with the *Bismarck* and, later, the *Tirpitz* must be continuous, sustained operations.'

Act boldly against convoys – keep heavy British escorts tied down but don't get into action unless it serves the primary mission and can be done without excessive risk – if battle becomes unavoidable, conduct it with full force – operate deliberately and carefully – such were the conflicting demands laid upon the Fleet Commander. How often was Lütjens going to have the heavy responsibility of deciding when to forgo an irretrievable tactical opportunity and when to take it. His mission was far from simple.

6

Another Postponement and Last Liberty

'Anxiety to get into our first battle,' wrote a 24-year-old petty officer, 'reached fever pitch, and tension was kept high by numerous rumours that we were about to go into action.'

By the end of April the *Bismarck* was provisioned for three months at sea. This meant that, among other things, she had embarked enough pork and beef to feed a city of 250,000 inhabitants for one day. On the twenty-eighth, Lindemann reported to the Oberkommando der Kriegsmarine, Naval Group North, Naval Group West, and the Fleet Commander that his ship was fully operational in terms of men and material. In the War Diary, he noted: 'The crew, from whom it is impossible to keep our approaching departure secret – war correspondents, prize crews, and B-Dienst[1] teams come aboard daily – still does not know that our departure has been postponed. Everyone is working on the final preparations with enthusiastic energy. I fear a considerable setback in morale if the delay is long.' Then again:

The first stage of the ship's life since her commissioning on 24 August 1940 has come to a successful conclusion. Our goal has been attained in eight months, only 14 days more than the original schedule (Easter) allowed, and that was only because we had to wait in Hamburg for six weeks because the Kiel Canal was blocked and ice was creating a problem.

The crew can be proud of this feat. It was achieved because the desire to come to grips with the enemy as soon as possible was so strong that I had no hesitance in making extraordinary

[1] Funkbeobachtungsdienst (radio intelligence)

demands on the crew over long periods of time, and because the ship and her systems suffered no major malfunction or damage, despite heavy demands and very little time in port. The level of training is equivalent to that attained by big combatants preparing for the annual battle practice inspection in a good peacetime year. Even though my crew, with few exceptions, has had no combat experience, I have the comforting feeling that, with this ship, I will be able to accomplish any mission assigned to me. This feeling is strengthened by the fact that, in combination with the level of training achieved, we have – for the first time in years – a ship whose fighting qualities are at least a match for any enemy.

The delay in our departure, whose approximate date obviously could not be kept from the crew, is a bitter disappointment to everyone concerned.

I will use the waiting time the same way as before, to acquire a still higher degree of training, but I will allow the crew more rest, and give more time to divisional exercises and the external conditioning of the ship, activities that have understandably had to be severely restricted in recent weeks.

It was announced that the fleet staff would embark in the *Bismarck* on 12 May and conduct a practical test of its collaboration with the ship's command in a clear-for-action drill at sea the following day. The staff numbered approximately 65 men. It consisted of the Fleet Commander, Admiral Günther Lütjens, his chief of staff, Kapitän zur See Harald Netzbandt, with whom he had been close friends for years, three other senior officers, the fleet engineer, the fleet surgeon, the officer in charge of the B-Dienst, and a few junior officers, plus petty officers and men.

The fifty-one years old, Lütjens was an undemonstrative man, tall and thin, with dark, serious eyes. He entered the Imperial Navy as a cadet in 1907 and first saw the world from the heavy cruiser *Freya* that same year. After completing the required courses at the Naval School and graduating twentieth out of a total of 160 midshipmen in his class, in 1909 he had his first sea duty in a position of responsibility in a big ship. That tour was followed by many years in the sort of training assignments with which he was to be repeatedly entrusted, officer training and development of the torpedo-boat flotillas. Thus, from 1911 to 1912 he was the officer in charge of naval cadets in the heavy cruiser *Hansa*. During the First World War he served in torpedo boats, winding up as a commanding officer and half-flotilla leader of the Flanders Torpedo Boat Flotilla. In the years following the war, he commanded torpedo-boat flotillas, served on the Naval Staff in Berlin, and was captain of the *Karlsruhe*. In the year 1937, as a rear-admiral, he became Chief, Torpedo Boats. Soon after the Second World War broke out, Lütjens, then a vice-admiral, was in command of reconnaissance forces in the North Sea. As a deputy of the Fleet Commander, he led the covering forces, the *Scharnhorst* and *Gneisenau*, during the invasion of Norway. In July 1940 he assumed command of the fleet and was promoted admiral in September of the same year. In February and March 1941, he gained operational experience striking at British supply lines in the previously mentioned Atlantic sortie of his flagship *Gneisenau* and the *Scharnhorst*. This experience proved useful to him in a new operation aboard the mighty *Bismarck*.

Throughout his career Lütjens was seen by both his superiors and his peers as a highly intelligent, able, and courageous man of action. Although his serious, dry disposition and reserve made it difficult for his more outgoing comrades to get close to him, this forbidding exterior concealed a noble and chivalrous character. When he spoke, which he did in a quick and lively manner, it was evident that his thought processes were equally lively.

On the morning of 13 May the fleet staff conducted the

tests on board, as had been announced, and inspected and tried out the ship's internal communications facilities. A morning was ample time for that. When at noon the staff disembarked to return to Gotenhafen in the tender *Hela*, the newcomers among our crew were an experience richer. They had seen how, just as in times past a commander led his troops into battle, so now, in the Nelson tradition, the Fleet Commander would exercise command in action. He would be as close to death as anyone else on board. He would have no more of a rear echelon in which to take refuge than would a corpsman.

In many ways, it must have seemed to the greenhorns in the crew that their ship belonged less to the world of war than to the world of modern industry. Many of them worked in confined spaces, far from the light of day, their eyes on pressure gauges and indicators, their hands on valves and levers, as they struggled to keep a wandering pointer at the proper place on a dial. Bound to their stations, they would have to manipulate their precision instruments with cool deliberation, even in the heat of battle. Their world was not that of the infantryman, who can release tension during an attack by such satisfying means as firing his rifle; it was a stationary world of highly specialized technology. The hardest test of their physical and psychological endurance, of course, would come in actual combat.

By order of the Fleet Commander, that same afternoon the *Bismarck* again exercised at refuelling over her bow with the *Prinz Eugen*. Lütjens was particularly concerned that the ships be letter-perfect at this manoeuvre, because of the circumstances to be anticipated in the operational zone. In the event the enemy should appear when the *Bismarck* had fuel lines over her bow, she was to be released immediately from the tanker so that she could make her way unhindered.

On 14 May we carried out reconnaissance and combat evolutions with the light cruiser *Leipzig*, which was then training in the Gulf of Danzig. The reconnaissance was conducted by our aircraft, whose crews took the opportunity to get in some more practice by 'attacking' one another. In the midst of these exercises one of the cranes used for hoisting in aircraft suddenly broke down and all practice came to a premature end. Since repair of the crane was urgent and could not be done with the means available in the ship, we went in to Gotenhafen, where it was to be offloaded. This was by no means our first experience with a malfunctioning crane. Indeed, in the War Diary Lindemann described our cranes as 'extremely susceptible to damage and unreliable.' He reported this new incident to higher headquarters, adding that he could not yet predict when his ship would be back to a state of operational readiness. In the wardroom First Officer Oels and the electrical engineer, Korvettenkapitän (Ingenieur-wesen) Wilhelm Freytag, resumed their grumbling about the sorry state of our cranes, but this time the trouble was remedied surprisingly fast. We had gone to all the trouble of offloading oil so that the ship could pass through the shallows at the entrance to Gotenhafen Harbour, but it proved unnecessary to remove the crane. A mechanic from the crane's manufacturer came aboard and repaired the damage in about an hour. Meantime, however, Group North had reacted to Lindemann's message by postponing our departure for Exercise Rhine for at least three days.

In those beautiful May days of 1941 we were only too glad to be able to spend our free hours ashore. We found Gotenhafen rather dreary, however. Originally named Gdynia and later called Gdingen by the Prussians, it was a small fishing village until after the First World War, when it was incorporated into Poland and developed into a naval base and commercial port. It had 130,000 inhabitants when in 1939, following the conquest of Poland, the Germans named it Gotenhafen and began to convert it into a major naval base. Being beyond the range of enemy bombers at the outset of the war, it made an ideal base for ships in battle training.

We preferred to go to Danzig or to Zoppot, which was still closer but, because of wartime conditions, rather deserted. The beach and pier at Zoppot invited visits. Both these places were easy to reach by rail, and my good friend Kapitänleutnant (Ingenieurwesen) Emil Jahreis, nicknamed 'Seppel', and I spent many happy hours together in one or the other. Bar-hopping in Danzig one evening, we were asked by an acquaintance, 'When won't we see you again? Of course, we know you can't say. One day you just won't come, and then maybe we'll read about you in Wehrmacht reports.'

Another time, after a tour of the bars in Zoppot, we returned to our hotel very late. When we woke up, the sun told us that the *Bismarck* must have long since sailed for her at-sea exercises. Springing out of bed, we made for Gotenhafen with lightning speed. Would we have the unde-served good luck to find a neighbourly tug in the harbour? We did. As we neared the *Bismarck*, which had stopped for us, we saw, standing on the upper deck, where we would have to go alongside, a man we had no great desire to see at that moment: Hans Oels who, as First Officer, was primarily responsible for the discipline of the ship. His only words were, 'The captain awaits you on the bridge.'

'Well,' said Lindemann, with a kindly smile, when we rather sheepishly appeared on the bridge, 'go on about your duties!'

Seppel Jahreis from Öttingen, Bavaria – he loved life and was always cheerful. In those last weeks in

Gotenhafen, however, a change came over him. He became unusually quiet and seemed depressed. I had the feeling that a foreboding of what was to come weighed on him. Shortly before we put to sea for Exercise Rhine, he had to change his action station. Jahreis, the turbine engineer, took over damage control. It was a fateful change. His successor in the engine room survived the sinking of the ship.

7
Hitler Comes Aboard

On 1 May, the Fleet Command received a telephone call from Hitler's naval aide, Fregattenkapitän Karl Jesko von Puttkamer, advising that the 'Führer' intended to inspect the *Bismarck* and *Tirpitz* at Gotenhafen on the fifth. That day, Hitler, Feldmarschall[1] Wilhelm Keitel, von Putt-kamer, Oberst[2] von Below, Hitler's Luftwaffe aide, and the rest of the party arrived in Gotenhafen Roads aboard the *Hela*. Grossadmiral Raeder was conspicuously absent. Hitler, looking somewhat pale, and Keitel, followed by Lütjens and Lindemann, reviewed the crew who were mustered on the upper deck in greeting. The party then inspected some of the ship's equipment, which gave the responsible officers a chance to brief the 'Führer' in their own areas. Hitler remained for an especially long time in the after gunnery computer space, where an extremely capable gunfire-plotting officer, Oberleutnant zur See Friedrich Cardinal, explained how the various intricate-looking devices controlled gunfire. Keitel as well as Hitler seemed to be much impressed by Cardinal's presentation, but neither asked any questions.

After touring the ship, Hitler, Lütjens, and a small group adjourned to the admiral's cabin. There, Lütjens told of his experiences in action against British commerce in the Atlantic with the *Scharnhorst* and *Gneisenau*, expressed optimism about an operation of this type with the *Bismarck*, and explained his immediate intentions. He

[1] Field Marshal
[2] Colonel

considered it an advantage that in the *Bismarck*, which was more powerful than the *Scharnhorst* class, he would no longer be forced to avoid well protected convoys. This, however, did not solve his most difficult problem: getting his force out into the Atlantic without being spotted by the enemy. When Hitler suggested that, apart from anything else, the numerical superiority of the British fleet presented a great risk, Lütjens pointed to the *Bismarck*'s superiority over any single British capital ship. Her hitting and staying power were so great that he had no apprehension on that score. After a pause, he added that breaking out to the high seas would not by any means be the end of our worries. Quite clearly, torpedo planes from British aircraft carriers were a great danger that he would have to reckon with all the time he was in the Atlantic. Little did he know how directly his words bore on the impending fate of his flagship.

Apart from his remark about the superiority of the British fleet, Hitler remained silent throughout Lütjens's presentation. This was probably no surprise to Lütjens. He must have been aware that Hitler, who was strictly a landsman, knew nothing whatever about the unique features of war at sea. Whenever the big ships were at sea, Hitler worried that they might be lost, which would be bad enough, and that their loss would damage his prestige, which would be still worse. While he viewed commerce-raiding as a deviation from the proper mission of warships, he often assessed its risks more realistically than did the experts. Be that as it may, he remained remote from matters concerning the sea and naval warfare. This characteristic was demonstrated that day aboard the *Bismarck*, when Hitler, who was very much interested in military technology, could not find a single word to say about this masterpiece of naval construction and weapon technology. He was not moved to comment.

At this time the Seekriegsleitung was afraid that Hitler might suddenly forbid any ocean operation for the *Bismarck*, a fear it had had in similar cases. Could that have been the reason why Lütjens did not tell Hitler that she was scheduled to sail in two weeks' time? Had he and Raeder decided to keep quiet about it? Quite possibly so, because Raeder did not report the departure of the *Bismarck* and *Prinz Eugen* until 22 May, by which time the ships had been at sea for four days and were nearing the Denmark Strait, having entered the North Sea long before. Even with the operation that far under way, to get approval for it to continue, he would still have to overcome Hitler's very considerable reservations. In the end, Hitler grudgingly allowed him to have his way.

After the presentation in the admiral's cabin, luncheon was served in the wardroom. Hitler's preference for meatless fare being known, it was a vegetarian, one-course meal, during which he said hardly anything. Afterwards, however, he started to talk. It was almost a monologue; only occasional comments came from others. I was seated a long way from the high-ranking people, but from what I could hear, Hitler spoke first about the German minority in Romania. He said that he intended 'to haul these people back into the Reich in short order' if the government in Bucharest did not stop 'harassing' them. On the subject of the United States, he expressed his belief that there was no question of her coming into the war. He declared that the Americans remembered the First World War and the unpaid debts of their former allies only too well: they were hardly likely to get themselves involved in another such undertaking and would gladly renounce sacrificing their soldiers in Europe again.

Lindemann disagreed with this point of view. He said he was not by any means prepared to write off the possibility that the United States would enter the war.

Fregattenkapitän Oels was obviously extremely embarrassed by this contradiction, as it were, of the 'Führer': misgiving showed all over his face. At the end of these proceedings, Lütjens stood up and made a brief address. He talked about how the war at sea was going and the tasks that lay before the *Bismarck*. The objective, he said, was and always would be to beat the British wherever they showed themselves. There was no response.

During the four hours that Hitler was aboard, the 'Führer's standard' waved over the *Bismarck*.

8

Departure from Gotenhafen

On 16 May 1941, Lütjens reported that the *Bismarck–
Prinz Eugen* task force would be ready for Exercise Rhine
on the eighteenth. Accordingly, Group North ordered
him to enter the Great Belt at nightfall on the nineteenth.
At about the same time, two freighters moved into the
Atlantic to act as scouts, and a store ship and five tankers
steamed for the Norwegian Sea and the Atlantic where
they would resupply the task force.

Aboard the *Bismarck* on 18 May Lütjens went over the
operational details of the exercise with Lindemann and
Kapitän zur See Helmuth Brinkmann of the *Prinz Eugen*.
It was decided that, if the weather was favourable, they
would bypass Korsfjord and make directly for the Norwegian Sea to rendezvous with the *Weissenburg*; then, if
possible, go on through the Denmark Strait. There, they
would be under cover of the Arctic fog yet, with the help
of radar, able to maintain high speed. If enemy cruisers
and auxiliary cruisers should appear in our path, they
might have to be attacked. Paramount, however, was the
preservation of the *Bismarck* and *Prinz Eugen* so that they
could spend maximum time in the area of operations.
They were to proceed independently to the island of
Rügen, where the task force would be formed on the
morning of 19 May.

His operation order of 22 April shows that Lütjens
favoured the route through the Denmark Strait; from the
outset, he gave it priority over any other. Hadn't he done
pretty well when he broke out through the Denmark Strait

in the *Gneisenau* in early February? Why shouldn't the poor visibility that prevails there most of the year help him again? Apparently, that was how Lütjens thought – although I do not know for certain.[1] In any case, he apparently just took no notice of Group North's recommendation that he use the Iceland–Faeroes passage. That command had warned against use of the Denmark Strait for what it viewed as very good reasons: its channel was relatively narrow, which made it easier for the enemy to watch; it would be simpler for the British to maintain contact in the north, because their forces there could draw their southern patrols into the search, which would not work in reverse; time and fuel would be saved if, immediately after leaving Norway, Lütjens took the nearer and shorter southern course; and on the southern course he would be able to gain a greater lead over the British ships that would sortie from Scapa Flow when word of the attempted German breakout was received.

The intensification of preparations for the approaching operation, the embarkation of the fleet staff with all its gear, the bunker-cleaning to which the entire crew was assigned on 17 May – all these developments made it clear that our departure from Gotenhafen was imminent.

Bunker-cleaning – a filthy job! A petty officer and a seaman, armed with a fresh-air pipe to enable them to breathe and a safety lamp, had to go into each bunker to clean out the sludge. They collected the muck in buckets, which were then passed from hand to hand, via the upper deck, to barges made fast alongside. Many a bucket reached the upper deck empty, its black contents having wound up on the men's working uniforms somewhere along the way. But after twenty-four hours the job was

---

[1] There being nothing in writing on this matter, I asked Vizeadmiral Helmuth Brinkmann if this was the case but he could not recall that Lütjens gave his reasoning.

done, and the bunkers were spanking clean and ready to take on a new supply of fuel.

Liberty was cancelled as of noon 17 May. Towards midday on the eighteenth the *Bismarck* left the wharf at Gotenhafen. The fleet band stationed on the upper deck struck up 'Muss i denn', the tune traditionally played on large warships leaving for a long cruise. I must admit that I was more than a little surprised by this musical advertisement that Exercise Rhine had begun. I think it highly doubtful that either our Fleet Commander or our captain knew we were to have this musical programme. In all likelihood, it did not occur to any responsible officer that such a thing would happen, and therefore nothing was done to stop it. The bandmaster, aware that our departure was imminent, probably just automatically chose that song without giving the matter another thought. We did not put to sea immediately, however, but dropped anchor in the roadstead, in view of Gotenhafen. Great masses of provisions and fuel oil still had to be taken aboard. Although thousands of tons of fuel flowed into our bunkers, we could not fill them completely, because a hose ruptured, causing the fuelling operation to be called off so that the mess could be cleaned up. By that time, our schedule forced provisioning to be brought to an end. The ship was not far short of being fuelled to capacity, and no one then suspected how important this shortfall would become. The *Bismarck* sailed at 0200 on 19 May.

The crew was in the state of tense anticipation that comes when a long period of preparation is finally over and the action for which it was designed is about to begin. Their faith in their captain and their ship was boundless, even though they knew nothing about the operation on which they were embarking. Now, they heard Lindemann announcing over the loudspeakers that we were going to conduct warfare against British trade in the North Atlantic

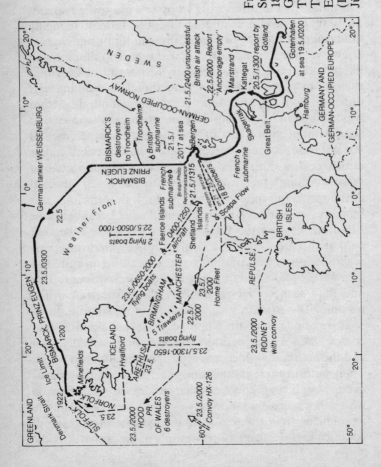

From 1700, German Summer Time, on 18 May to 2000, German Summer Time, on 23 May. The beginning of Exercise Rhine. (Diagram courtesy of Jürgen Rohwer.)

for a period of several months. Our objective was to destroy as much enemy tonnage as possible. This message confirmed what the men had long suspected. Their apprehension about the unknown was replaced by certainty. Below, the gentle vibration of the engines reminded them of the tremendous power that made their ship a deadly weapon.

Our passage to the west, under a cloudy sky, with medium wind and seas, was uneventful. Escorted by the destroyers *Z-23* and *Friedrich Eckoldt* and preceded by Sperrbrechers, the task force sailed as a unit after leaving Rügen and reached designated positions on schedule. Around 2230, the *Hans Lody*, carrying the commander of the 6th Destroyer Flotilla, Fregattenkapitän Alfred Schulze-Hinrichs, joined the formation and we steamed north through the Great Belt. To maintain the secrecy of our mission, the commander of the Baltic security forces announced that the Great Belt and the Kattegat would be closed to commercial traffic on the night of 19–20 May and the following morning.

Next day, when we were in the Kattegat, the *Hans Lody* sounded our first aircraft alarm. We in the *Bismarck* assumed that we had been sighted by British reconnaissance planes. However, they turned out to be our own fighters, of whose arrival we had not been informed.

In contrast to the preceding day, 20 May was clear and sunny. It was perfectly beautiful. The shimmering green sea, corded with the light blue of many small swells, stretched to the far horizon. As we passed the small, flat island of Anholt to port, the tall, slender lighthouse on its northeastern end was clearly visible. This radiant weather might have been seen as a good omen for our operation. If only we hadn't had to steam in such clear view of the Swedish coast and among innumerable Danish and Swedish fishing boats. They seemed to be everywhere, these little white craft with their chugging motors, some of them bobbing up and down beside us. Not only that but steamers from all sorts of countries were passing through the Kattegat. If this wasn't a giveaway of what we were doing here, what was? Surely the appearance of our task force in Scandinavian waters would attract attention that might well work to our disadvantage. Would Sweden's neutrality, which at that time was benevolent towards Germany, avert the military damage that the vigilant Norwegian underground was certainly eager to inflict on us? It was not exactly a secret that the Norwegian underground was in touch with London. But more than that. As our Seekriegsleitung was well aware, Stockholm and Helsinki were hotbeds of British intelligence, and British naval attachés there reported all known German ship movements and other German military operations to London. Indeed, we knew that on 15 March 1941, the British naval attaché in Stockholm informed the Admiralty that an organization had been set up to observe ships passing through the Great Belt and that its reports could reach him in twelve hours.

It ran through my head that enemy agents were being handed a unique opportunity to identify and report our task force just as it was putting to sea. On top of that, the weather was perfect for aerial reconnaissance. I could not see how Exercise Rhine could possibly be kept secret. I became still more concerned when around 1300 the Swedish aircraft-carrying cruiser *Gotland* came in view to starboard against the Swedish coast. For a while, she even ran on a parallel course with us! Assuming that the *Gotland* would inform the Swedish Admiralty that we had been sighted, Lütjens radioed Group North. 'At 1300 aircraft-carrying cruiser *Gotland* passed in clear view, therefore anticipate formation will be reported.' The commander in chief of Group North, Generaladmiral

Rolf Carls, replied: 'Because of the strictly neutral conduct of Sweden, I do not think the danger of being compromised by the Swedish warship is any greater than from the already present, systematic enemy surveillance of the entrance to the Baltic.'

But if Lütjens did fear that we had been dangerously compromised, it was he, not Carls, who was right. Captain Ågren, of the *Gotland*, immediately reported our passage to the nearby Kullen signal station.

9

A British Naval Attaché in Stockholm

Early in 1941, a few high-ranking officers in the Swedish intelligence service privately cáme to the conclusion that a weakening of Germany would be greatly to the advantage of their country. They considered the German invasion of Denmark and Norway an outrageous attack on the sovereignty of all Scandinavia, and, after February 1941, worked closely with the Norwegian underground. Some of their contacts with this movement were through the Norwegian government-in-exile's military attaché in Stockholm, Colonel Roscher Lund, who had become a friend and trusted informant of the British naval attaché there, Captain Henry W. Denham.

On the evening of 20 May, Roscher Lund learned from Major Törnberg,[1] chief of staff to the head of the Swedish intelligence service, that, during the day, two large German warships and several merchantmen had passed through the Kattegat on a northerly course under air cover. He hastened to the British embassy, where he was told that Denham was at a certain restaurant in the city.

---

[1] Roscher Lund never divulged the name of this officer. He spoke of him as his 'source'. His identity has, however, been established by Ludovic Kennedy, *Pursuit*, p. 19, and Patrick Beesly, *Very Special Intelligence*, which states on p. 75: 'There were, however, certain Swedes who were passionately sympathetic to their conquered cousins, the Norwegians, and to the British. One such was a Major Törnberg, Chief of Staff to the head of the Swedish Secret Service. He was friendly with the Norwegian Military Attaché, Colonel Roscher Lund and with the British Naval Attaché, Captain Henry Denham, who since his arrival in Stockholm in the previous year had worked hard at making friends and influencing people.'

He pursued him there and gave him the important news. Both returned immediately to the embassy, and Denham cabled the Admiralty in London: 'Kattegat today 20th May. At 1500 two large warships, escorted by three destroyers, five escort vessels, ten or twelve aircraft, passed Marstrand course north-west 2058/20.' On 23 May, Denham wrote Roscher Lund a letter of thanks:

Your very valuable report of enemy warships in the Kattegat two days ago, has enabled us to locate in the fjords near Bergen on 21st

one Bismarck battleship
one Eugen cruiser.

Naturally there is no harm in your making use of this to enlighten your source.

Thank you so much for your very helpful efforts – let us hope your friend will continue to be such a valuable asset.

Törnberg had seen the *Gotland*'s sighting report in the Admiralty in Stockholm and immediately advised Roscher Lund of its contents, but for security reasons he did not reveal the source of his information. It was routine for the *Gotland* to report the presence of foreign warships in or near Swedish territorial waters. On 20 May she was at sea on a training cruise, but whether her presence at precisely the spot where the German task force passed was fortuitous or whether it was arranged by the intelligence service is a question that has not been clarified to this day.

Of course, at the time, I did not know of these events, but even so, it did seem to me on 20 May that there had been far too many opportunities for our formation to be sighted and, when I thought about what this might do to our mission, I felt that a shadow had fallen over it. I doubt that I was the only one in the ship who had such thoughts, yet none of my younger shipmates, at any rate, said anything about it. What good would it have done? Nothing could be changed. The only thing to do was hope for the best. No one in the *Bismarck* had any inkling of the rapidity with which the news would reach the British Admiralty or of the energetic and successively wider-reaching steps the sea lords would take.

10

Grimstadfjord and the Journey North

Around 1600[1] on 20 May, we were escorted through our own minefields by the 5th Minesweeping Flotilla, which was under the command of Korvettenkapitän Rudolf Lell. When we arrived at our rendezvous with the flotilla, we were dismayed to find a number of merchant ships waiting to take advantage of the cleared channel. Their presence was liable to endanger the security of Exercise Rhine and, therefore, was extremely unwelcome. However, it gave the Swedish observers and their British friends the impression that our task force and the merchantmen were operating together. As has been said, they so stated in their reports. Consequently, in London the Admiralty put a lot of effort into puzzling over what the Germans could be intending to do with such a combination of ships and how they might counter whatever it was.

When we left the minefield, the minesweepers were detached and the *Bismarck* and *Prinz Eugen*, still escorted by destroyers, steered a zigzag course at 17 knots to avoid submarines. The south coast of Norway came into view during a magnificent summer sunset. The outlines of the beautiful, austere landscape, with the black silhouettes of its mountains raised against the red glow of the sky, enabled me to forget for a moment all about the war.

Following the line of the coast, we turned westward.

[1] This was German Summer Time (one hour ahead of standard Central European Time), which I have used throughout. It was the same as double British Summer Time used in the British ships and in all British accounts of the operation. I chose to adopt it in order to synchronize with British literature on this subject, even though the clocks in the *Bismarck* were set on Central European Time at noon of 23 May and remained so to the end.

We would resume our northerly course after we had rounded the southwestern tip of Norway. Between 2100 and 2200 we passed through the southernmost channel in the Kristiansand minefield, then proceeded at a speed of 27 knots. At all times half the guns were manned.

I was off duty that evening and went to see the film that was showing in the wardroom, *Play in the Summer Wind*. We carried enough films to keep us entertained for the several months we were to be at sea but, after that evening, Exercise Rhine kept us so busy that we were never able to put on another programme.

Little did we know, as we watched the only movie shown on the *Bismarck* during the operation, that, on the coast near Kristiansand, Viggo Axelssen, a member of the Norwegian underground, and some of his friends were watching our formation. To make it difficult for enemy submarines to estimate her range and speed, the *Bismarck* had white waves painted behind the dark grey of her bow and stern, and three black-and-white stripes, one of them angled, on her hull and superstructure. The *Prinz Eugen* wore similar camouflage. Looking through his binoculars, Axelssen saw our bow wave and realized that we were steaming at high speed. Very little later, from a hiding-place nearby, he and his companions radioed a coded sighting report that was interpreted in London as confirmation of Denham's report.

Early the next morning the *Bismarck* went to general quarters. From then on, we would have to be on guard against British submarines, especially during the hours of twilight. Shortly after 0700 four aircraft came into view – mere specks against the sun. Were they British or our own? So quickly did they vanish that we wondered if we had imagined them. It was impossible to say, and the supposed sighting was soon crowded out of our minds by other events.

Not long thereafter, we reached the rocky cliffs near Bergen and before noon ran past barren, mountainous countryside and picturesque, wooden houses to enter Korsfjord under a brilliant sun. The *Bismarck* went into Grimstadfjord, south of Bergen, and anchored at the entrance to Fjörangerfjord, about 500 metres from shore. The *Prinz Eugen* and the destroyers went farther north, to Kalvanes Bay, where they took on fuel from a tanker. With the thought that, in the hazy visibility of these northern waters, our black-and-white stripes might stand out and betray us, both we and the *Prinz Eugen* painted over our camouflage with the standard 'outboard grey' of German warships.

Apart from that activity, we simply waited for the day to pass. The sun shone continuously and many members of the German occupation forces in Norway, understandably eager to see the new *Bismarck*, came out to visit us. One episode gave everyone who witnessed it a hearty laugh. A soldier, who apparently had run out of tobacco and assumed that we would have a great store of it, got a boat and came out to the *Bismarck*. As his cockleshell bobbed up and down beside the giant battleship, our men lowered down to him on strings so many cigarettes and so much tobacco that, unless he shared his booty with his comrades, he had enough to smoke for a year!

We were quite close inshore and could feast our eyes on terra firma, from which many Norwegians stared at us. I couldn't help wondering how many of them were looking with something more than idle curiosity.

Two Messerschmitt-109 fighters flew cover over the *Bismarck* all day, and I can still remember the feeling of security they gave us. A little after 1300 the antiaircraft watch sounded the alarm, but the *Bismarck* was not attacked and our guns did not go into action. The British plane that may have caused this alarm had an objective other than an attack. At 1315 Flying Officer Michael Suckling of RAF Coastal Command, near the end of his reconnaissance mission, was circling 8,000 metres above us in his Spitfire when he spotted and photographed 'two large German warships'. Later that same day, thanks to Flying Officer Suckling, the British were able to identify a *Bismarck*-class battleship and an *Admiral Hipper*-class cruiser[2] in the vicinity of Bergen – thanks were also due to Roscher Lund, as is shown in Captain Denham's congratulatory letter to him of 23 May. And we, in our ignorance, were just happy that nothing came of the alarm. I did not learn of Suckling's success until the summer of 1943, when I was a prisoner of war in Bowmanville, Ontario, Canada. One morning I picked up the paper to which I subscribed, *The Globe and Mail*, and there on the front page was an enlargement of Suckling's photograph of the *Bismarck* at anchor in Grimstadfjord. I have never forgotten my astonishment.

As we lay at anchor the entire day, I was perplexed – this is not hindsight, I remember it very clearly – as to why the *Bismarck* did not make use of what seemed like ample time to refuel, as did the *Prinz Eugen*. Of course, I did not know that the *Bismarck*'s operation orders did not call for her to refuel on 21 May, but I did know that we had not been able to take on our full load in Gotenhafen, and I thought it was imperative to replenish whenever possible, so as to put to sea on an operation of indeterminate duration with a full supply of fuel.[3]

[2] The *Prinz Eugen* belonged to the *Admiral Hipper* class.
[3] Histories of the *Bismarck* allude to a 'contradiction' between our stopover in Norway and the intention Lütjens expressed in Gotenhafen on 18 May to continue across the Norwegian Sea without stopping to join up with the *Weissenburg* (*see* Jochen Brennecke, *Schlachtschiff Bismarck*, 4th edition, pp. 66, 278; Ludovic Kennedy, *Pursuit*, p. 40). I do not see that there was any contradiction. According to the *Bismarck*'s War Diary, at the commanders' conference Lütjens said that he intended to continue if the weather was 'favourable'. Perhaps he defined what he

At 1930 the *Bismarck* weighed anchor and headed north to join the *Prinz Eugen* and the destroyers outside Kalvanes Bay. The formation then continued on its way. As we slid past the rocky promontories at moderate speed, I was in a small group of younger officers on the quarterdeck. We wanted to enjoy the Norwegian scenery at close range before we put out into the Atlantic. While we were standing there, the chief of the fleet staff's B-Dienst team, Korvettenkapitän Kurt-Werner Reichard, passed by, a piece of paper in his hand. Eager for news from his interesting duty station, we asked him what he had and he readily told us. It was a secret radio message from B-Dienst headquarters in Germany, according to which early that morning a British radio transmission had instructed the Royal Air Force to be on the lookout for two German battleships and three destroyers that had been reported proceeding on a northerly course. Reichard said that he was taking the message straight to Lütjens. I must admit that we found this news somewhat of a damper because we junior officers had no idea that the British were aware of Exercise Rhine. Now we felt that we had been 'discovered', and that was something of a shock. Surely, I immediately began to theorize, Lütjens would now change his plans. For instance, he might go into the Greenland Sea and stay there long enough for the British

---

meant by 'favourable'. I was not present at the conference, but I take it that he meant he would continue without a halt only if the visibility were poor enough to give him a chance of making the critical passage between the Shetlands and Norway without being observed by enemy aerial reconnaissance. If I am correct, our entry into the fjords in the beautiful sunshine of 21 May was precisely in accordance with his original intention. Indeed, he could not have done anything else.

The fact that, in spite of the fighter cover we requested and were given during our day at anchor, a high-flying British reconnaissance plane photographed us and the *Prinz Eugen* has nothing to do with it. After all, Bergen and its surroundings were within reach of British short-range aerial reconnaissance.

to relax the intensity of their search. The whole business of making an 'undetected' breakthrough pressed into my thoughts and once again I reviewed what seemed to me to be the breaches of security to which we had been sub-jected since leaving Gotenhafen: casting off from the wharf at Gotenhafen to the strains of 'Muss i denn'; our passage through the – despite its name – narrow Great Belt; the swarms of Danish and Swedish fishing boats in the Kattegat; being in plain view from the coast of Sweden; the Swedish aircraft-carrying cruiser *Gotland*; passing so close to the Norwegian coast near Kristiansand; the sunny, clear day at anchor in Grimstadfjord, with the soldiers coming and going. How could Exercise Rhine really have been kept secret? Might it not have been better to enter the North Sea by way of the Kiel Canal and rendezvous with the *Weissenburg* when the timing was best, without touching at Norway? There would have been a risk of detection on this route, too, but probably much less than in our day-long cruise through the narrows of the Kattegat and Skagerrak. But what good did it do to speculate now? In any event, we did not let Reichard's news get us down and decided to keep our knowledge to ourselves. Passing it on to our men would have not helped anyone.

At this hour there was still a visitor on board, whom Lindemann graciously permitted to leave on the pilot boat after the ship put to sea. Around noon that day the telephone rang in the office of Oberfeldarzt[4] Dr Otto Schneider, who was then stationed in Bergen, and a familiar voice said, 'Would you like to visit your brother Adalbert on the *Bismarck*? We don't know what she's doing, but she's lying in a nearby fjord at this very minute.' He did not have to think twice about the answer

---

[4] Major, Army Medical Corps

and soon he and two companions were under way in a speedboat. 'After a short, fast ride,' he later wrote, 'we turned into a bay and saw a bewitching sight. Before us, the *Bismarck* lay like a silver-grey dream from *The Thousand and One Nights*. In spite of her mighty superstructure, gun barrels, and armour, her silhouette was a thing of beauty, almost as though it were worked in filigree.' Then he saw his brother waving for him to come on board. After a joyous, hearty greeting Otto mentioned, not without pride, that the speed of the boat that brought him out was 32 knots, only to hear in reply, 'We can do that with the *Bismarck*, too, and a little more, besides! We're faster than anything stronger and stronger than anything faster, so really nothing can happen to us, and our assignment is just like life insurance.' For Otto Schneider this was an interesting indication of the technological capability and superiority of the *Bismarck*. He found the morale of both officers and men to be outstanding in every respect. 'Until now, up to the time we got to Norway,' several officers told him, 'our operation was nothing but a pleasure cruise.' In the wardroom, over which in retrospect Otto Schneider sensed 'an almost eerie, spooky atmosphere,' they discussed the operational and tactical aspects of the ship's forthcoming mission, although they knew hardly anything about it. In any case, his brother Adalbert absolutely radiated optimism. In his brother's stateroom, Otto admired a photograph of Adalbert's three small daughters. Later, he was invited to have dinner with Adalbert. The brothers also wrote some joint postcards, which Otto offered to take back to Bergen. By the time those cards reached their addressees, the fate of the *Bismarck* had long since been sealed, and the messages were like greetings from the other side of the grave. That night, as they cruised past the rocky cliffs, Adalbert and Otto talked about this and that operation, such as the airborne assault on Crete, but not a word, of course, was said about Hitler's imminent attack on the Soviet Union, because they had no idea it was about to take place. Otto asked how Adalbert, confident as he was, evaluated the danger of the ship being attacked from the air. Adalbert answered with a smile that her defences and armour protection made her almost invulnerable to air attack. When they were training in the Baltic, he said, the Luftwaffe had not been able to score a single hit! For the approaching breakout, Adalbert only wanted there to be as much rain and fog as possible. He apparently knew nothing whatever about the state of British radar.

Then it was time for Otto to say good-bye to his brother and also to the captain who had made this visit possible. When he reported to the latter, Lindemann stood alone, leaning against the forward command post. They shook hands and Schneider looked into a pale, calm face with deep-set eyes. 'Looking back,' Otto Schneider said later, 'I believe that at this moment Lindemann was well aware of the great dangers that the *Bismarck* faced and I think he considered my prospects of ever seeing my brother again very slight. It seemed that he and the Oberkommando der Kriegsmarine differed in their estimates of the situation.'

Had the message relayed by Reichard from B-Dienst headquarters contributed to Lindemann's mood? Had it caused him to regard the evening of 21 May as the last possible chance to make what he regarded as the necessary change in the task force's breakout tactics? And did he realize, with a heavy heart, that such a change, the power to make it lying, as it did, within the jurisdiction of the fleet commander, was scarcely to be expected in view of Lütjens's personality?

Meanwhile, the weather had worsened and the sky became completely overcast. A sharp wind from the southwest chased heavy rain clouds before it and raised whitecaps in the waters of the fjords. Foggy haze hung between the mountains. At about 2300 we turned away from the rocky shoreline, the destroyers in the lead, followed by the *Bismarck* and the *Prinz Eugen*, and resumed our war watches. When we began to head north, shortly before midnight, the wind was blowing out of the south-southwest at Force 4. Looking back, we saw alternating white, yellow, and red lights flickering in the clouds over the mainland. Group North informed us later in the day that five British planes had flown between the cliffs 10 kilometres north of Bergen and dropped flares and bombs over Kalvanes Bay. Their attack was the result of Flying Officer Suckling's midday reconnaissance, of which we were still unaware. The beams of the searchlights ashore and the flashes of the antiaircraft batteries had heightened the light effects in the sky. I did not learn until very much later that, because of the weather, the British could make out hardly anything and dropped their bombs simply on suspicion.

According to plan, around 0400 on 22 May, Lütjens released the destroyers that had shielded our formation from British submarines. We were in the latitude of Trondheim, and I can still see the three ships disappearing towards the coast in the morning mist. For the first time I felt that we really had left home and Exercise Rhine had begun. From now on, the *Bismarck* and the *Prinz Eugen* were alone.

As I write this story, I have to remind myself repeatedly that the young officers on board that morning had no knowledge whatever of the defensive measures that the British were then taking against Exercise Rhine. However, having been told by Reichard the previous evening about the alerting of the British air force, I assumed that the enemy's naval forces would also be looking for us.

And the mere thought of that inspired a prickly anxiety over what being in these narrow waters, the outposts of British sea power, under those conditions might entail. On the other hand, it was not long since the intercepted British radio order had gone out, so the probability of our being rediscovered soon was slight.

At 0930 or so, Lütjens was informed by Group North that, according to B-Dienst, neither the sailing of his task force nor the British orders to search for 'the battleships' had produced any perceptible consequence, other than intensified British aerial reconnaissance in the north-eastern sector. Group North believed that the enemy was concentrating its search of Norway and the Norwegian Sea too far to the south to find our task force. Thus, it appeared that this leg of our journey had not been detected by the enemy.

Steaming at 24 knots in hazy weather under an overcast sky, the task force reached a position approximately 200 nautical miles from the Norwegian coast, in the latitude Iceland–Norway, at about noon. Weather conditions, which seemed settled, were just what Lütjens hoped to encounter when he attempted to break out into the Atlantic through the northern passage. Accordingly, he advised the *Prinz Eugen* that he intended to proceed through the Denmark Strait, adding that, in the event the weather cleared up, which would reduce the task force's prospects for a breakthrough, he would first rendezvous with the *Weissenburg*.

At 1237, the *Bismarck* sounded her submarine and aircraft alarms – a periscope-sighting had been reported. The task force turned to port and steered a zigzag course for half an hour, but nothing transpired and at 1307 it resumed its former course. The weather was still favourable; in fact, it seemed inclined to become our best ally. By 1800 it was raining and a southwesterly wind was blowing at Force 3. Visibility fell to between 300 and 400 metres, and patches of fog appeared. A damp cold gripped us, and the *Bismarck* glistened all the way to her foretop under a silvery sheen of moisture. It was a wonderful sight. In order to maintain contact and station, both ships turned on their signal lights or small searchlights every now and again, and, when the fog was particularly thick, the *Bismarck* shone her big searchlights astern to help the *Prinz* keep station. We were now in the northern latitudes, where the nights are almost as light as the days, so we could stay in a tight formation and maintain 24 knots even in poor visibility. Our passage was truly ghostly, as we slid at high speed through an un- known, endless, eerie world and left not a trace. The setting might have been created for the 'perfect' breakout.

Low, dark rain clouds driven by a steady wind from astern ran with us like sheltering curtains. They were moving faster than we were, and it was only because there were so many of them that, as one overtook us, it was quickly replaced by the next, giving us virtually unbroken protection from hostile eyes. Despite the dampness, when I was not on watch I went for a stroll on the quarterdeck. The fleet staff's meteorologist, Dr Heinz Externbrink, happened to be doing the same thing, and I fell in with him. I could not resist asking him if he agreed that we should increase speed, so that we could keep up with the clouds and take advantage of their cover for as long as possible. He replied: 'You've no idea how many times I've suggested that to Lütjens. I've warned him repeatedly that if we don't do so we'll have to count on unpleasantly good visibility in the Denmark Strait. But he won't budge. He simply rejects the idea without giving any reasons.' Externbrink was worried sick, and the next day proved that his fears were not groundless.

After 2300 on this 22 May, Lütjens received three very

important radio messages from Group North. The first, practically a repetition of the one he'd received that morning, read, 'Assumption that breakout has not yet been detected by the enemy reconfirmed.' The second, based on aerial reconnaissance of Scapa Flow, stated: 'Partly visual reconnaissance Scapa 22.5. Four battleships, one possibly an aircraft carrier, apparently six light cruisers, several destroyers. Thus no change from 21 May and passage through the Norwegian Narrows not noticed.'[5] Didn't 'no change' once more confirm that the *Bismarck* and the *Prinz Eugen* had left Norway without being detected? What renewed confidence Lütjens must have gained from that! Wasn't his intention to break through in the north without delay absolutely correct? And at 2322 he ordered a course change to the west: a course toward the Denmark Strait.

Shortly thereafter, the third signal arrived. In it, Group North reported that no operational commitment of enemy naval forces had yet been noted and that in the past days our U-boats had scored great successes south of Greenland. The landings in Crete, which we had begun on 20 May, were going according to plan and, in view of the sinking of several British cruisers off Crete, an *early* appearance of our fleet on the Atlantic sea lanes promised to inflict serious new damage on the British position at

[5] A pencilled note regarding this report in MGFA-DZ III M 307/5, 'Preparatory Directives and Operational Orders of the Seekriegsleitung,' page 281, reads: 'This visual reconnaissance must be very strongly doubted on the basis of *later* knowledge. The matter in which it was relayed is not apparent to me. Should it have caused the fleet commander to attempt the breakthrough into the Atlantic, without pausing in the north, it can only be described as fateful. LNB MVO (signature illegible).' Later, in October 1942, the Naval High Command commented in its MDV 601 on the results of this Luftwaffe reconnaissance flight: 'Subsequent determinations allow it to be taken for certain that the visual reconnaissance of 22 May, according to which four battleships lay in Scapa Flow, was in error.'

sea.[6] Naturally, this message strengthened Admiral Lüt-jens's resolve – indeed, it made him feel indirectly ordered – to carry on with Exercise Rhine without the slightest delay.

The truth of the matter was that our departure from Norway had been noticed by the enemy, and the German report on the ships at Scapa Flow was wrong. We were soon to discover all that the hard way.

[6] Admiral Carls noted in the War Diary of Group North: 'I gave this latter information to the fleet, not only because I expected its speedy appearance in the Atlantic to have the result indicated, but because the danger to ships in the north when they do not have the cover of darkness will increase with every delay. I also wanted to indicate that, if the Fleet Commander still had a choice between the Denmark Strait and a southern passage, the latter appeared preferable to me because it would be shorter and quicker.' But Lütjens did not really have a choice, because when he received this message he was already in the latitude of the Denmark Strait.

11
Alarm in Scapa Flow

As early as the beginning of May, the British noted an increase in German aerial reconnaissance in the far north and over Scapa Flow. The commander in chief of the British Home Fleet, Admiral Sir John Tovey, suspected that this activity portended another German surface operation in the Atlantic. His first precautionary measure was to instruct the cruiser *Suffolk*, which was patrolling the Denmark Strait, to keep a sharp watch for a possible German attempt to break out. At the same time, he ordered the cruiser *Norfolk*, flagship of the commander of the First Cruiser Squadron, Rear-Admiral W. F. Wake-Walker, and then lying at a base in Iceland, to relieve the *Suffolk* as necessary.

In the early hours of 21 May Denham's report of the sighting of German warships on a northwesterly course in the Kattegat reached Tovey aboard his flagship *King George V* at Scapa Flow. He immediately attached great significance to this report and began speculating as to what ships were involved, what they were up to, and what was the purpose of the accompanying merchantmen.[1] The admiral thought of the *Bismarck*, of whose recent trials in the eastern Baltic the British Intelligence service had kept him advised. Naturally, he could not be certain that she was one of the 'large warships' sighted, but it seemed wise to base his plans on the assumption that she was. If it turned out that his assumption was false – well, so much the better!

Tovey and his staff worked out four possibilities as to

[1] Since Denham's message made no mention of merchantmen, Tovey was probably told about them in a separate message.

what might be the mission of the reported combination of ships:

The warships were escorting a supply convoy to Norway, and when the latter reached its destination, they would return to Germany.

The warships were escorting the merchant ships to the north, in order to use them for replenishing during their own operations.

The warships were escorting the merchant ships northwards in preparation for a landing in Iceland or the Faeroes, for which they would provide cover.

The warships were escorting the merchant ships only as a secondary mission, their prime one being to get out into the Atlantic.

All these mental gyrations were brought on by our purely accidental meeting with some merchant ships at the entrance to the channel through the Skagerrak minefield!

Since the last of the four hypotheses would be the most threatening to him and at the same time the one the Germans could most quickly implement, that is what Tovey prepared for. He reckoned that any measures he took to counter that threat would be bound to serve as some defence against a landing in Iceland or the Faeroes, if that was what the Germans intended. But which of the five possible routes to the Atlantic would they choose this time? There was the Denmark Strait between Iceland and Greenland, which, in May, was narrowed by pack ice from 200 nautical miles wide to probably 60 nautical miles; the passage between Iceland and the Faeroes, 240 miles wide; the passage between the Faeroes and the Shetlands, 140 miles wide; the Fair Island Channel between the Shetlands and the Orkneys; and the narrow Pentland Firth, between the Orkneys and the coast of Scotland, which for practical purposes could be counted out.

After carefully weighing the pros and cons, Tovey concentrated on the Denmark Strait, but did not ignore the three more southerly routes. At his immediate disposal were the battleships *King George V* and *Prince of Wales*, the battle cruiser *Hood*, the heavy cruisers *Suffolk* and *Norfolk*, eight light cruisers – including the *Galatea*, flagship of the commander of the Second Cruiser Squadron, Rear-Admiral A. T. B. Curteis – and twelve destroyers. Upon receipt of Denham's report, the Admiralty also assigned him the aircraft carrier *Victorious* and the battle cruiser *Repulse*. The *Prince of Wales* and *Victorious* had been in commission for only two months and were not fully combat-ready.

Tovey at once deployed his ships to meet the new situation. He ordered the *Norfolk* and the *Suffolk* to patrol the Denmark Strait together, rather than alternately, sent three cruisers to watch the passage between Iceland and the Faeroes, and divided the rest of his force into two task groups: the *Hood* and the *Prince of Wales* under the command of Vice-Admiral Lancelot Holland; the *King George V*, the *Repulse*, and the *Victorious* under his own command.

In the midst of all this planning, the interpretation of Suckling's photography arrived: so it was the *Bismarck*! She and a *Hipper*-class cruiser in the fjords near Bergen. Tovey's hunch had not played him false. The same evening he sent Holland's task group and six destroyers to watch the passages into the Atlantic, especially those north of 62° latitude. In order to avoid wasting fuel on superfluous searches, he decided not to take his own group to sea until it had been determined that the *Bismarck* and her accompanying cruiser had left Norway. He then had almost twenty-four hours of anxious waiting because the bad weather of 22 May was as great a handicap to British aerial reconnaissance as it was an advantage to the German ships, which that day were steaming across the Norwegian Sea. Late in the afternoon of 22 May a plane left the Orkneys on a daring, low-level reconnaissance flight across the water and over the hilly coast of Norway. That evening Tovey got the report he wanted: the German ships had left Norway. At 2200 he put to sea on a northwesterly course to cover the breakout routes south of the Faeroes.

Winston Churchill cabled President Franklin D. Roosevelt:

Yesterday, twenty-first, *Bismarck*, *Prinz Eugen*, and eight merchant ships located in Bergen. Low clouds prevented air attack. Tonight [we find] they have sailed. We have reason to believe a formidable Atlantic raid is intended. Should we fail to catch them going out, your Navy should surely be able to mark them down for us. *King George V*, *Prince of Wales*, *Hood*, *Repulse*, and aircraft-carrier *Victorious*, with ancillary vessels, will be on their track. Give us the news and we will finish the job.[2]

[2] Winston Churchill, *The Second World War*, Vol. III, p. 272.

12
Lütjens's Operational Decisions

At midnight on 22 May, as British and German forces converged on the northwestern passages into the Atlantic, it is interesting to compare the premises on which the two commanders were basing their actions.

Tovey had had the German task force identified, knew it had left Norway, and anticipated that it would try to enter the Atlantic through the Denmark Strait.

Lütjens knew that the opening stage of Exercise Rhine had become known to the enemy. The several signals he received from Group North on 22 May, however, led him to believe that his northward passage had not been detected and that most of the British Home Fleet was still concentrated at Scapa Flow.

It should here be pointed out that Lütjens, his staff officers, and the diaries of both the fleet and the ship having been lost in the *Bismarck* on 27 May, the considerations and estimates that determined tactical decisions after we left Grimstadfjord on the evening of 21 May cannot be known for certain. Neither the surviving turbine engineer, Kapitänleutnant (Ingenieurwesen) Gerhard Junack, nor I, in charge of the after fire-control station, knew what was going on in the minds of the fleet and ship commands. Like everyone else, we could follow closely only the events that took place in the immediate vicinity of our duty stations. All we knew about Exercise Rhine was what Lindemann had told the ship's company over the loudspeakers on 19 May. Even such basic matters as the route we were planning to take and where we might stop, being components of a secret operational plan, were not made known to the junior officers ahead of time. And none of the warrant officers, petty officers, or men on the fleet staff who might have had even marginal knowledge of what the command of the task force was thinking survived.

Lütjens's taciturnity probably ensured that deliberations at his level were restricted to a very small circle, anyway. Finally, the fact that we were at general quarters almost continually from the time we entered the Denmark Strait on 23 May until the end on 27 May made conversation among the officers next to impossible.

The tactical conduct of the operation must, therefore, be based primarily on the *Bismarck*'s War Diary as it was reconstructed from whatever material was available at installations ashore. Obviously a document so produced cannot be entirely satisfactory because, for example, it cannot show whether the embarked B-Dienst team or shipboard radio and listening equipment provided Lütjens with information that Group North and Group West did not have and, if so, what that information was. Nor can the reconstructed diary show why and how new decisions brought about by significant developments in the course of the operation were reached.

13

First Contact with the Enemy

Early on the morning of 23 May, in foggy, rainy weather, the *Bismarck* and *Prinz Eugen* entered the Denmark Strait. Around 0800 the wind, which had been blowing from the south-southwest, veered to the north-northeast, and thus again came from astern on our new, westerly course. Around noon a new weather forecast from home promised that weather favourable for our undetected passage of the strait would continue on the twenty-fourth: 'Weather 24. Area north of Iceland, southeasterly to easterly wind, Force 6-8, mostly overcast, rain, moderate to poor visibility.' In spite of this welcome message, in the afternoon visibility increased to 50 kilometres, but before long intermittent heavy snow caused it to vary considerably between one point on the horizon and another: to port, in the direction of Iceland, heavy haze hung over the ice-free water; on our bow, in the direction of Greenland, there were shimmering, bluish-white fields of pack ice and the atmosphere was clear. The high glaciers of Greenland stood out clearly in the background, and I had to resist the temptation to let myself be bewitched by this icy landscape longer than was compatible with the watchfulness required of us all as we steamed at high speed through the narrowest part of the strait, with our radar ceaselessly searching the horizon. We would not have welcomed this clear visibility even if we had not been expecting intensified British reconnaissance. I could not help thinking of the warnings Externbrink had given Lütjens.

Suddenly, at 1811, alarm bells sounded throughout the *Bismarck*: vessels to starboard! The task force turned to port but the 'vessels' revealed themselves to be icebergs.

Ice spurs and ice floes piled one on top of another frequently led young men, unaccustomed to recognizing objects at sea, to report nonexistent ships and submarines. Excusable, but dangerous, because when a man had made several incorrect observations he might be afraid to report any sighting. But that wasn't all. Sometimes the air over the glaciers of Greenland caused mirages that fooled even the old sea dogs. When that happened, the officers on the bridge were liable to see ships and shapes that were not there.

Shortly before 1900 we entered the pack ice. From then on, we had to steer a zigzag course through heavy ice floes that could have damaged our hull. In an area three nautical miles wide, visibility ahead and to the edge of the ice to starboard was now completely clear. To port, there was haze in the distance and, in front of the haze, there were patches of fog.

It was 1922 when the *Bismarck*'s alarm bells sounded again. This time our hydrophones and radar had picked up a contact on our port bow. I stared through my director but could not see anything. Perhaps the contact was hidden from me by the ship's superstructure. Our guns were ready to fire, awaiting only the gunfire-control information. It never came. Whether the 'contact' was a shadow on the edge of a fog bank or a ship bow-on or stern-on, perhaps very well camouflaged, we saw it too fleetingly to fire on it. Our radar registered a ship heading south-southwest at very high speed and plunging into the fog. As the contact moved out of sight, the shadowy outline of a massive superstructure and three stacks was discernible for a few seconds. That was the silhouette of a heavy cruiser – as we learned later, the *Suffolk*. Thereafter the hydrophone and radar bearing of the vanished enemy soon shifted astern and the range increased. With exemplary speed, the B-Dienst team in the *Prinz Eugen* deciphered the radio signal by which the *Suffolk* had

From 1800 to 2400, German Summer Time, on 23 May. Breakout through the Denmark Strait. (Diagram courtesy of Jürgen Rohwer.)

reported us in the course of her turn: 'One battleship, one cruiser in sight at 20°. Range seven nautical miles, course 240°.' Lütjens reported to Group North the sighting of a heavy cruiser. When shortly afterwards we saw the *Suffolk* clearly and for some time, she was at the limit of visibility. Her small silhouette revealed that she was trailing us astern.

There was another alarm in the *Bismarck* at 2030 and 'full speed ahead' was ordered. Our forward radar had made a new contact. Over the loudspeakers, Lindemann informed the crew, 'Enemy in sight to port, our ship accepts battle.' Looking through my director in the indicated direction, at first I could see nothing at all. Then the outline of a three-stack heavy cruiser emerged briefly from the fog. It was the *Norfolk*, summoned by the *Suffolk*, with which we had collided, so to speak, and which had suddenly discovered her alarming proximity to our big guns. Flashes came from our guns, which were now trained on her, and in a moment we could see the splashes of our shells rise around the cruiser, which laid down smoke and turned away at full speed to disappear into the fog. According to the *Norfolk*'s after-action report, three of our five salvoes, all that we could fire in so short a time, straddled their target. A few shell fragments landed on board but no hits were scored. The *Norfolk* stayed hidden in the fog for a while, then reappeared astern to join the *Suffolk* in shadowing us. The word was passed to our crew, 'Enemy cruisers are sticking to our course in order to maintain contact.'

It now developed that the jolts caused by the firing of our big guns had put our forward radar out of action and, since the *Bismarck* was in the lead, our task force was blind to any threat from ahead. In order to overcome this disability and also to have the ship with the heavier guns near the shadowers astern, Lütjens ordered a 'number

change', which meant that the *Prinz Eugen*, her forward
radar intact, would take the lead. In the Kriegsmarine
number changes were routine evolutions: the ship in the
rear pulled out of the line and increased speed, while the
leading ship slowed down until the overtaking one had
taken her place at the head of the line. That was supposed
to happen this time, but instead of a routine manoeuvre
we had a little excitement. Lindemann happened to be
inspecting my battle station and asking questions about
this and that, when he received a report from a talker on
the bridge. Hurrying forward, he was confronted with an
alarming sight: the *Bismarck* and the *Prinz Eugen* were on
a collision course! Without waiting to get back to the
bridge, he had his orders to the helm relayed – and the
danger passed.

Thus the thing we most wanted to avoid, an encounter
with British naval forces, had happened at the very
beginning of Exercise Rhine. As I have probably emphasized enough already, such an encounter was highly
undesirable because an undetected breakout was so important to the success of our commerce warfare in the
Atlantic. We younger officers still did not know that
Tovey was expecting us to be in this area and had
strengthened his surveillance of the Denmark Strait two
days earlier. Nor did we know that there had been no
German aerial reconnaissance of the strait since a Focke-
Wulf had flown over it four days before, on 19 May, and
had not observed anything unusual. Not only being unaware of these things but counting on the fact that our
departure from Norway was still a secret, this sudden
encounter with British cruisers came as a shock to me,
especially as it was reasonable to assume that there would
be other enemy ships in these rather narrow waters. But at
the same time, I regarded it as only the opening act, and
naturally we were confident that we would be able to ward

off the threat. Lütjens's next moves were aimed at either shaking off our pursuers or sinking them.

Now, the *Suffolk* and the *Norfolk* were both maintaining contact with us from astern and at the limit of visibility – the *Suffolk* to starboard, where visibility was good; the *Norfolk* to port, where there were long stretches of fog. Most of the time, I had a good view of the *Suffolk* and occasionally could see them both. Since at least the tip of a mast was always visible on the horizon, it gradually dawned on us that these annoying hangers-on must have better means of maintaining contact than optical instruments.

Through dark grey seas and white wave crests, the pursuit continued. At almost 30 knots we sped through the half-light of the Arctic night, through fog banks, rain squalls, and snow squalls, every now and again adding to the cover the elements gave us by laying down smoke. In an attempt to shake off our pursuers, we changed course and sought the shelter of every patch of haze; but it did no good. The British cruisers were continuously informed of our position, course, and speed, which they radioed to Tovey. Their reports were intercepted by our B-Dienst team and in five minutes were laid before Lütjens. They read like a minute-by-minute account of the movements of his task force – this phase of his operation was an open book to Tovey. What a depressing beginning for Exercise Rhine!

Lütjens decided to take the offensive. Around 2200, under cover of a rain squall, he had the *Bismarck* make a 180-degree turn. He intended to surprise the *Suffolk* by suddenly running out of the squall and attacking her when she came into view, but when we emerged, there was no enemy to be seen. It looked as though the cruiser had seen through our manoeuvre in time; in any case, she had turned and moved away from us at high speed. For a while we pursued her, in the hope of getting her in sight. Then

Lütjens gave up, not wanting to be drawn too far back to the east, no matter what the enticement. He ordered the *Bismarck* to turn back and resume her former position in the task force. The *Suffolk* eventually caught up with us, but Lütjens did not take the offensive again. He assumed that it would not turn out any differently, and he was undoubtedly correct.

We had another excitement when the word was passed, 'Aircraft off port beam!' In the far distance, a Catalina flying boat, evidently from Iceland, was banking as it searched the area; then, apparently unsuccessful, it turned away and disappeared. We could see it clearly outlined against the sky, but for its crew the grey hulls of the *Bismarck* and *Prinz Eugen* probably blended into the leaden hue of the Arctic sea.

Shortly before midnight our task force was enveloped in a heavy snow storm, into which our followers soon ran. Visibility shrank to a nautical mile, and the cruisers' signals ceased. On our bridge the atmosphere was tense: perhaps there would be no more. Were we to be lucky for once? But the respite lasted only three hours. Lütjens concluded that the British had an efficient long-range radar system, a conclusion that threw his whole concept of surface warfare in the Atlantic into a disturbing new dimension.

In fact, only shortly before, the *Suffolk* had had a modern radar installed, by means of which she could reconnoitre up to 24,000 metres. It was blind only in a small sector astern of the ship, where its impulses were blocked by the ship's superstructure. The *Norfolk* had to get along with an older and less efficient radar.

Although we continued to hope that somehow we would succeed in shaking off our shadowers, we were haunted by concern as to what other ships they might have called on to join them.

14
The Hood *Blows Up*

The early morning of 24 May brought radiantly clear weather and moderate seas. Steaming in the same order as the previous evening, the *Prinz Eugen* in the lead, the *Bismarck* in her wake, we were following a southwesterly course at a speed of 28 knots. Below, in the three turbine rooms, a warrant officer (machinist), two petty officers, and six stokers were on duty at all times. The warrant officer, the senior petty officer, and one stoker stood on the control platform, the second petty officer and the other five stokers tended the auxiliary engines and the fresh-water generator. Every lever and every control had to be examined again and again to make sure that the 150,000 horsepower propulsion plant was performing precisely as it should. Because of the high steam pressures at speeds such as we were then making, the slightest error in handling could have catastrophic consequences. And everyone on board sensed that the hours to come would bring great decisions.

The watch on the bridge and all the lookouts paid particular attention to the southeastern horizon, from which direction other enemy units were most likely to come. And we were certainly not disappointed.

Not long after 0500, the hydrophones in the *Prinz Eugen* picked up ship noises to port, and at 0509 Group North radioed that shortly before 0500 the *Suffolk* had again reported our position, course and speed to Scapa Flow. It must have been around 0545, the rising sun having already lit up the horizon, when the smoke plumes of two ships and then the tips of their masts came into view on our port beam. General quarters was sounded on the *Bismarck*. Through my director, I watched as the masts in the distance grew higher and higher, reached their full length, and the silhouettes of the ships below them became visible. I could hear our first gunnery officer, Korvettenkapitän Adalbert Schneider, speaking on the fire-control telephone. His hour had come, and all our thoughts and good wishes were with that competent, sensible man. How was it that a young seaman in the *Bismarck* had summed up his own and his comrades' feelings? 'Next to the captain, the first gunnery officer, Korvettenkapitän Schneider, has all my respect and confidence!' Now I heard Schneider saying he thought the approaching ships were heavy cruisers and giving targeting information on the lead one; I heard our second gunnery officer, Korvettenkapitän Helmut Albrecht, who was in the forward control station, expressing first mildly, then definitely, doubt that the ships were heavy cruisers and saying that he thought they were battle cruisers or battleships. Then the turrets were trained, the 38-centimetre guns loaded, and all we needed was the Fleet Commander's permission to fire.

Meanwhile, the enemy ships were rapidly closing their original range of more than 30,000 metres. I estimated that they were steaming at about the same speed we were, 28 knots. To approach nearly bow-on as they were doing, appeared to me absolutely foolhardy; it reminded me of an enraged bull charging without knowing what he's up against. But, since the British admiral obviously knew that, his impetuous approach must, I thought, have something to do with gunnery. Presumably, he wanted to close the range rapidly, so as to get out of the way of plunging fire.[1] But there was not time to ponder such considerations

---

[1] Captain S.W. Roskill writes in *The War at Sea*, Vol. 1, p.398: 'Admiral Holland must also have considered whether it would be to his advantage to fight the enemy at long or short ranges. He had no information regarding the ranges at which the *Bismarck* would be most vulnerable to the gunfire of his own ships, but he did know that the *Prince of Wales* should be safe from vital hits by heavy shells from maximum gun range

at this moment. Whatever the British tactic was, the exciting reality was that the ships were getting nearer and nearer to us.

The clock showed 0553. The range, I figured, was less than 20,000 metres. There were flashes like lightning out there! Still approaching nearly bow-on, the enemy had opened fire. *Donnerwetter!* Those flashes couldn't be coming from a cruiser's medium-calibre guns. Certain that we would immediately return the fire, I braced myself for 'Permission to fire' and the thunder of our guns that would follow. Nothing happened. We in the after station looked at one another in bewilderment. Why weren't we doing something? The question hung in the air. Schneider's voice came over the telephone. 'Request permission to fire.' Silence. Schneider again: 'Enemy has opened fire,' 'Enemy's salvoes well grouped,' and, anew, 'Request permission to fire.' Still no response. Lütjens was hesitating. The tension-laden seconds stretched into minutes. The British ships were turning slightly to port, the lead ship showing an extremely long forecastle and two heavy twin turrets. On the telephone I heard Albrecht shout, 'The *Hood* – it's the *Hood*!' It was an unforgettable moment. There she was, the famous warship, once the largest in the world, that had been the 'terror' of so many of our war games. Two minutes had gone by since the British opened fire. Lindemann could restrain himself no longer and he was heard to mutter to himself, 'I will not let my ship be shot out from under my ass.' Then, at last, he came on the intercom and gave the word, 'Permission to fire!'

---

down to about 13,000 yards, and that the *Hood* should become progressively more immune from such hits as the range approached 12,000 yards and the enemy shell trajectories flattened. At long ranges the *Hood*, which lacked heavy horizontal armour, would be very vulnerable to plunging fire by heavy shells. There were, therefore, strong arguments in favour of pressing in to fight the *Bismarck* at comparatively short ranges.'

Both the German ships concentrated their fire on the *Hood*, while she, deceived, as our enemies often were, by the similarity of design of all our ship types, was firing at the *Prinz Eugen*, in the belief that she was the *Bismarck*. The captain of the other British ship, which turned out to be the battleship *Prince of Wales*, realizing what had happened, began firing at the *Bismarck*, despite Admiral Holland's order to concentrate fire on the leading German ship. About four minutes after the firing began and after six salvoes had been aimed at the *Hood*, Lütjens ordered the *Prinz Eugen* to take the *Prince of Wales*, which he referred to as the *King George V*, under fire. Having been ordered to keep our old fellow travellers, the *Norfolk* and *Suffolk*, under continuous observation in case they launched torpedoes at us, I could no longer watch what was going on off our port beam. I had to depend on what I could hear over the fire-control telephone.

Lindemann's permission for us to fire was immediately followed by our first heavy salvo. The *Bismarck* was in action, and the rumble of her gunfire could be heard as far away as Reykjavik, the capital of Iceland.[2] I heard Schneider order the first salvo and heard his observation of the fall of the shot, 'short'. He corrected the range and deflection, then ordered a 400-metre bracket.[3] The long salvo he described as 'over', the base salvo as 'straddling', and immediately ordered, 'Full salvoes good rapid'. He had thus laid his battery squarely on target at the very outset of the engagement.

I had to concentrate on watching the *Suffolk* and *Norfolk*, but I must say I found it very difficult to deny

[2] In 1953, as the chargé d'affaires ad interim of the Federal Republic of Germany, I was invited to a state dinner at which the foreign minister of Iceland, Bjarni Benediktsson, told me that he was in Reykjavik and clearly heard the sound of the battle.
[3] The lateral fall of shot was corrected by adjusting the bearing.

myself glimpses of the morning's main event. The cruisers, still twelve to fifteen nautical miles astern, followed on our course, a little to one side of our wake. There was no evidence that they were preparing to launch a torpedo attack. The *Suffolk* fired a few salvoes, but they fell hopelessly short. Wake-Walker in the *Norfolk* appeared to have left the battlefield completely in the hands of the senior officer, Holland, in the *Hood*. I continued to hear Schneider's calm voice making gunnery corrections and observations. 'The enemy is burning,' he said once, and then 'Full salvoes good rapid'. The forward gunnery computer room was telling him at regular intervals, 'Attention, fall.'

Ever since the action began, I had been wondering whether I would be able to distinguish the sound of the enemy's shells hitting us from the sound of our own firing – with all the noise that was going on, that might not always be easy. Then I heard Schneider again: 'Wow, was that a misfire? That really ate into him.' Over the telephone I heard an ever louder and more excited babble of voices – it seemed as though something sensational was about to happen, if it hadn't already. Convinced that the *Suffolk* and *Norfolk* would leave us in peace for at least a few minutes, I entrusted the temporary surveillance of the horizon astern through the starboard director to one of my petty officers and went to the port director. While I was still turning it toward the *Hood*, I heard a shout, 'She's blowing up!' 'She' – that could only be the *Hood*! The sight I then saw is something I shall never forget. At first the *Hood* was nowhere to be seen; in her place was a colossal pillar of black smoke reaching into the sky. Gradually, at the foot of the pillar, I made out the bow of the battle cruiser projecting upwards at an angle, a sure sign that she had broken in two. Then I saw something I could hardly believe: a flash of orange coming from her forward guns! Although her fighting days had ended, the *Hood* was firing a last salvo. I felt a great respect for those men over there.

At 0557 one of our observers had spotted a quick-spreading fire forward of the *Hood*'s after mast; the fourth salvo from the *Prinz Eugen* had set fire to ready ammunition. Four minutes later, a heavy salvo from the *Bismarck* hit the *Hood* and sent a mountain of flame and a yellowish-white fireball bursting up between her masts and soaring into the sky. White stars, probably molten pieces of metal, shot out from the black smoke that followed the flame, and huge fragments, one of which looked like a main turret, whirled through the air like toys. Wreckage of every description littered the water around the *Hood*, one especially conspicuous piece remaining afire for a long time and giving off clouds of dense, black smoke.

Another observer, on duty in the charthouse as an assistant to Korvettenkapitän Wolf Neuendorff, the navigator, described what he saw:

'Straddling,' boomed out of the loudspeaker. I was standing with Kapitän Neuendorff in front of the chart on which we were continuously recording our course. We put our instruments down and hurried to the eye-slits in the forward conning tower, looked through, and asked ourselves, what does he mean, straddling? At first we could see nothing but what we saw moments later could not have been conjured up by even the wildest imagination. Suddenly, the *Hood* split in two, and thousands of tons of steel were hurled into the air. More than a thousand men died. Although the range was still about 18,000 metres, the fireball that developed where the *Hood* still was seemed near enough to touch. It was so close that I shut my eyes but curiosity made me open them again a second or two later. It was like being in a hurricane. Every nerve in my body felt the pressure of the explosions. If I have one wish, it is that my children may be spared such an experience.

In my director I now saw the after part of the *Hood* drift away and quickly sink. Her forward section sank slowly, and soon there was nothing to be seen where the pride of the Royal Navy, the 48,000-ton[4] 'mighty *Hood*', had so suddenly suffered the fate Admiral Holland had in mind for the two German ships. From the time the firing began, only six minutes passed before a shell from the *Bismarck* penetrated the *Hood*'s armour protection at a point never definitely established and detonated more than 100 tons of gunpowder in the ammunition room of one of her main turrets. How reminiscent of what happened to the battle cruisers *Queen Mary*, *Indefatigable*, and *Invincible* at the battle of Jutland in 1916! The *Hood* met her end in the midst of battle. She left only three survivors in the ice-cold waters, and they were picked up by a British destroyer and landed at Reykjavik.

At their battle stations, our men were kept informed of the course of the action by the ship's watch. They heard, 'Enemy in sight' – 'Opponent has opened fire' – they waited to hear the response of our own guns. A few minutes later it came, and each salvo made the ship shudder. Salvo after salvo was leaving the *Bismarck*'s guns and her engines were running smoothly, when the men below heard, '*Hood* is burning', and, a little later, '*Hood* is exploding'. They just stared at one another in disbelief. Then the shock passed and the jubilation knew no bounds. Overwhelmed with joy and pride in the victory, they slapped one another on the back and shook hands. Their superiors had a hard time getting them back to work and convincing them that the battle wasn't over and that every man must continue to do his duty.

When the *Hood* had gone, our heavy guns were ordered to 'Shift to left target'. That meant combining our fire with that of the *Prinz Eugen* which, along with our own medium guns, had been firing at this target for some

---

[4] Full-load displacement in 1941

From 0530 to 0620, German Summer Time, on 24 May. The battle off Iceland. (Diagram courtesy of Jürgen Rohwer.)

Labels within diagram:

N

0620 SUFFOLK

0620 BISMARCK PRINZ EUGEN

0537

0543

BISMARCK opens fire on HOOD

0620 NORFOLK

bearings taken on British radio signal

enemy sighted optically

PRINZ EUGEN

0555

0559

0601

0609

last salvo

Change of target to PRINCE OF WALES

0620

Evasive manoeuvres from torpedo tracks

0530 PR. OF WALES

HOOD

0537

0543

hits on PRINCE OF WALES

0553 HOOD + PR. OF WALES open fire

0558 HOOD burning

0601

HOOD blows up

0603 PRINCE OF WALES turns away

0609

0620

minutes. The *Prince of Wales*, which, in obedience to
Admiral Holland's last command, was turning 20 degrees
to port when the *Hood* blew up, had to change direction
to avoid the wreckage of her vanished leader. She was
then at approximately the same range and on the same
course as the *Hood* had been. Consequently, Schneider
could continue the action without adjusting the firing
data. Because our courses were converging, the range
soon closed to 14,000 metres and the *Prince of Wales* was
taking shells from both the German ships. By this time I
was back watching for a torpedo attack from the *Norfolk*
and *Suffolk*, listening over the telephone to Schneider's
firing directions. The action did not last much longer.
Clearly it was telling on the *Prince of Wales* and she
turned away to the southeast, laying down a smoke screen
to cover her withdrawal. When the range increased to
22,000 metres, Lütjens gave the command to cease firing
on the *Prince of Wales*. She, too, must have been hard hit,
how hard we had no way of knowing at the time.
Nevertheless, I will tell here what we learned later.

The *Prince of Wales* took four 38-centimetre hits from
the *Bismarck* and three 20.3-centimetre hits from the
Prinz Eugen. One 38-centimetre shell struck her bridge
and killed everyone there except the captain and the chief
signal petty officer. Another put her forward fire-control
station for the secondary battery out of action, and a third
hit her aircraft crane. Number four penetrated below the
waterline, did not explode, and came to rest near one of
her generator rooms. Two 20.3-centimetre shells went
through her hull below the waterline aft, letting in some
600 tons of water which flooded several compartments,
including a shaft alley; the third entered the loading room
of a 13.2-centimetre gun and came to rest there, without
exploding. Besides the damage done by these hits, the
Prince of Wales was suffering from increasingly frequent

trouble with her main turrets, which had been in operation for only two months, so that she was able to get off scarcely a salvo with its full load of shells.

It was in the stars that the shell that struck the bridge of the *Prince of Wales* would not explode until it had passed through, a fact that later brought me the friendship of one of its victims. Lieutenant Esmond Knight, Royal Naval Volunteer Reserve, an actor by profession and a painter and ornithologist by avocation, was keeping lookout through a pair of German Zeiss binoculars. His station was in the unarmoured antiaircraft fire-control position above the bridge, and he was protected only by his steel helmet. He heard something like 'a violently onrushing cyclone,' then someone said, 'Stretcher here, make way.' He had the feeling that he was surrounded by corpses and he smelled blood. People were approaching him and asking, 'What happened to you?' He looked in the direction of the voices and saw nothing – a shell splinter had blinded him. In 1948, after a visitor to Germany brought me greetings from him, he wrote me, 'I was blind for a year, but now I am back in my old profession at the theatre, which makes me very happy.' In 1957 I was a surprise guest in the episode of the BBC's television programme 'This is Your Life' that was devoted to Esmond Knight. That is when we met for the first time, and we have been friends ever since.

But back to the *Bismarck*.

Today, I greatly regret that, especially from this time forward, I was not a party to Lütjens's deliberations, his conferences within the fleet staff, and his conversations with Lindemann, and did not even have any means of hearing about them secondhand. Nothing of them reached me in the after fire-control station. I can only record the statements of survivors to the effect that Lütjens and Lindemann had a difference of opinion regarding breaking off the action with the *Prince of Wales*. Apparently, Lindemann wanted to pursue and destroy the obviously hard-hit enemy, and Lütjens rejected the idea. Lütjens may have feared that if he continued the action he would be drawn in a direction from which other heavy British units might be advancing. German aerial reconnaissance had not, at that time, provided him with accurate information on the disposition of the British Home Fleet. Therefore, he would be running the risk of getting into more action, using up more ammunition, and, of course, having his own ships damaged – none of which prospects he could have welcomed in view of his principal mission, 'war against British trade'. He would have viewed it as necessary to forgo the destruction of another British battleship, which must have been tempting to him also. But the chances are that his reserve prevented him from explaining his decision to Lindemann. 'Differences of opinion' generally result in arguments and, according to one survivor, there was an argument between Lütjens and Lindemann about breaking off the action. It is not clear what the survivor meant by an argument, but it is highly unlikely that there were loud words in the presence of third parties. In view of the personalities of the men involved, it seems certain that whatever took place would have been conducted with military formality. The only thing definite about this is that someone overheard an officer of the fleet staff telling Fregattenkapitän Oels over the telephone that apparently Lindemann had tried to persuade Lütjens to pursue the *Prince of Wales*. According to other reports, there was 'heavy weather' on the bridge for a while. It seems likely that the 'argument' was more evident in the atmosphere than in an exchange of words.[5]

---

[5] In the *Bismarck Episode*, p. 85, Russell Grenfell reports another disagreement on the bridge: 'It became known afterwards that there had been a hot and prolonged argument between the German Admiral

In any event, the men below found it absolutely incomprehensible that, after the destruction of the *Hood*, we did not go after the *Prince of Wales*. They were upset and disappointed.

The battle of Iceland was over and we had used astonishingly little ammunition: the *Bismarck*'s 38-centimetre guns had fired 93 shells and the *Prinz Eugen*'s 20.3-centimetre guns had fired 179. Many shells fell close to the *Prinz*, but she was not hit; the *Bismarck* received three 35.6-centimetre (14 inch) hits. My action station was high up and in the tumult of the battle, I was not aware of any incoming hits, but the men in the spaces below found them easily distinguishable from the firing of our own guns. 'Suddenly,' a petty officer (machinist) wrote of our first hit from the *Prince of Wales*, 'we sensed a different jolt, a different tremor through the body of our ship: a hit, the first hit!'

That first hit, forward of the armoured transverse bulkhead in the forecastle, passed completely through the ship from port to starboard above the waterline but below the bow wave. It damaged the bulkheads between Compartments XX and XXI and Compartments XXI and XXII and left a one-and-a-half metre hole in the exit side. Before long we had nearly 2,000 tons of seawater in our forecastle.

The second hit struck beneath the armoured belt alongside Compartment XIV and exploded against the torpedo bulkhead. It caused flooding of the forward port generator and power station No. 4, and shattered the bulkheads between that room and the two adjacent ones, the port No. 2 boiler room and auxiliary boiler room. Later, it

---

Lütjens in the *Bismarck* and the Captain of the ship, Lindemann, the latter arguing strongly for a return to Germany, the Admiral insisting on a continuance westward.' I regard this account as greatly exaggerated. Nothing has ever suggested to me that Lindemann did any more than urge that the action with the *Prince of Wales* be continued.

was discovered that this hit had also ripped up several of the fuel tanks in the storage and double bottom.

The third shell severed the forepost of one of our service boats, then splashed into the water to starboard without exploding or doing any other apparent damage. The crew of an unarmoured antiaircraft gun nearby was very lucky; although the hit sent splinters of the boat flying in every direction, none of them was injured. Happily, no one was hurt by any of the hits we took at this time.

Our damage-control parties[6] and machinery-repair teams made a detailed inspection of the damage that had been done by the two serious hits and set about making what repairs they could.

Forward, the anchor windlass room was unusable and the lower decks between Compartments XX and ·XXI were flooded. Consequently, the bulkhead behind Compartment XX was being subjected not only to the pressure of static water, but, on account of the big hole in our hull, to that created by our forward motion. To keep it from giving way, a master carpenter's team shored it up while the action was still going on. After the action, a work party led by the second damage-control officer, Oberleutnant (Ingenieurwesen) Karl Ludwig Richter, attempted to enter the forward pumping station through the forecastle

---

[6] We had six twenty-six-man damage-control parties – one each for Compartments I-IV, V-VII, VIII-X, XI-XIII, XIV-XVII, and XVIII-XXII. Each party was led by a warrant officer (machinist), who was assisted by a petty officer. The petty officer of each team assigned most of his men to important points in the area under his supervision but always kept from four to six men with him to take care of emergencies. In the event of a hit or any severe shock, each man checked the various tanks and spaces assigned to him and reported by telephone to the petty officer. The latter gave all the reports of his team to the warrant officer, who relayed a consolidated report to the command centre in Compartment XIV on the upper platform deck, where the First Officer received it. Thus, the ship's command was informed of damage in the shortest time possible.

in order to repair the pumps so that the contents of the forward fuel storage tanks could be transferred to the service tanks near the boiler rooms. But the pumps in Compartment XX were under water, those in Compartment XVII did not help much, and the valves in the oil lines in the forecastle were no longer serviceable. When an effort to divert the oil via the upper deck also failed, we realized that the 1,000 tons of fuel in the forward tanks were not going to be any use to us. Lütjens turned down Lindemann's suggestion of heeling the ship first to one side and then the other and reducing speed in order to allow the holes in our hull to be patched. Later, however, we did slow to 22 knots for a while, which at least allowed matting to be placed over the holes, and the flow of water into the ship was reduced.

Eventually, we had to shut down power station No. 4, in Compartment XIV. We still had sufficient energy for all our action stations, but our 100 per cent reserve capacity was cut in half. The damage-repair parties stuffed the shattered bulkheads in the port No. 2 boiler room and the auxiliary boiler room with hammocks to keep the water in check.

As a result of the flooding, the *Bismarck* was down 3 degrees by the bow and had a 9-degree list to port. The tips of the blades of her starboard propeller were already turning above water. The leader of Damage-Control Team No. 1, Stabsobermaschinist[7] Wilhelm Schmidt, was ordered to flood the flooding and trimming tanks in Compartments II and III, and this improved the situation somewhat.

The lasting effect of the hits in Compartments XIV and XXI was that, mainly because of water pressure on the forward bulkheads, our top speed was restricted to 28 knots. We were now leaving a broad streak of oil in our wake, which was undoubtedly going to help the enemy's

[7] Chief Warrant Officer (Machinist)

reconnaissance and pursuit. The oil was leaking from the service tanks in Compartment XIV and possibly also from the storage tanks in Compartments XX and XXI.

After the 'all clear' was sounded around 0830 the off-duty officers assembled in the wardroom to congratulate our first gunnery officer on the sinking of the *Hood*. Schneider was his friendly and unassuming self as we gathered around to empty a glass of champagne in his honour. His brilliant success made us forget for a few minutes any worries we had about the *Suffolk* and *Norfolk* hanging on to us and the hits we had suffered. None of us grasped the gravity of the damage we had sustained and certainly no one suspected that this would be our last big gathering in the wardroom during Exercise Rhine. Quite obviously, the *Bismarck* was holding her breakout course into the Atlantic and those of us assembled had no reason to think that our operation would not continue according to plan. If anyone doubted the correctness of the Fleet Commander's decision to go on, he did not say so.

At 0632, the battle being over, Lütjens reported to Group North: 'Battle cruiser, probably *Hood*, sunk. Another battleship, *King George V* or *Renown*, turned away damaged. Two heavy cruisers maintain contact.' Atmospheric conditions in the waters off Greenland were so poor that this message was not received in Wilhelmshaven until 1326. When the minutes passed and it was not acknowledged, Lütjens had it repeated continually. At 0705 he enlarged upon it in a brief report, which also failed to reach Group North, 'Have sunk a battleship at approximately 63°10′ North, 32°00′ West.' At 0801, Lütjens advised the Seekriegsleitung of the damage he had received, adding 'Denmark Strait 50 nautical miles wide, floating mines, enemy two radars' and 'Intention: to proceed to St. Nazaire, *Prinz Eugen* [to conduct] cruiser warfare.'

15
Lütjens's Alternatives

The dispatch of his third radio signal, at 0801 on 24 May, shows that within an hour or so after the action off Iceland, Lütjens had decided to make for St Nazaire. That was too soon for him to have had a complete picture of the damage the *Bismarck* had suffered or, most important, of what shipboard repairs we would be able to make. The time of his signal shows further that even as we in the wardroom were rejoicing in the assumption that the operation would continue as planned, he had already informed the Seekriegsleitung that such was not his intention. Not until noon, when we changed course from southwest to south, did the news go around, to the officers' considerable surprise.

Before that, I had been wondering, as I'm sure the other officers had too, what Lütjens's decision would be when he knew the full extent of our damage and could tell how, if at all, the enemy's situation had changed. I, of course, had no idea what redeployment of his forces Tovey might consider necessary, but Lütjens had probably already received information on this subject from the B-Dienst in the *Bismarck* and *Prinz Eugen* and in Germany. Therefore, I was sure he would have weighed all the factors he would have to take into consideration in deciding whether to continue the operation immediately, to disappear into the Atlantic and make emergency repairs, to make for a tanker and resupply, to make for a port in western France, to return to Norway, or even to return home.

The only thing clear to me at the moment was that our

operation had not gone at all according to our hopes: our breakthrough was anything but undetected, in fact we had been in a battle. It was true that we had scored a tactical victory over two warships, but we had lost the element of surprise, which was so important to the success of our commerce raiding on the high seas. On top of that, even though the battle was over, we still had our unwelcome companions astern. Would we be able to shake them off – now that our speed had been reduced?

I then took to wondering whether we had any chance of commerce raiding after our breakthrough under the eyes of the enemy. What ships would the enemy bring against us and how long would it take to get them there? What was the fleet staff thinking? What did Lindemann think, and what suggestions had he made to Lütjens? Question after question came to mind, but there was no one from whom to expect answers. They would have to be deduced from the execution of Lütjens's new decisions.

The answer came around midday, in the form of our change of course to the south. So, Lütjens had decided to make for western France. But what had so suddenly moved him to try to reach port when he had just decided against the highly promising pursuit of the wounded *Prince of Wales* in order to conduct commerce warfare – the commerce warfare he now had obviously decided not to pursue?

Although, when he ordered our course change, Lütjens could hardly have been absolutely certain what repairs could be made on board, he must have known how alarming the damage was: two holes in our hull, 2,000 tons of water in our forecastle, our speed reduced by 2 knots, the threat that two of our boilers would have to be shut down, 1,000 tons of fuel oil inaccessible in our forward storage tanks, the steady leakage of fuel, and the loss of some of our electric power. It would not have taken him long to realize that little could be done about these things aboard ship and, therefore, decide to look for a port. But that was not all. It was no secret in the ship that Lütjens was much impressed by the excellent performance of the radar carried by the two British cruisers. That the *Suffolk* and *Norfolk* had been able to stay in contact at long range through the rain, fog, and snow of the Denmark Strait made him think that the British definitely had a technological superiority in this area. This is why he mentioned 'enemy two radars' in his radio signal to the Seekriegsleitung at 0801. Furthermore, he was probably disheartened by the fact that the few salvoes fired at the *Norfolk* the night before had put the *Bismarck*'s forward radar out of action. Shipboard repair of the radar was obviously impossible.

Around 1000, in the course of a semaphore exchange with the *Prinz Eugen*, it came to light that several radio signals sent by Group North in the previous two days had not been received by the *Bismarck*. The *Prinz Eugen* then passed the messages on to us by visual means. They contained information about the enemy in the Atlantic, mostly the position and course of escort groups, but also what U-boat attacks were doing to them. Lütjens had not suffered any operational disadvantage by not having this information, but the fact that the *Prinz Eugen* had received the signals and his flagship had not must have given him still another cause for concern. His own radio signal of 0632 about the sinking of the *Hood*, in spite of being repeated several times, had apparently not been received by Group North. The two incidents may have shaken his faith in the *Bismarck*'s radio operators and equipment, upon whose flawless functioning during a month-long operation in the Atlantic he had to rely heavily.

Why did Lütjens choose to make for St Nazaire, 2,000 nautical miles away? He could have gone back to Norway, via the south coast of Iceland. Bergen was only 1,100 nautical miles away and Trondheim was 1,300. Or, he could have returned to Norway by way of the Denmark Strait, on which course Trondheim was 1,400 nautical miles distant.

Viewed in terms of the weather, the Denmark Strait, with its generally poor visibility, should have been the most inviting. But hadn't Lütjens just discovered that in spite of poor visibility the British maintained contact? Might not going back through the strait be a repetition of the pursuit, this time in the opposite direction? The *Suffolk* and *Norfolk* were still very near us. What forces would they call up this time? The British Home Fleet had been alerted. Where were Tovey's other big ships, anyway? All Lütjens knew was that they were somewhere between us and Scapa Flow. And mustn't he have remembered how he had been misled by Group North only two days ago – 'Assumption that breakout has not yet been detected by the enemy reconfirmed,' they had told him, and then sent him an erroneous report on the ships still at Scapa Flow. The appearance of the *Hood* and *Prince of Wales* had told him a different story. On the evening of 23 May, Group North had informed him that the weather had made aerial reconnaissance of Scapa Flow impossible that day. The picture, as he saw it, could not have been exactly rosy: any information he had about the enemy was suspect; our top speed had been reduced; it was light both day and night in northern waters at this season; the British would probably be making aerial reconnaissances over the Norwegian Sea; we were leaving a telltale trail of oil in our wake; the effectiveness of British radar and radio direction finders had been demonstrated; a second attempt to get out into the Atlantic, after completing repairs, would be even riskier than the first. It would be much better not to return to Norway.

A reconstruction of the overall situation made later by the Oberkommando der Kriegsmarine showed that the best thing the Fleet Commander could have done was go back through the Denmark Strait. But that was hindsight and was based on knowledge of where the British naval forces were deployed, which Lütjens, naturally, did not have.

Although St Nazaire was 600 nautical miles farther away than Trondheim, we would be on a southerly course, where there would be more hours of darkness, and we would not be in narrow waters. On the high seas we would have a better chance of shaking off our pursuers, and we might be able to get some support from our U-boats or to fuel from one of our tankers positioned in the Atlantic. Other things in favour of St Nazaire were that it had a dry dock large enough for the *Bismarck* and it would be a good point of departure for operations against enemy commerce in the Atlantic.

That Lütjens regarded his visit to St Nazaire as an interruption of Exercise Rhine and not its end, I can only surmise, but his actions up to this point make it almost certain that he did: he had not hesitated to go on with the operation after the day in Grimstadfjord, even though the enemy was known to be alerted; he had maintained course after the first encounter with the British cruisers in the Denmark Strait, instead of reversing it, as he did in a similar operation with the *Gneisenau* and *Scharnhorst* three months earlier; he had broken off the pursuit of the *Prince of Wales* in favour of carrying out his principal mission of commerce warfare. The rumour that the operation would be 'continued' after the repairs there went around the ship in the course of the day.

These speculations about St Nazaire lead back to Lütjens's rejection of Lindemann's suggestion that we reduce speed and heel the ship so that the holes in our hull could be patched. I have not been able to find out why Lütjens did this, nor do I know precisely when he and the captain had this exchange. It must, however, have been after Lütjens decided to make for St Nazaire, because, once he had done so, there would have been no point in doing anything that would delay our getting into port. It might, of course, have been possible for us to do an at-sea repair job on the two shell holes and thus restore our ability to steam at top speed. But would that have made sense when the loss of the two boilers in our forward boiler room, which seemed imminent and actually occurred barely twenty-four hours later, could easily have cancelled out the advantage? Would it have been worth the risk of reducing speed, perhaps for a considerable length of time, while we were still within range of our shadowers, who were in a position to get help from powerful ships? The wisdom of doing so would have been questionable for many reasons and, if Lütjens viewed the pros and cons as I have presented them, I can sympathize with him.

16

Parting with the Prinz Eugen

Shortly before 1000, Lütjens ordered the *Prinz Eugen*, which had been steaming ahead of the *Bismarck*, to drop back and examine the battleship's trail of oil. As the ships passed one another during this change of station, Lindemann asked Brinkmann, his classmate at the Naval School, to signal the results of his observations. The slick was still visible, Brinkmann reported, and was spreading over the surface of the water so rapidly that it was impossible to estimate, even approximately, its extent. The giveaway streak seemed to want to stay with us, and give us away it did, because before long a Sunderland flying boat began cruising back and forth over our wake, beyond the range of our antiaircraft guns. It notified the *Suffolk* that we were trailing oil and kept her informed of the situation. When the *Prinz Eugen* had completed her inspection of the oil slick, she took the lead again and resumed her radar search of the area ahead.

Throughout the morning of the twenty-fourth the *Suffolk* and *Norfolk* hung on and around noon the *Prince of Wales*, directed by a Catalina flying boat, renewed contact at extreme range. The cruisers detected every change of course and speed we made and immediately passed on the information by radio. We had come to accept the three ships as our standing escort. Morale on board did not suffer, however. On the contrary, the crew was optimistic, or seemed to be, that somehow we would shake them off.

Group North, still knowing nothing of any action off

Iceland,[1] signalled Lütjens at about 0830 that it assumed he intended to drive off his shadowers so that the *Prinz Eugen* could refuel, and above all that he would try to lure the enemy to our U-boats. It also noted that, at 1200, operational control of Exercise Rhine would pass to Group West – a transfer that took place on schedule. Other signals received in the course of the morning relayed to the Fleet Commander information B-Dienst had collected about the success the British were having in keeping up with us. This merely reconfirmed to him that his task force was under constant surveillance by the *Suffolk*, *Norfolk*, and *Prince of Wales*.

Somewhere about 1100 the weather suddenly worsened and the sea rose. Rain squalls began to alternate with haze, and broad banks of fog loomed ahead, but now and again the sun broke through. Visibility varied between eighteen and two nautical miles. Difficult as it was for the British shadowers, operating at a distance of around 30,000 metres, they never lost contact.

Shortly before 1400 Lütjens reported to the Seekriegs-leitung and to Group West: '*King George V* and a cruiser keep contact. Intention: if no action, to attempt to lose them after dark.' Obviously, he was still mistaking the *Prince of Wales* for her sister ship, the fleet flagship *King George V*. And the reason he mentioned only one cruiser was that the *Norfolk*'s course took her through fog banks and she was lost to sight for considerable periods of time, which was the case when the message was sent.

In a semaphore message sent to the *Prinz Eugen* some twenty minutes later, Lütjens amplified what he had told Group North at 0801: 'Intend to break contact as follows: *Bismarck* will take a westerly course during a rain squall. *Prinz Eugen* will hold course and speed until forced to

[1] Lütjens's radio signal of 0632, reporting the action, had not yet reached Group North; the repeat sent at 0705 never did get there.

change or for three hours after separating from the *Bismarck*. Then released to fuel from the *Belchen* or *Lothringen*, thereafter to conduct cruiser warfare. Execute on code word *Hood*.'

Lütjens explained his other intentions in a radio signal to the Commander in Chief, U-Boats, who already knew from our shadowers' radio messages where the task force was. The latter was instructed to position whatever boats he had in the west in a line south of the southern tip of Greenland. Lütjens planned to lead his British shadowers over the waiting U-boats on the morning of 25 May. The positioning of the U-boats, relatively far to the west of us, indicates that, in order to escape enemy aerial reconnaissance as long as possible, Lütjens intended to steam well out into the Atlantic before turning in a great southwesterly curve towards St Nazaire. He still thought he had enough fuel for such a detour. At 1508 he gave the Seekriegsleitung and Group West more details about the action off Iceland: '*Hood* destroyed at 0600 this morning in a gunnery action of less than five minutes. *King George V* withdrew after being hit. *Bismarck*'s speed reduced. Down by the bows a result of a hit in the forecastle.'

About this time an aircraft came into view astern. At first, it was taken for a Dornier flying boat and, later, some of the men said that it even gave the German recognition signal in answer to our calls. I have not been able to learn the source of this rather questionable assertion. When the plane closed to around 4,000 metres, however, our antiaircraft officer, Kapitänleutnant Karl Gellert – my good friend from officer candidate and gunnery schools, with whom I had spent a lot of my free time – clearly recognized it as an American boat. It was a Catalina. He immediately sounded the aircraft alarm and almost simultaneously our antiaircraft batteries opened up. The Catalina withdrew. Several times thereafter it

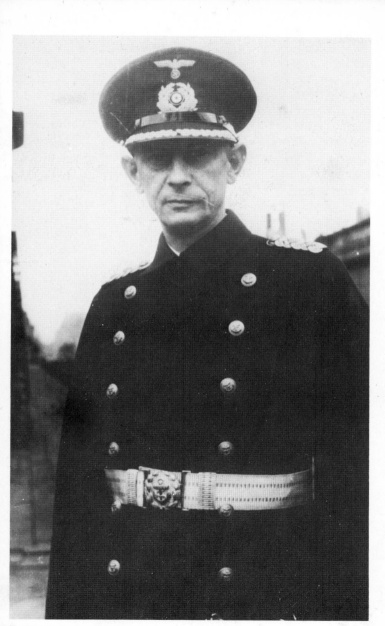

Kapitän zur See Ernst Lindemann.

Looking aft over the *Bismarck* on the slipway at Blohm & Voss. She is complete up to her armoured deck, where an octagonal hole awaits the installation of the armoured barbette for 38-centimetre turret Bruno. The barbettes for turret Caesar and for all six 15-centimetre turrets are in place. (Photograph courtesy of Württembergische Landesbibliothek, Stuttgart)

The *Bismarck* is shown almost complete to her upper-deck level. Barbettes for the main and secondary batteries have been installed. (Photograph courtesy of Württembergische Landesbibliothek, Stuttgart)

The author as a Leutnant zur See aboard the light cruiser *Königsberg* in 1934. He served as a range-finder officer in the *Königsberg* and in her sister, the *Karlsruhe,* thus beginning a career in gunnery. (Photograph from the author's collection)

Because he was not physically very strong, Ernst Lindemann was accepted into the Imperial German Navy 'on probation,' a status that had not been changed even when he had twenty years of naval service behind him. (Photograph courtesy of Hans H. Hildebrand)

The author, adjutant to the
Bismarck's commanding
officer and fourth gunnery
officer, shown here as an
Oberleutnant zur See.
(Photograph from the
author's collection)

After being christened by Frau Dorothea von Loewenfeld, granddaughter of Prince Otto von
Bismarck, the *Bismarck* begins her slide down the ways. Just as the champagne bottle
smashed against her bow, a huge sign was lowered to reveal her name and the family crest
on her bow was uncovered. Before the ship was completed, the crest was removed and the
straight stem was replaced by a flared 'Atlantic' bow. (Photograph courtesy of
Württembergische Landesbibliothek, Stuttgart)

The ensign is hoisted for the first time on the *Bismarck,* formally placing her in commission in the Kriegsmarine. The horizontal and vertical stripes and the Iron Cross in the upper lefthand corner are reminiscent of the white ensign flown by ships of the Imperial German Navy. In the background is the ocean liner *Vaterland,* which was launched earlier the same day. (Photograph from Bundesarchiv, Koblenz)

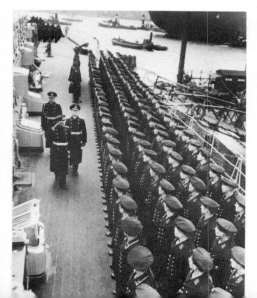

Kapitän zur See Lindemann, followed by the First Officer, Fregattenkapitän Hans Oels, and the author, reviews one of the ship's divisions during commissioning ceremonies. (Photograph from Bundesarchiv, Koblenz)

In the course of her construction, the *Bismarck* went into a giant floating dry dock at Blohm & Voss so that work could be done on her external hull fittings. (Photograph from Bundesarchiv, Koblenz)

While the *Bismarck* was in dry dock, her three propellers, which were almost five metres in diameter, were installed. The workman sitting on the hub of the starboard propeller gives an idea of its size. In the foreground are the ship's twin rudders, her Achilles' heel. (Photograph from Bundesarchiv, Koblenz)

A view of the tower mast and bridges from the forward upper deck, taken while the ship was still outfitting at Blohm & Voss. The platform jutting out from the open bridge was for navigating in such confined waters as canals. It could be folded aft when not in use. Just forward of the two 15-centimetre gun turrets is a group of men in training. In the immediate foreground is turret Bruno. (Photograph from Bundesarchiv, Koblenz)

The forward superstructure of the *Bismarck*. The first level at left is the open bridge. Just aft and to the right is the armoured conning tower containing the protected wheelhouse and forward fire-control station. On the next level is a twin 3.7-centimetre anti-aircraft gun mount. Just above it is the admiral's bridge. On top of the tower mast is the foretop fire-control station. Two of the three directors in each of these fire-control stations can be seen protruding through the roofs. The rotating range-finder cupolas have not yet been fitted. (Photograph from Bundesarchiv, Koblenz)

A view of the forward main-battery turrets from the forecastle. Just aft of and above turret Bruno is the open navigation bridge and the armoured conning tower. The enclosure with large windows is the admiral's bridge. Aft of the wave-breaker, to starboard, a detachment of men is assembled. On the wharf, to port, is one of the Blohm & Voss workshops. (Photograph from Bundesarchiv, Koblenz)

The dark colour on the *Bismarck's* gun barrels is red lead. It was normally applied when the barrel's grey paint blistered and peeled from the heat of extensive firing and had to be scraped. The rings around the guns hold a cable connecting a coil (visible at the muzzle) to an instrument in the turret which measures each shell's time of flight. (Photograph from Ferdinand Urbahns)

Provisions being brought up to the ship's galley from the meat locker below. The *Bismarck's* cold-storage spaces could hold 300 sides of beef and 500 dressed pigs. (Photograph from Ferdinand Urbahns)

A tailor at work in the *Bismarck* during routine hours. When general quarters was sounded, the tailors, like everyone else, would go to assigned battle stations. (Photograph from Ferdinand Urbahns)

The *Bismarck* had a complete cobbler's shop. (Photograph from Ferdinand Urbahns)

The steam press in the *Bismarck*'s laundry. (Photograph from Ferdinand Urbahns)

A mess cook ladles food from a giant cauldron into pots that were then carried to the mess decks of the *Bismarck*. (Photograph from Ferdinánd Urbahns)

Members of the *Bismarck*'s crew at mess. The large pot was used to bring hot food from the central galley. (Photograph from Ferdinand Urbahns)

The *Bismarck* made fast to the main outfitting wharf of Blohm & Voss, Hamburg, which she left for the first time on 15 September 1940. After initial trials, she returned to the yard on 9 December 1940 to get her 'finishing touches.' She had to remain there until 6 March 1941 because the Kiel Canal was blocked by a sunken ship. (Photograph courtesy of Blohm & Voss)

On 15 September 1940, the *Bismarck* cast off from the wharf at Blohm & Voss and got under way for the first time. She is seen here going down the Elbe with the aid of a tug. (Photograph courtesy of Württembergische Landesbibliothek, Stuttgart)

The *Bismarck* going down the Elbe on her first voyage. At one point, she collided with the lead tug *Atlantik* but sustained no damage. (Photograph from the author's collection)

Immediately after coming aboard the *Bismarck*, her commanding officer receives a salute from the ship's honour guard. Behind Lindemann is the author, wearing the aiguillette of adjutant to the commanding officer. (Photograph from Bundesarchiv, Koblenz)

The *Bismarck* shows her rakish, modern lines in Kiel Bay in late 1940. A censor slightly altered her appearance by removing the radar antenna from her foretop range-finder cupola. (Photograph courtesy of Blohm & Voss)

The *Bismarck* returns up the Elbe in December 1940 to complete her yardwork at Blohm & Voss. Her range-finder cupola and radar antenna have been installed above the foretop, but the cupola has not yet been mounted on top of her forward fire-control station. (Photograph courtesy of Blohm & Voss)

Korvettenkapitän (V) Rudolf Hartopf, chief administrative officer of the *Bismarck,* and his assistant, Oberleutnant (V) Günther Tischendorf, supervise the loading of provisions at Scheerhafen in March 1941. 'V' (Verwaltungs) designated an administrative officer. (Photograph from Ferdinand Urbahns)

The *Bismarck*'s camouflage is touched up at Scheerhafen in March 1941. (Photograph from Ferdinand Urbahns)

The heavy cruiser *Prinz Eugen* steaming at high speed on her trials before joining the *Bismarck* for exercises in the Baltic. Only a practised eye could tell the silhouettes of the two ships apart. (Photograph courtesy of Robert O. Dulin, Jr.)

Lindemann reviews machinist petty officers. The geared wheel on the sleeve of the man at the end of the front row indicates his rating. The device on his collar shows that he is a petty officer, first class. (Photograph from Bundesarchiv, Koblenz)

Kapitän zur See Harald Netzbandt, Admiral Lütjens's chief of staff. (Photograph courtesy of Hans H. Hildebrand)

tried to maintain contact at close range, but was driven off by our fire. Around 1630 it disappeared for good – as we know today, because of engine trouble.

We entered another heavy rain squall. Visibility declined and Lütjens, deciding that the moment had come for us to leave the *Prinz Eugen*, gave the signal, 'Execute *Hood*'. It was about 1540. The *Bismarck* increased speed to 28 knots and turned to starboard, in a westerly direction. But our breakaway did not succeed. We were out of sight for a few minutes, then ran out of the squall, right back into the sight of one of our pursuers. We simply completed a circle and, coming up from astern at high speed, rejoined the *Prinz Eugen* some twenty minutes after we'd left her. By visual signal, we told her, '*Bismarck* resumes station here, as there is a cruiser to starboard.' Almost three hours later, when we were in a fog bank, Lütjens repeated the code word *Hood*. We executed the same manoeuvre as before and separated ourselves from the *Prinz Eugen*, this time for good. Turning first to the west and then to the north, we ran into a rain squall, pretty confident that the enemy had not observed the dissolution of our task force. The second gunnery officer of the *Prinz Eugen*, Kapitänleutnant Paul Schmalenbach, later described the parting:

The signal to execute the order for the two ships to separate is given for the second time at 1814. As the *Bismarck* turns away sharply, for the second time, the sea calms. Rain squalls hang like heavy curtains from the low-lying clouds. Watching our 'big brother' disappear gives us a melancholy feeling. Then we see him again for a few minutes, as the flashes of his guns suddenly paint the sea, clouds, and rain squalls dark red. The brown powder smoke that follows makes the scene even more melancholy. It looks as though the ship is still turning somewhat northward.

In the fire of his after turrets, we see clearly again the outline of the mighty ship, the long hull, the tower mast and stack, which

now look like one solid, sturdy building, the after mast, at the top of which the Fleet Commander's flag must be waving. Yet, because the distance between the two ships is rapidly increasing, it can no longer be made out. On the gaff below, waves the battle ensign, still recognizable as a dot.

Then the curtain of rain squalls closes for the last time. The 'big brother' disappears from the sight of the many eyes following him from the *Prinz*, with great anxiety and the very best of wishes. According to orders, which could still be transmitted by signal light, the *Prinz Eugen* reduces speed. We are to act as a decoy, proceeding on the same course as before at a somewhat lower speed, in order to help the *Bismarck*, whose speed has been impaired, to escape from the British shadowers.

We in the *Bismarck* also had heavy hearts as we parted with the faithful *Prinz*. Only reluctantly did we leave her to her own destiny. In retrospect, it must be considered fortunate that we did, for against the concentration of heavy British ships that we later encountered we could not have been of much help to one another. Had we not separated, we probably would have lost the *Prinz Eugen* as well as the *Bismarck* on 27 May. As it was, she was able to reach the port of Brest undamaged on 1 June.

Opposite page: From 0600, German Summer Time, on 24 May to 0400, German Summer Time, on 25 May. Movements of the opposing forces between the battle off Iceland and the loss of contact with the *Bismarck* early on 25 May. (Diagram courtesy of Jürgen Rohwer.)

17

Direct Course for St Nazaire

The *Bismarck*'s gunfire, to which Schmalenbach refers, was being directed at our persistent shadower, the *Suffolk*. We met her in the course of our turn, and opened fire at a range of 18,000 metres. She immediately turned away and laid down smoke, but the *Prince of Wales*, which was farther away from us, opened up with her big guns. We turned to our originally planned southerly course and continued the gunnery duel with the *Prince of Wales*. But the extreme range at which we fought, 28,000 metres, coupled with the glare of the sun on the surface of the water and the clouds of stack smoke, made observation from the main fire-control centre in the foretop so difficult that Schneider was able to fire only single salvoes at long intervals. Since the enemy was astern of us, he eventually ordered me to take over the fire control. Apparently he thought that I, in my station aft, could see better. Such was not the case. The range was too great for me to make reliable observations, either. I told Schneider this, and after a few salvoes had been fired at my direction we got the order to cease fire. Neither side scored a hit in this sporadic exchange of salvoes. At 1914 Lütjens, still under a misapprehension about the identity of the British battleship, reported to the Seekriegsleitung, 'Short action with *King George V* without result. *Prinz Eugen* released to fuel. Enemy maintains contact.'

Since leaving the *Prinz Eugen*, the fact that we were alone gradually sank into our consciousness and there was mounting tension as we wondered what surprises the coming hours and days might bring us. Some things we did not even have to wonder about. If for no other reason than to make up for the shame of losing the *Hood*, the British would do everything they possibly could to bring an overwhelming concentration of powerful ships to bear on us. How many and which would they be? Where were they at the moment and in what combination? These uncertainties created tension and were the most important objects of our speculation. A great deal, if not everything, would depend on our shaking off our shadowers and getting as far as possible along the projected great curve towards western France without being observed. Our fuel supply being tight because of the 1,000 tons cut off in the forecastle, we reduced speed to an economical 21 knots. With a little luck, we would reach St Nazaire without having to fight.

Shortly before 1900 Lütjens received Group West's answer to the radio signal he had sent early that morning saying that he intended to take the *Bismarck* to St Nazaire and to release the *Prinz Eugen* to conduct cruiser warfare. Group West concurred and had already made arrangements for the *Bismarck* to be received at St Nazaire and also at Brest. The auxiliary arrangements at Brest had been made in case it became impossible for any reason for the *Bismarck* to go in to St Nazaire.

Group West made the suggestion that, in the event enemy contact had been shaken off, the *Bismarck* make a long detour en route to port, obviously hoping that this would wear out the British pursuers. It was not a bad idea, and it is more than likely that Lütjens had considered doing just that. What Group West did not know was that the *Bismarck*'s fuel situation had been changed by the damage she had suffered – a fact that had not been reported. Therefore it must have been surprised to receive Lütjens's radio signal of 2056: 'Shaking off contact impossible due to enemy radar. Due to fuel steering direct for St Nazaire.'

Why Lütjens considered our fuel situation so much more serious on the evening of 24 May than he had at midday, I do not know. Perhaps he had finally accepted the fact that there was no way we could draw on the fuel oil stored in the forecastle.

The Fleet Commander's decision to make 'direct for St Nazaire' had immediate and important results. The Commander in Chief, U-Boats, supposing his instructions to form a line of U-boats south of Greenland to be thereby cancelled, adjusted his dispositions to the *Bismarck*'s new course towards France. Appropriate instructions were sent to the *U-93*, *U-43*, *U-46*, *U-557*, *U-66*, and *U-94*. The *U-556* was ordered to act as a scout.

18
Attack by Swordfish Torpedo Planes

Since the fruitless action with the *Prince of Wales*, which took place a little after 1900 on 24 May, the *Bismarck* had held steady on her southerly course. Before long a report came over the ship's loudspeakers that there was probably an aircraft carrier in the area. All our antiaircraft gun crews immediately went on full alert.

Then, around 2330 – it was still light as day[1] – several pairs of aircraft were seen approaching on the port bow. They were beneath a layer of clouds and we could see them clearly, getting into formation to attack us. Naturally, we did not know it then, but they were from the *Victorious*, the carrier that accompanied Tovey's force out of Scapa Flow on the evening of 22 May. Tovey's objective was to intercept the German task force southwest of Iceland, in the unlikely event that, after Admiral Holland's attack with the *Hood* and *Prince of Wales*, interception would still be necessary. It was.

Aircraft alarm! In seconds every antiaircraft gun on the *Bismarck* was ready for action. One after the other, the planes came towards us, nine Swordfish, torpedoes under their fuselages. Daringly they flew through our fire, nearer to the fire-spitting mountain of the *Bismarck*, always nearer and still nearer. Watching through my

[1] It was light as day at midnight because, as pointed out earlier, we were on German Summer Time (one hour ahead of standard Central European Time). At 35° west longitude, about where we were during the air attack, German Summer Time was more than four hours ahead of the true local time. This means that when German Summer Time showed midnight, it was not a true 2000. At our position, approximately 57° north latitude, the sun does not go down until after 2000.

director, which, having been designed for surface targets, had a high degree of magnification but only a narrow field, I could not see all the action. I could see only parts of it, and that only so far as the swirling smoke of our guns allowed. But what I could see was exciting enough.

Our antiaircraft batteries fired anything that would fit into their barrels. Now and again one of our 38-centimetre turrets and frequently our 15-centimetre turrets fired into the water ahead of the aircraft, raising massive water-spouts. To fly into one of those spouts would mean the end. And the aircraft: they were moving so slowly that they seemed to be standing still in the air, and they looked so antiquated. Incredible how the pilots pressed their attack with suicidal courage, as if they did not expect ever again to see a carrier.

In the meanwhile, we had increased speed to 27 knots and begun to zigzag sharply to avoid the torpedoes that were splashing into the water. This was an almost impossible task because of the close range and the low altitude from which the torpedoes were launched. Nevertheless, the captain and the quartermaster, Matrosenhauptge-freiter[2] Hans Hansen, who was steering from the open bridge, did a brilliant job. Some of the planes were only two metres above the water and did not release their torpedoes until they had closed to 400 or 500 metres. It looked to me as though many of them intended to fly on over us after making their attack. The height of impu-dence, I thought.

The enemy's tactics were such that torpedoes were coming at us from several directions at the same time and, in trying to avoid one, we were liable to run into another. Back and forth we zigzagged. All at once the sharp, ringing report of an explosion punctuated the roar of our

[2] Seaman

guns and the *Bismarck* gave a slight shudder. At the moment, I was only aware that whatever had caused it must have taken place forward of my duty station. Although I silently cursed what I supposed was a torpedo hit, my immediate reaction was that it had not done much harm. Undoubtedly launched at close range, it could not possibly have reached its set depth – it would have been dangerous to us if it had – but had probably struck in the area where our armour belt was strongest: at the waterline amidships. That armour, I was sure, would not be bothered by a little aerial torpedo. Nonetheless, I took a careful look at the speed and rudder-position indicators. They showed that the engines and rudder were intact – thank God!

What had happened? A torpedo, perhaps the last one launched, and a surface runner at that, had struck the armour belt amidships on the starboard side and exploded, creating a tall waterspout. It was delivered by a pilot who left his wingman and came in, unnoticed by us, in the glare of the setting sun. The concussion of the hit hurled Oberbootsmann[3] Kurt Kirchberg, who was handling ammunition in the immediate vicinity of the explosion, against something hard. He was killed instantly: the first man to die aboard the *Bismarck*. We sewed up his corpse in sailcloth and laid it in a boat. His death made a deep impression on all his shipmates in that he was the only fatality, but it was especially distressing to those who had come to know him as a strict but capable and understanding superior.

Below, the explosion made it seem as though the ship had been thrust sideways with much greater force than had been the case when the shells hit that morning or than was created by the recoil of our own guns. Our

[3] Warrant Officer

damage-control and fire parties lost no time in inspecting their areas of responsibility and phoning in their reports to the damage-control centre. In the record time of three minutes the ship's command knew the situation in every sector. Hardly any material damage had been done, although Oberartilleriemechaniker[4] Heinrich Juhl and five other men had broken bones.

Shortly before the attack began, Matrosengefreiter[5] Georg Herzog, of the port third 3.7-centimetre mount, spotted three planes to port and sang out, 'Three aircraft approaching at 240 degrees.' 'I had the feeling,' he said later, 'that the British were putting their all into this attack and were coming in with exceptional daring to deliver their torpedoes. It seemed to me that they came within 15 metres of the ship before they turned away.'

Matrosengefreiter Herbert Manthey, of the starboard fifth 2-centimetre mount, noticed that, at first, the incoming planes tried to make a concentrated attack on our port side, then they separated to attack from different directions. When he asked Oberleutnant zur See Sigfrid Dölker, his section commander, about this he was told that three squadrons of torpedo planes had participated in the attack. Our constant zigzagging to avoid torpedoes had greatly complicated his efforts to bring his guns to bear. And towards the end of the attack he heard the explosion to starboard.

Morale in the ship after the attack, whose end was easily told by the cessation of antiaircraft fire, was outstanding. The crew felt even better when they heard that five enemy aircraft had been shot down. In fact, none had been.

Although we weathered it quite well, it cannot be said that we came out of the Swordfish attack unscathed.

[4] Warrant Officer (Ordnance Engineer)
[5] Seaman Apprentice

When we increased speed to 27 knots, water pressure increased correspondingly and that, together with our violent zigzags, caused the matting in the forecastle to rip, and water began rushing in again. The result was that we were still more deeply down by the bow. Furthermore, vibration from our gunfire enlarged the gash in the bulkhead between port boiler room No. 2 and the adjacent electric power station, which had flooded after the shell hit that morning, to such an extent that the boiler room also flooded and had to be given up. We reduced speed and steamed at 16 knots long enough for the matting in the forecastle to be made watertight again. Meanwhile, we resumed course towards St Nazaire.

Sometime after midnight Lütjens reported home, 'Attack by torpedo planes. Torpedo hit on starboard,' and around 0200, 'Torpedo hit not important.'

Soon after the air attack, we became engaged in a brief sea fight, again with the *Prince of Wales*, which had reappeared on the horizon. She fired two salvoes from around 15,000 metres. Schneider answered two or three times with our big guns, but fading light made observation difficult for both sides. The British battleship steamed out of sight and the intermezzo was over.

19

The Admiralty Steps Up the Pursuit

The air attack on the *Bismarck* was the last of the measures that Tovey had planned before leaving Scapa Flow on the evening of 22 May. Despite the impressive performance of the *Suffolk* and *Norfolk* in maintaining contact, the German task force had not been destroyed nor had its speed been so drastically reduced that it would be possible, without doing anything else, to bring other big ships up against it. Nor were there any such ships near enough to be brought up right away. For Tovey and the Admiralty, the failure as such was bad enough, but the loss of the *Hood* made it doubly hard to bear. The *Hood* was not just any battle cruiser. To the Royal Navy, and indeed to the nation, she was the incarnation of British sea power. Wake-Walker had succeeded Holland as senior naval officer on the scene, and his laconic report, '*Hood* has blown up', hit London like a bolt of lightning. If it had been necessary to sink the *Bismarck* before, the loss of the *Hood* made it even more so.

On the evening of 23 May, Tovey with the Home Fleet, consisting of the *King George V*, the *Victorious*, the *Repulse*, several cruisers, and some destroyers, was about 550 nautical miles southeast of the German task force. He had chosen a course to the northwest so that he would be in a position to intercept the German ships whether, after the expected action with Holland's force, they went back through the Denmark Strait or, although heavily damaged, continued to make for the Atlantic. Now, everything was different, and Tovey had very little hope of being able to engage the German task force as long as it continued to the southwest at high speed.

What would the German Fleet Commander do in the changed circumstances? As Tovey saw it, Lütjens was likely to do one of three things: rendezvous with a tanker off the west coast of Greenland or near the Azores; if the *Bismarck* had been damaged in the action with Holland's ships – there were no reports that she had – seek out a port in western France for repairs; return home. Not only was Germany the best place for repairs to be made but, more important, the return of the heroes would give the German propaganda machine material that it could use to excellent effect – the alternative that Winston Churchill later declared would have been the best for the Germans. The three courses of action being equally probable, Tovey decided to compromise and take a course towards the southern tip of Greenland. In doing this, he hoped to guard against what was in his eyes the most dangerous eventuality: the German ships getting out into the Atlantic, where they would be able to interdict supply routes vital to Great Britain. And where the *Bismarck* could inflict damage that he of all people would rather not think about.

In London, the Admiralty reacted to the morning's catastrophic report by making a number of important and far-reaching decisions. There were at this time ten convoys in the North Atlantic, escorted by battleships, cruisers, and destroyers. To rob them of their protection when a German task force was at large would expose them to deadly danger, but it was a risk that had to be taken. All that mattered was to deploy against the *Bismarck* every warship then in the Atlantic or anywhere nearby – and deployed they were, every one of them.[1]

---

[1] See Appendix C

Vice-Admiral Sir James Somerville's Force H, consisting of the battle cruiser *Renown*, the aircraft carrier *Ark Royal*, the cruiser *Sheffield*, and six destroyers, was at Gibraltar, waiting to escort a troop convoy. It was released from this mission and instructed to proceed north for operations against the German task force. The cruiser *London*, which was escorting a convoy from Gibraltar to Great Britain, received orders to change course to intercept the *Bismarck* and *Prinz Eugen*. The cruiser *Edinburgh*, which only shortly before had captured a German blockade-runner near the Azores, was also and without regard to her fuel supply deployed against the German formation. Hundreds of nautical miles to the northwest, the battleship *Ramillies* was instructed to leave the convoy she was escorting and take a course to intercept the German task force. Thousands of miles to the west, in Halifax, the battleship *Revenge* was directed to take over the escort of the convoy the *Ramillies* had left. West of Ireland, the battleship *Rodney*, which was en route to the United States for repairs, was escorting the troop transport *Britannic* across the Atlantic. She, too, received orders to begin operations against the *Bismarck* and *Prinz Eugen*. Three destroyers were assigned to screen her on this new mission. Among them was the *Tartar*, on whose bridge the previous evening Sub-Lieutenant Ludovic Kennedy, the officer of the watch, had received from the hands of a signalman the *Norfolk*'s first report of having sighted the German task force in the Denmark Strait. Ludovic Kennedy, whose book *Pursuit* tells the story of the search for the *Bismarck*, is the son of Captain E. C. Kennedy, who had met a seaman's death as commander of the *Rawalpindi* in action against the *Gneisenau* and *Scharnhorst* in November 1939, when I was fourth gunnery officer of the *Scharnhorst*, the same billet I now held in the *Bismarck*.

Within six hours of the loss of the *Hood*, the British had deployed against us four battleships, two battle cruisers, two aircraft carriers, three heavy cruisers, ten light cruisers, and twenty-one destroyers. And so there began a chase which, in terms of the area involved (more than a million square nautical miles) and the number and strength of the ships engaged, is perhaps unique in naval history.

20
Contact Shaken Off

In the afternoon of 24 May Lütjens learned from Group West that the *Renown*, *Ark Royal*, and a *Sheffield*-class cruiser – in other words, Force H – had sailed from Gibraltar the previous evening, course not known. What Group West did not know, and therefore could not tell Lütjens, was that these ships had left Gibraltar on a convoy-escort mission but had subsequently been redirected against our task force. Lütjens would have assumed the latter objective, anyhow. Whether or not our B-Dienst team gave him any more information about the enemy that same afternoon, I do not know.

It was not until around noon the next day that the Fleet Commander told us anything at all about the drastic measures the British were taking, and then he told us only in general terms. Up to that time every man had made up for the lack of information by using his own imagination. I recall that my imaginings were very vague. It was just that some things were not known. That way, we could still have our moments of hope and, should a critical situation arise, we would deal with it as before, to the best of our ability. Our young crew was inherently optimistic and, surely, the preservation of optimism for as long as possible could only be to the good. An exact awareness of the enemy armada being assembled would have had anything but a healthy effect on the ship's morale.

Midnight gave way to Sunday, 25 May, Admiral Lütjens's birthday, and over our loudspeaker system the ship's company offered him congratulations. Darkness had fallen and our shadowers, the *Suffolk*, *Norfolk*, and *Prince of Wales*, were once again forced to rely on the *Suffolk*'s invaluable radar. Since late the day before, all three of them had been off our port quarter, the *Suffolk* at times being as little as ten nautical miles away from us.[1]

Lütjens, undoubtedly having been informed that our listening devices and radar showed no hostile ships to starboard, evidently decided it was high time to try to break contact. Shortly after 0300, we increased speed and turned to starboard. First, we steered to the west, then to the northwest, to the north, and, when we had described almost a full circle, we took a generally southeasterly course in the direction of St Nazaire. I was not aware of these manoeuvres, either because I was in my completely enclosed control station and in the darkness did not notice the gradual turn, or because I was off duty at the time. The manoeuvre carried out the intention that Lütjens had radioed to the Seekriegsleitung the previous afternoon and that had grown increasingly urgent, 'Intention: if no action, to attempt to break contact after dark.'

Fate seemed to have a birthday present for the Fleet Commander. The *Suffolk*, steering a zigzag course as a defence against possible U-boat attacks, had become accustomed to losing contact with us when she was on the outward leg of her course and the range opened, but regaining it as soon as she turned back towards us. At

[1] It seems curious that Admiral Wake-Walker kept all three of his pursuing ships off the *Bismarck*'s port quarter, the *Suffolk*, with her superior radar, nearer to the *Bismarck* than the *Prince of Wales* and *Norfolk*. At first, he intended to have the *Prince of Wales* engage the *Bismarck* with gunfire from time to time, in the hope that the defensive manoeuvres the latter would be forced to take would draw her to the east, the direction from which Tovey's task force was approaching. But this plan did not work out and was soon abandoned. Keeping his three ships to port enabled Wake-Walker to command them as a unit, but how seriously he considered the risk that the German battleship might be able to slip away to starboard, I am unable to say.

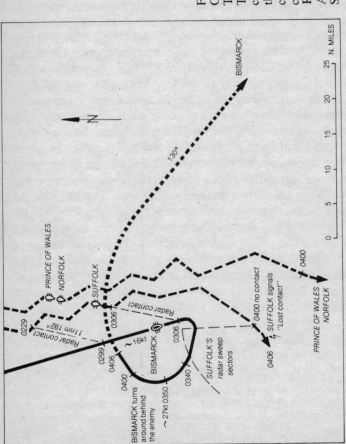

From 0229 to 0406, German Summer Time, on 25 May. The *Bismarck*'s changes of course that led to the loss of contact. (Diagram courtesy of Jürgen Rohwer and Vice-Admiral B. B. Schofield.)

0330 she expected to regain the contact she had lost at 0306. She did not.

Lütjens's great chance had come! But he didn't recognize it. He must have believed that, despite his manoeuvres, the *Bismarck*'s position was still known to his shadowers. He cannot have been aware that by transmitting messages he might be enabling the enemy's direction finders to renew contact with her. After all, his position had been known to the *Suffolk* and *Norfolk* ever since he first encountered them more than twenty-four hours earlier, and radio signals, even long ones, would not really tell the enemy anything new about the position of his flagship. Therefore, he saw no reason for maintaining radio silence, or even any need to use the Kurzsignalverfahren,[2] which at that date was still immune to direction-finding.

It cannot be definitely determined, but this must be how he thought because at around 0700 he radioed Group West, 'A battleship, two heavy cruisers continue to maintain contact.'[3]

When the *Suffolk* was unable to renew contact with the *Bismarck*, she and the *Norfolk*, going on Wake-Walker's assumption that the battleship had broken away to the west, changed course in an attempt to pick her up again. Therefore, by 0700, they had been steaming for several hours in first a southwesterly then a westerly direction. If the *Suffolk*'s radar, with its range of 24,000 metres, could not regain contact with the *Bismarck* at 0330, what chance did it have of doing so at 0700, by which time the *Bismarck* had been steaming for hours in a southeasterly direction? As for the battleship whose presence Lütjens reported, around 0600 the *Prince of Wales* turned to a southerly course in compliance with orders that she join

[2] Short-signal procedure.
[3] This message reached its destination at 0908.

the *King George V*. Therefore, she also had moved too far away from the *Bismarck* to know the latter's position at 0700.

Shortly after 0900 Lütjens radioed to Group West:

Presence of radar on enemy vessels, with range of at least 35,000 metres,[4] has a strong adverse effect on operations in Atlantic. Ships were located in Denmark Strait in thick fog and could never again break contact. Attempts to break contact unsuccessful despite most favourable weather conditions. Refuelling in general no longer possible, unless high speed enables me to disengage. Running fight between 20,800 and 18,000 metres . . . *Hood* destroyed by explosion after five minutes, then changed target to *King George V*, which after clearly observed hit turned away making smoke and was out of sight for several hours. Own ammunition expenditure: 93 shells. Thereafter *King George* accepted action only at extreme range. *Bismarck* hit twice by *King George V*. One of them below side armour Compartments XIII-XIV. Hit in Compartments XX-XXI reduced speed and caused ship to settle a degree and effective loss of oil compartments. Detachment of *Prinz Eugen* made possible by battleship engaging cruiser and battleship in fog. Own radar subject to disturbance, especially from firing.[5]

In the first four sentences of this signal Lütjens reported the perplexing new dimensions that during his passage of the Denmark Strait he had seen looming for the operation of our heavy ships in the Atlantic.

In the course of the past hours Group West got a completely different and correct impression of the scene around the *Bismarck*. Reports sent out by the British shadowers and received by Group West after the dissolution of our task force had, at first, shown some confusion on the part of the enemy. They were still reporting contact with both the *Bismarck* and *Prinz Eugen* at 2230, 24 May,

---

[4] Lütjens overestimated the range of the *Suffolk*'s radar by 11,000 metres.

[5] This signal reached its destination at 0942.

in spite of the fact that the ships had separated shortly after 1800. From 2230 until 0213 the next day, they reported contact with the *Bismarck* alone, then their reports ceased. When several hours passed and no more reports of contact were picked up, it seemed clear that contact had been broken, and at 0846 the Group signalled Lütjens: 'Last report of enemy contact 0213 *Suffolk*. Thereafter continuation of three-digit tactical radio signals but no more open position reports. Have impression that contact has been broken.'

How incomprehensible it must have been for Group West, after 0900, to receive two radio signals from Lütjens reporting that the enemy was still in contact. Why did he still believe his position was known, when even Group West had the impression that contact had been broken? There are four conceivable explanations, in one of which, or in a combination of which, the answer must lie.

First, perhaps the *Bismarck* was still detecting enemy radar pulses, and that made Lütjens think that contact had been maintained. Besides her three radar sets, the *Bismarck* had a radar detector, a simple receiver designed to pick up incoming pulses of enemy radar. Upon receiving such pulses, the detector allowed the wavelength, the frequency and strength of the pulse, and the approximate direction of the sender to be determined. Precise direction-finding, however, was not possible. If such incoming pulses were actually still being picked up at 0700 that day, they could not have been useful to the originating ships, since the pulse reflections had to return to the shadowers' radar transmitter to be registered. For if, as previously mentioned, the range had already become too great for the reflections from the *Bismarck* to return to the *Suffolk*'s radar at 0330, because of the ship's diverging courses, by 0700 the range must have been much too great. Possibly the *Bismarck*'s operators were picking up weak radar pulses beyond effective range of the radar transmitter – in the case of the *Suffolk*, 24,000 metres. Merely to receive a pulse, however, does not necessarily mean that the sender has fixed the target's position. Radar operators must be especially careful to observe and evaluate the strength of an incoming pulse. The ability to do that requires expert training and practice, and whether the *Bismarck*'s radar operators had those qualifications, I cannot say. I am not an expert in this area. In any case, it should be borne in mind that all radar was still in its infancy and there was not much experience to go on. I leave the question open. I think that by 0700 on 25 May our distance from the *Suffolk*, *Norfolk*, and *Prince of Wales* must have been too great for us to pick up even weak pulses from them. Moreover, the three erstwhile shadowers assumed that the *Bismarck* had turned to the west and therefore adjusted their search patterns in that direction. Would they not have used their radar to search the area ahead of them, to the west, rather than behind them, to the east, where the *Bismarck* really was? It is difficult for me to believe that radar pulses were still being picked up by the *Bismarck* at 0700.

Second, the interception of enemy radio traffic might have given Lütjens the impression that his position was still known. It may be that the signals of his shadowers were still so strong that it did not occur to him that there had been any change in their proximity. The possibility is purely theoretical. Nothing concrete concerning it has come to my attention.

Third, it is possible that during these hours our B-Dienst team gave Lütjens information that he took or had to take as an indication that the enemy was still in contact. Had the B-Dienst misinterpreted British tactical signals or operational transmissions? Did it play any other role in this connection? That possibility cannot be excluded.

Fourth, Lütjens might have been so deeply under the spell of what he took to be the superiority of British radar that he was no longer able to imagine anything else. Can the two radio messages he sent on the morning of 25 May therefore have a purely psychological explanation, his feeling of resignation? As stated, it is conceivable. In view of the first four sentences of his second signal, it is even probable.

To draw a convincing conclusion from four such diverse alternatives is difficult. I would, however, like to exclude the first. The second and third I can neither assert nor exclude. Not having any direct knowledge of how Lütjens reacted during the most critical phase of the operation so far, from the beginning of the pursuit by the *Suffolk* and *Norfolk* in the Denmark Strait to the morning of 25 May, I am not in a position to transfer the fourth alternative from the realm of the conceivable into that of the believable. In my view, a veil must remain over the reason why Lütjens supposed that the *Bismarck*'s position was known and therefore did not regard the enemy's ability to take a fix on a radio signal as a new and serious danger to his ship.

After 1000 the *Bismarck* did observe radio silence, and Group West then realized that the signal it sent to Lütjens at 0846 had shown him his error concerning enemy contact. But his attempt to correct his mistake by maintaining radio silence was not enough to repair the damage done by the dispatch of his two radio signals.

21

The British Compute the Bismarck's *Position*

Around 1030, barely an hour and a half after Lütjens sent his second message, Tovey received an urgent signal from the Admiralty informing him that the radio bearing of a ship, supposedly the *Bismarck*, had been picked up at 0852. It gave him the relevant bearings but did not include a determination of our position. This information was omitted because, before he left Scapa Flow, Tovey said he wanted such computations to be done in his flagship.

The bearings the Admiralty sent him were not ideal, however, because they stemmed from stations in Great Britain and, for the most part, ran parallel. Therefore, they did not furnish any reliable points of intersection, and the computations then made in the *King George V* were far from unequivocal. Faced with a choice of positions in which the *Bismarck* might be found, Tovey decided that the most northerly was the most probable. That position was, in fact, so far north that Tovey concluded the *Bismarck* was going home through the Norwegian Sea. When he transmitted it to his ships, most of them, with the *King George V* in the lead, turned to the north or northeast on courses that led away from the *Bismarck*'s true position.

Were we to have two chances of escape in one day, 25 May?

The Admiralty soon began to have doubts about the *Bismarck* steering a northerly course and that afternoon recalculated the coordinates with the help of a fix on another signal sent by Lütjens. As a result, it sent Tovey a more southerly position for the *Bismarck*, one that definitely showed her to be heading for the Bay of Biscay. Tovey meantime had had his computations re-examined and realized that a grave error had been made that morning. After another exchange of thoughts with the Admiralty, more hesitation, and briefly taking a compromise course to the east, he let himself be persuaded that the *Bismarck* was steering for the west coast of France. Accordingly, shortly after 1800 he turned to the southeast. For seven hours the *Bismarck* had been enjoying his gift of space and time, and now he was 150 nautical miles behind her on course for St Nazaire. At 0400 that day, he was 100 nautical miles ahead of her in that direction.

22
A Fateful Sunday

Around the noon hour on 25 May Lütjens spoke to the ship's company. The summons to assemble near the loudspeakers came on short notice and reached me while I was watch officer in the forward control station. I dismissed the men on watch with me so that they could listen to the talk but, not wanting to leave the guns completely uncovered, I remained at my station.

According to the *Bismarck*'s reconstructed War Diary,[1] Lütjens said:

Seamen of the battleship *Bismarck*! You have covered yourselves with glory! The sinking of the battle cruiser *Hood* has not only military, but also psychological value, for she was the pride of England. Henceforth, the enemy will try to concentrate his forces and bring them into action against us. I therefore released the *Prinz Eugen* at noon yesterday so that she could conduct commerce warfare on her own. She has managed to evade the enemy. We, on the other hand, because of the hits we have received, have been ordered to proceed to a French port.[2] On our way there, the enemy will gather and give us battle. The German people are with you, and we will fight until our gun barrels glow red-hot and the last shell has left the barrels. For us seamen, the question now is victory or death!

I can still see the leading petty officer who operated one of my directors returning dejectedly from the loudspeaker and still hear him remarking that it was really all over. He

---

[1] This reconstruction is based on statements made by survivors landed in France by the *U-74* and the weather ship *Sachsenwald* during their debriefing by Group West in Paris at the beginning of June 1941.

[2] Here the survivors' memories must have played them false. Lütjens can hardly have said anything about being ordered to proceed to a French port. It was his own decision to head for St Nazaire.

and the others who heard the address regarded our chances of getting through to France as practically nil. The enemy, they told me the admiral had said, is concentrating his entire high-seas fleet, not only the ships in home waters, but those in any part of the Atlantic. In the face of such a mass, the fate of the *Bismarck* could only be victory or defeat.

The undertone of the men's remarks was clear. They had used both words, 'victory' and 'defeat'. Yet, before them they saw only defeat. It was not easy to reassure and calm them. I said something to the effect that perhaps things really wouldn't be that bad and reminded them of our lightning victory over the *Hood*.Why shouldn't we do something else like that? But a shadow hung over the men: after all, it was the Fleet Commander who had said those things.

Kapitänleutnant (Ingenieurwesen) Gerhard Junack later reported that after Lütjens's address dejection spread throughout the ship, and it was obviously generated at the top. Staff officers began to wear unfastened life jackets. Senior ship's officers declared in the presence of their juniors that they now saw no way out. Senior petty officers appeared at their duty stations with open life jackets, although to do so was against regulations. The division officers tried harder than anyone to counter the contagious depression and had some success in cheering up their men. But the high morale that permeated the ship in the preceding days was irretrievably lost.

Junack continued: 'Whether the Fleet Commander simply made a bad choice of words or whether the crew sensed his innermost fears must remain an open question. Needless to say, all the later rumours about people refusing to obey orders and so forth were invented out of thin air. Morale was low, however, and who can judge what tactical effects that had?'

Stabsobermaschinist Wilhelm Schmidt said: 'It is under-standable that immediately after this address some of the crew were depressed. The men were so young, some of them had come directly from the training centres and had been on board only six weeks. We warrant and petty officers, trusting in what fighting power we had left and in timely intervention by our long-range bombers, did every-thing we could to revive and sustain the men's morale.'

And a few other voices. A junior gunnery officer: 'The Fleet Commander should not have described the situation so baldly.' A seaman gunner: 'My comrades seemed downhearted and said that the Fleet Commander spoke well, but they interpreted his words to mean that we were already lost.' A machinist: 'The address had a depressing effect on the crew. Since morale was very high before the speech, the general opinion was that it would have been better if we had not been told anything about the situation we were in.' A machinist petty officer: 'The Fleet Commander's words had a devastating effect on us. They were taken to mean that we were sentenced to death, whereas we had already reckoned when we would arrive in France. No one looked at anyone else, for fear of betraying any weakness in himself. Deep depression en-veloped the whole crew.'

Quite obviously, Lindemann immediately perceived what the Fleet Commander's words and tone were bound to do to the spirit of his crew. There were already whispers that the two had their differences. About an hour after Lütjens spoke, the captain made a brief address over the loudspeakers, in which he said exactly the opposite: we would put one over on the enemy and soon reach a French port. Also, in conversations with groups of men, he did his best to counteract the effect of Lütjens's words. He suc-ceeded in dispelling the gloom. The men went back to their duties cheerfully. 'I remember,' a survivor wrote me, 'how their faces brightened after the captain's address; they showed that the men had got their courage back.'

Junack's impression that, after Lütjens's address, the dejection seeped down from the top, confirms that our crew, being very young on the average, was overwhelmingly optimistic by nature. At first, some of the younger men were not particularly depressed by the Fleet Commander's warnings. Later they made such comments as, 'We were all young and believed in victory,' or 'The Fleet Commander's address didn't give us the slightest idea that anything could happen to this powerful ship.' Another youngster had to overhear a conversation between two older members of the ship's company before he understood 'that worse awaited us and that the near future was not nearly as rosy as it appeared to us young sailors.'

The *Bismarck*'s reconstructed War Diary concludes: 'After this address by the Fleet Commander, which made the crew aware of the situation of the ship and the intentions of its command, the morale of the crew, outstanding until then, suffered a certain setback.'

Information regarding the latest dispositions of the British fleet, on which his address was based, was evidently given to Lütjens by the B-Dienst at home and perhaps also by our own B-Dienst team. He continued to get this kind of information and periodically had the crew told about it. 'Intercepted and decoded radio signals must have kept our leadership very well informed as to British positions and intentions,' remarked a survivor. Thus the crew learned, among other things, that Force H had left Gibraltar; that the British battleship damaged by us in the action of 24 May was not the *King George V*, but the *Prince of Wales*; and that the *Bismarck* was now being sought and pursued by the *King George V*, *Rodney*, *Ramillies*, and *Repulse*, plus cruisers and destroyers, eager to avenge the loss of the *Hood*.

In the course of the day Lütjens received two personal messages from home. One was from Raeder: 'Hearty congratulations on your birthday. After the last great feat of arms, may more such successes be granted to you in your new year. Commander in Chief of the Navy.' The other, dry and aloof, came from the 'Führer', 'Best wishes on your birthday. Adolf Hitler.'

During my off-duty time that afternoon I went up to the bridge to have a chat about what was going on with whomever I could. I also hoped to find out some details of the situation, which Lütjens had only outlined in general terms. The officer of the watch was Kapitänleutnant Karl Mihatsch, the Division 7 officer. Even today I can see us standing side by side on the starboard side of the bridge, our mighty ship running through a following sea with the wind from astern.

Mihatsch knew no more than I did, so we could talk only in general terms. We both thought that in spite of the enemy's intensified efforts to intercept us, we had a good chance of reaching St Nazaire. We reckoned that the lead we had over the main British force plus the fact that we could still do 28 knots gave us a better than fifty-fifty chance. We were fully aware that, besides the pursuers coming up astern and Force H to be expected ahead, other ships, if not formations, would be approaching from other directions. It all depended on which ships they were and how fast, where they were at the moment, and what radius of operations they had left. Only one thing could not be allowed to happen under any circumstances: the *Bismarck* must not lose speed or manoeuvrability. If that were to happen, the slow but heavily armed British ships presently astern would be able to close and concentrate more fire power on us than we would be able to withstand. Of course, the most serious threat was an air attack, such as we had experienced from the *Victorious* the evening before. But was there an aircraft carrier close enough to launch an attack? That was the really big question. We decided, rather lightheartedly, that we had little to fear from other quarters: we regarded submarines, which in any case we were not likely to meet until we got near the French coast, as a secondary danger that did not seriously enter our calculations. And so ended our little 'council of war'. It did not produce anything sensational, but it was good to talk to someone, and we parted with contented optimism.

Late in the morning the word went round the ship like a streak of lightning: Contact has been broken! Broken after thirty-one long, uninterrupted hours! It was the best possible news, a real boost to confidence and morale. Exactly how this blessing had come about and where the British ships were at the moment, we did not know. Other things we did not know were that around 0400 Tovey's task force had intersected our course 100 nautical miles ahead of us and two hours later the *Victorious* and four cruisers had done the same behind us; and, since 0800 we had been standing to the east, away not only from both those formations, but also from the cruisers. *Suffolk* and *Norfolk*, which were looking for us to the west. We probably would not even have wanted to know that much detail. Content with the momentary respite, we kept expressing to one another the hope that we would not catch sight of the enemy again before we got to St Nazaire.

As the time since Lütjens's address increased and the long day passed into night, the thoughts of those who were not up to date on the enemy situation came to be dominated by the idea that contact had been broken and there was only an extremely small chance that it would be reestablished. The very pleasant contrast between the sound of guns on Saturday and the calm of Sunday contributed to this feeling. So, too, did human nature, which allows pessimism to fade fast and offers us the welcome support of hope.

What significance did 25 May have for the continuation of Exercise Rhine? No exciting actions took place and by nightfall we had not seen a single enemy either on the sea or in the air, nor did we throughout the night of 25–26 May. But, it could hardly have been a more fateful day:

In the morning the enemy lost contact with us – Lütjens didn't realize it and sent two radio messages – Group West informed him of its impression that contact had been broken – Lütjens accepted this finding and instituted radio silence – the enemy took a bearing on the two messages he did send, but, their coordinates having been incorrectly evaluated in the *King George V*, our pursuers turned in the wrong direction – Tovey's loss of time and space was our gain – in the afternoon Tovey returned to the correct course – the British net drew together again – preparations were made for an air search for the *Bismarck* at her supposed position – our prospects of reaching St Nazaire rose in the morning and sank in the afternoon, but were still real at the end of the day.

23
The Bismarck's *Dummy Stack*

On the afternoon of 25 May, we devised a small stratagem whose purpose was to make our adversaries, when next we met them, mistake us for a British battleship. *King George V*-class ships had two stacks, so orders were given to build a second stack for us.

Even with such a change, our silhouette would, of course, give us away to an expert observer on the surface. But we expected that the next enemy to spot us would be in the air. From there it is not easy to recognize ship types, and a second stack could cause real confusion. If it did nothing else, our camouflage would cost the enemy recognition time, especially if visibility worsened, and time became increasingly valuable as our fuel supply became increasingly precarious. So small a thing as delaying our being recognized would be a gain because, once we were recognized, we might be forced, in self-defence, to steam at high speed or to steer an evasive course, either of which measures would strain our fuel supply. Everything, literally everything, counted – and not the least was the fact that the longer it took Tovey's ships to find the right course, the better was the chance that one or another of them would run low on fuel and have to give up.

Our dummy stack seemed to me to be a feeble trick because, for one thing, unless our ship's command knew what visual recognition signals the British exchanged when they met, it would not be effective. Perhaps they did know them. I cannot say. Not only that, but British battleships operating on the high seas were usually escorted by destroyers and the *Bismarck* had no screen, which would certainly make any enemy scout think twice. However, a feeble trick was better than none at all.

Lütjens must have bitterly regretted not having taken the opportunity to fuel in Grimstadfjord or from the *Weissenburg* after we got under way. Ever since it had been determined that part of our fuel supply was inaccessible, more than twenty hours earlier, the *Bismarck* had had to proceed at an economical 20 knots. Had we been making the 28 knots of which her engines were capable, we would have been 160 nautical miles nearer to St Nazaire and under cover of the Luftwaffe. We would not have had to worry about camouflaging ourselves, either.

With sheet metal and canvas, we built a dummy stack and painted it grey to match the real stack. It was to be set up on the flight deck forward of the hangar. Men from the workshops went at this unaccustomed task with enthusiasm until darkness fell; for them, it was a welcome change from the routine of long war watches.

Our chief engineering officer, Korvettenkapitän (Ingenieurwesen) Walter Lehmann, who took a personal interest in the dummy stack, naturally wanted to see for himself how his men were going about their task. From the first, he had established a close and confidential relationship with them. It was reinforced by the bull sessions he held, preferably near turret Dora, whenever anyone did something wrong. He would take the culprit aside and, to put him at his ease, growl, 'No formalities!' As a survivor put it, 'You had to walk round the turret with him and could say whatever was on your mind.' In Gotenhafen, while liberty was cancelled in preparation for our departure, a young stoker learned that his mother was dying. He was heartbroken. A sympathetic comrade took him to Lehmann. The boy blurted out, 'Please, Papa,' then, overcome by emotion, fell silent. 'Now tell Papa,'

Lehmann said, 'it doesn't matter, what's got you down?'
Before long, all his men were calling him 'Papa
Lehmann'.

So Papa Lehmann came and took a look at what was
going on with the stack. 'We really must,' he said, 'fix it so
that it will smoke as it should.' The ship's command took
up his jesting idea, and word was passed over the loudspeakers. 'Off-duty watch report to the First Officer's
cabin to draw cigars to smoke in our second stack!' The
hilarity that this order caused did a lot to raise morale.

When the dummy stack had been completed it was left
lying on the deck. It was not to be rigged until the order
was given. In the meanwhile, I helped to compose several
English-language Morse signals for use in the event of an
enemy contact.

Lehmann's big worry that day was not so much the fuel
shortage created by the oil in the forecastle being cut off,
as it was the danger of saltwater getting into the boilers.
As a result of the flooding in port No. 2 boiler room, the
feedwater system of turbo-generator No. 4 had salted up
and the same danger was threatening power plant No. 3.
If seawater got into the boiler through the feedwater
system, unevaporated water might be carried into the
propulsion turbines along with the steam and, in no time
at all, destroy the turbine blades and lead to 'blade salad'.
Therefore the feedwater in all the turbo-generators must
be changed immediately. But our high-pressure boilers
took so much feedwater that we had trouble producing
enough to keep pace with the demand. An all-out effort to
make our four fresh-water condensers and auxiliary boiler
produce enough was successful and by the evening of 25
May the danger had passed.

In the afternoon we reduced speed to 12 knots to
facilitate the repair work still being done in the forecastle.
With much difficulty, men in diving gear climbed into the

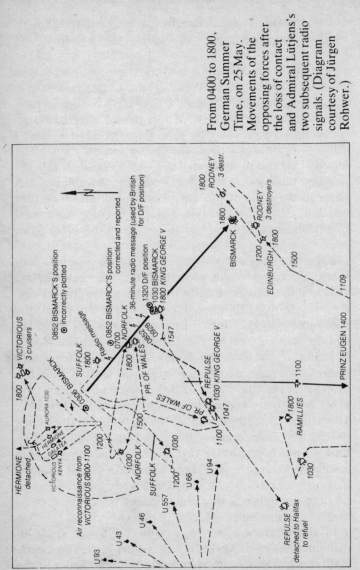

From 0400 to 1800, German Summer Time, on 25 May. Movements of the opposing forces after the loss of contact and Admiral Lütjens's two subsequent radio signals. (Diagram courtesy of Jürgen Rohwer.)

completely flooded forward compartments and opened the oil-tank valves, which gave us a few more hundred tons of fuel.

Marinebaurat[1] Heinrich Schlüter suggested that we jettison the forward anchors and anchor chains. His idea was to lighten the forward section so as to adjust the forward trim that we had since the flooding that began during the battle off Iceland. The ship's command rejected the suggestion, presumably because it forsaw that the anchors would be essential for manoeuvring our way in to St Nazaire.

Group West informed the Fleet Commander at about 1930 that the Luftwaffe was ready to cover the approach of the *Bismarck* in force: bombers as far out as 14 degrees west, reconnaissance planes to 15 degrees west, and long-range reconnaissance planes to 25 degrees west; and three destroyers were ready to meet her. The message advised him that the approaches to Brest and St Nazaire were under strict surveillance and, in an emergency, he would be able to go in to La Pallice. When he passed 10 degrees west longitude, he was to report it promptly.

At about 0430 on 26 May an announcement came from the bridge: 'We have now passed three-quarters of Ireland on our way to St Nazaire. Around noon we will be in the U-boats' operational area and within the range of German aircraft. We can count on the appearance of Condor planes after 1200.' Joy reigned throughout the ship and morale climbed.

[1] Naval Constructor

24
Catalinas from Northern Ireland

Like everyone else on board, I knew nothing of the reconnaissance activities in which the Royal Air Force's Coastal Command was engaged during the night of 25–26 May.

At the beginning of May 1941, seventeen U.S. Navy pilots were sent to Great Britain under the strictest secrecy – the United States was not at war with Germany at this time – and distributed among the flying-boat squadrons of Coastal Command. Their mission was to familiarize the Royal Air Force with the American-built Catalina flying boat, some of which had been put at the disposal of the British government under the provisions of the Lend-Lease Act. The arrangement was also to give the American pilots operational experience for the benefit of the U.S. Navy.

With a wingspan of 35 metres, the Catalina had what was at that time the unusually long range of 6,400 kilometres. At 0300 on 26 May, two of them left their base at Lough Erne in Northern Ireland on a far-reaching search into the Atlantic for the *Bismarck*. One of them was Catalina 'Z' of Squadron 209. Its pilot was a Briton, Flying Officer Dennis Briggs, its copilot an American, Ensign Leonard B. Smith. Around 1015, in poor visibility and low-lying clouds, Smith saw a ship that he took to be the *Bismarck*, but could not be absolutely certain. Briggs manoeuvred the plane into a position for better observation. From an altitude of 700 metres and at a distance of 450 metres abeam, Smith saw the ship again through a hole in the clouds. Was it the *Bismarck*? Minutes later, the Catalina began to transmit, 'One battleship bearing 240° five miles, course 150°, my position 49°33' north, 21°47' west. Time of origin, 1030/26.'

That message showed Tovey how narrowly the *Bismarck* had been missed the previous day: the *Rodney* and her destroyer screen had missed her by some 50 nautical miles, the cruiser *Edinburgh* by around 45 nautical miles. A flotilla of British destroyers had crossed the *Bismarck*'s wake at a range of only 30 nautical miles. Now the *King George V* was 135 nautical miles to the north, the *Rodney* 125 nautical miles to the northeast, and the *Renown* 112 nautical miles to the east-southeast of the German battleship, which was still 700 nautical miles from St Nazaire.

25

The Bismarck *is Rediscovered*

The *Bismarck* maintained course and speed towards the west coast of France. As the night past had been, the early morning hours of 26 May were quiet. At 1025 Group West radioed Lütjens that our own aerial reconnaissance had started as planned, but that weather conditions in the Bay of Biscay prevented air support from going out. Thus for the time being we could not expect air cover until we were close to shore.

Suddenly, around 1030, a call came from the bridge, 'Aircraft to port!' 'Aircraft alarm!' All eyes turned in the direction indicated and a flying boat was indeed clearly visible for a few seconds before it disappeared into the thick, low-lying clouds. As soon as it reappeared we opened well-directed antiaircraft fire. It turned away, vanished into the clouds, and was not seen again. We assumed that it was staying in the cover of the clouds so that it could continue to observe us and report our position, preferably unseen. For a while, the bridge considered sending our Arado planes up against the Catalina. But because of the risks that would be incurred in recovering the float planes in such heavy seas, Lindemann would not allow them to be launched.[1]

Our B-Dienst team speedily decoded the Catalina's reconnaissance report and at 1156 Group West radioed it

[1] The Arado-196 had a 760-horsepower Bayerische Motoren Werke engine, a cruising speed of 240 kilometres per hour, a maximum speed of 275 kilometres per hour, a rate of climb of 300 metres per minute, a ceiling of 5,300 metres, and an endurance of three to five hours. It was armed with one 2-centimetre cannon in each wing and two machine guns. Under each wing it had a rack for one 50-kilogram bomb.

to Lütjens as well: 'English aircraft reports to the 15th Reconnaissance Group: 1030, a battleship, course 150°, speed 20 knots. My position is 49°20′ north, 21°50′ west.'

We had been rediscovered.

Obviously, the big flying boat had come from a land base a long way away, which led me to assume that it might be a long time before there were any perceptible reactions to its report. But I soon found out that I was wrong. As early as 1200, only an hour-and-a-half after our encounter with the Catalina, Lütjens radioed Group West about the appearance of another aircraft: 'Enemy aircraft maintains contact; wheeled aircraft; my position approximately 48° north, 20° west.'[2]

A wheeled aircraft! So there must be an aircraft carrier quite nearby. And other, probably heavy, ships would be near her. Would cruisers or destroyers pick up contact before we ran into them? And were we now to experience a new version of our happily ended pursuit by the *Suffolk* and *Norfolk*?

We in the *Bismarck* had the realization forced upon us that another page had been turned. After thirty-one hours of almost unbroken contact, thirty-one hours of broken contact had now, perhaps for good, come to an end – an exactly equal number of hours, how remarkable! Did the carrier plane really signify a decisive turn of events? Morale sagged a little among those who could read the new signs.

Of course, we did not know then that the appearance of the carrier aircraft was not simply the visible result of the

[2] The position reported by Lütjens differs considerably from that reported by the Catalina shortly before. According to a subsequent reconstruction, both reports were in error as to our latitude, that of the Catalina by approximately 25 nautical miles, and that of the *Bismarck* by approximately 80 nautical miles. Such deviations can easily occur after long flights and cruises. (*See also* Ludovic Kennedy, *Pursuit*, pp. 154–55.)

Catalina's reconnaisance. We had no idea that the radio signals transmitted by Lütjens the morning before had led the enemy to us. The two signals, the second of which was especially useful to enemy direction-finding because of its length, became of interest when the operation was evaluated in Germany. At the time of their transmission, however, they were of no operational consequence. They only helped seal the fate of the ship and her crew.

The dummy stack still lay where it was built on the flight deck. It had not been rigged, and I have not heard a logical reason why not. If it was to serve its purpose, we would have had to set it up when we were out of sight of the enemy, so that the next time they saw us they would immediately think they were seeing a two-stack ship. Instead of playing our trick, we confirmed our identity by firing at the enemy aircraft. As we know today, we even spared him the trouble of making completely sure who we were! So we had decided in advance not to try our ruse or our prepared radio messages, and I could imagine only that this decision had something to do with the attitude of the fleet staff. They probably decided that the overall situation, which they sensed to be increasingly precarious, made it useless to try to camouflage ourselves. There was neither time nor opportunity to ask questions, so I kept my speculations to myself.[3]

[3] Jochen Brennecke, *Schlachtschiff Bismarck*, page 156, quotes the following excerpt from my private records: 'I do not know why at this time (1030, when we were rediscovered by the Catalina) the second stack built to mislead the enemy had not yet been set up or, in the same connection, why afterwards (between the disappearance of the Catalina

Opposite page: From 1800, German Summer Time, on 25 May to 1030, German Summer Time, on 26 May. After a day without sighting the enemy, the *Bismarck* was rediscovered at 1030, German Summer Time, 26 May. (Diagram courtesy of Jürgen Rohwer.)

During the afternoon a Catalina flying boat joined the wheeled aircraft that was holding contact with us. It was the partner of our discoverer, which had earlier been

---

and the appearance of a wheeled aircraft from the *Ark Royal*) it was not set up. On the contrary, our fire confirmed that we were the enemy. There is no way of knowing whether the aircraft would have been taken in by this stratagem ... .'

To this extract, Brennecke appends Footnote 267, in which Konteradmiral Hans Meyer (Retired) says: 'The whole business of the dummy stack is in my opinion a fantasy. The order to build a second stack was certainly given, but the situation that developed very soon made it clear that it could not be erected. *The very harsh criticism along the lines of, "Only he who gives up is truly lost," at least in connection with the dummy stack, I hold to be absolutely unjustified'* (my italics).

Surprised by this appraisal of a 'criticism' I had not made, I consulted the first edition of Brennecke's book, published in 1960, and found, on page 307: 'The mistaken attack [by aircraft from the *Ark Royal* on the evening of 26 May] on the *Sheffield* made one thing clear; the crucial value the second stack built on board the *Bismarck* could have had, if it had been set up. In the uncertainty that prevailed after this attack on the *Sheffield*, which did not look anything like the *Bismarck*, no British pilot would have dared attack a two-stack ship because the two-stack British ships *Renown*, *King George V*, and *Sheffield* were in the area. Perhaps the decisive hit [the hit on the *Bismarck*'s rudder later that evening] would not have been made. *Here, too, one might say, Only he who gives up is truly lost'* (my italics). Brennecke has deleted that passage, his own words, from his fourth edition. He simply attaches Meyer's negative evaluation to my words, which gave no occasion for it.

Furthermore, in the cited footnote Meyer says: 'Bad weather also came up. The dummy would have hardly been able to withstand the wind pressure. It was a matter of surface area. The situation might have been different if the ship had reached the open Atlantic, where only single aircraft were to be anticipated, not a battle at any moment, and where there would also have been time to tidy up the dummy. Presumably, the dummy was meant for this situation.' My reply to that is: When the dummy was being built on 25 May and the following day the wind was blowing from astern. It was strong but, on our course, the wind pressure was light and would not have had the effect that Meyer assumes. Secondly, the dummy was certainly not intended for use in the Atlantic. We had to get to St Nazaire by the quickest, i.e., the most direct, route. The order to build the stack proceeded, at least originally, from a feeling that we needed it immediately. After 24 May, most of the actions of the fleet staff and the ship's command were determined only by immediate needs.

obliged to break off the operation because of its fuel
supply. The Catalina circled back and forth over our wake
for a long time, out of range of our antiaircraft batteries.
Occasionally the planes tried to come closer to us, but
each time they were driven off by our flak. The bridge
announced that an aircraft carrier was in the vicinity and
all lookouts were to pay particular attention to the direction in which the wheeled aircraft disappeared, so that the
position of the carrier could be ascertained. The flying
boat vanished around 1800 but the carrier plane stayed
with us and was soon joined by the cruiser *Sheffield*, which
had newly arrived on the scene. At 1824, Lütjens reported
the *Sheffield*'s position to Group West, giving her course
as 115 degrees and her speed as 24 knots.

At 1903 he radioed Group West: 'Fuel situation urgent.
When can I count on replenishment?' The question must
certainly have puzzled its recipients. Knowing as little as
they did about the situation of the *Bismarck*, how could
they tell him when and where a supply tanker could be
deployed in the midst of the area of operations? It did not
become clear until later that Lütjens was only trying to tell
them that his fuel supply was critical. In order to keep his
transmission brief, he used the so-called short-signal book
for encoding, which permitted a report on the fuel situation to be given only in combination with a question about
replenishment.

26

Tovey's Hopes Are Pinned on the Ark Royal

In the meantime, several of the British ships were forced by their dwindling fuel supplies to abandon the pursuit towards the west coast of France. The *Prince of Wales*, the *Victorious*, their escorting destroyers, and the *Suffolk* dropped out of the race. The *Norfolk*, having been convinced from the start that the *Bismarck* was making for Brest, did not take the search course to the north, and was consequently in a quite favourable position. The *Rodney* was even more advantageously placed. She had proceeded on the same assumption as the *Norfolk*, but was too far to the south at the start ever to have joined in a pursuit to the north. The positions of the *Rodney* and *Norfolk* were only relatively favourable, however, because like the *King George V*, they were much too far behind the *Bismarck* on course for France to be any threat to her unless her speed were significantly reduced. When the hunt began, the *Ramillies* was not unfavourably placed, but she was withdrawn on account of her age and lack of speed.

At the moment, then, to attack the German battleship as soon as possible, Tovey had only Somerville's Force H, which was to the south. This task force and Tovey's had been steaming virtually towards one another since 24 May. In the beginning Tovey thought Force H was too far to the south to be able to take part in the pursuit. Now, it was the only force that was in a position to stop the *Bismarck*. And, that was certainly not because it included the *Renown* and the *Sheffield*. The loss of the *Hood* had shown the folly of pitting such ships against the *Bismarck* unless they had the support of heavier forces. It was upon the aircraft of the *Ark Royal* that he would have to rely. Their job was to cripple the *Bismarck* with their torpedoes so that Tovey's own big ships could come up for a decisive engagement – a situation that had to be created at once, because he was getting ever nearer to the effective range of the Luftwaffe. Tovey was aware that this was his one and only chance to avoid the barren alternative of calling off the days-long pursuit through the Atlantic. He had to remind himself that the attack by the planes of the *Victorious* on 24 May had not been successful, but their crews were young and inexperienced, whereas the *Ark Royal* had the best-trained and most experienced aircrews in the Royal Navy – with them, the prospects would be much better.

Since the morning of 25 May, Somerville had been going on the assumption that the *Bismarck* was heading for Brest. On the basis of running reports on the position of the German battleship, he launched ten of the *Ark Royal*'s Swordfish for reconnaissance on the morning of 26 May. Six other Swordfish, equipped with auxiliary fuel tanks to increase their range, joined them. They were to shadow the *Bismarck* once she had been found. Following their launching around 0830 nothing was heard from them for two hours. Then, around 1030, the radiomen in the *Renown* and *Ark Royal* recorded an incoming message: 'One battleship bearing 240° five miles, course 150°, my position 49°33' north, 21°47' west.' It did not come, as the people in the carrier hoped, from one of the Swordfish, but from the Catalina. This did not diminish the warmth of its welcome, and when the Catalina lost contact after being fired on by the *Bismarck*, it was a Swordfish that found the battleship again and maintained contact.

Thereafter Somerville's objective was an aerial torpedo attack on the *Bismarck*. The first opportunity to launch from the Ark Royal came in the early afternoon and, regardless of the stormy weather, fifteen Swordfish took off at 1450. Around the same time, he sent the *Sheffield* to maintain contact with the *Bismarck*, because, with the weather deteriorating, it seemed to him risky to depend on observation from the air. Unaware that the *Sheffield* had been given this mission, the skipper of the *Ark Royal*, Captain Loben E. Maund, told his pilots that there would not be any ship in view between the *Ark Royal* and the *Bismarck*. Consequently, when they detected a ship on their radar, they dived through the clouds and launched their attack. Only three of the pilots at the last moment recognized their faithful old target ship *Sheffield* and withheld their fire. Defects in their magnetic detonators caused most of the torpedoes that were launched to explode harmlessly upon entering the water. Fortunately, by putting on full speed, the *Sheffield* avoided the handful of torpedoes that ran well. Nevertheless the aircrews returned to the *Ark Royal* in a gloomy mood, and were consoled only by the promise that they would be launched again that evening. In spite of the gloom, the incident had its bright side in that it revealed the failure of the magnetic detonators. For the next attack, the Swordfish fell back on their old, reliable contact detonators.

For Tovey, who had not been told that the planes had mistaken the *Sheffield* for the *Bismarck*, the *Ark Royal*'s report of an unsuccessful attack was bitter news. He had little reason to think that another attack that same evening would be successful. Once more, he reviewed the whole situation. Unless the *Bismarck* could somehow be crippled on the night of 26 May, on the morning of 27 May she would have as good as escaped. In other words, an attack that evening would be the very last chance. Considering the continuing deterioration of the weather, he did not expect much from a night attack by the destroyers. Both the *King George V* and the *Rodney* were reaching the limits of their fuel endurance. Unless the next few hours brought a decisive change, the *King George V* would have to drop out of the race.

At 1820 Tovey signalled Somerville that if the *Bismarck*'s speed was not reduced by midnight, the *King George V* would have to turn away to refuel. The *Rodney*, he said, could continue the pursuit, without destroyers, if need be.

It was hard for Tovey to send that signal. For four days and nights, over 2,000 nautical miles, he had pursued the *Bismarck*, from the Denmark Strait almost into the Bay of Biscay, with a great body of ships. Should this tremendous effort really have been for nothing?

At 1740 the *Sheffield* made out the German battleship at the limit of visibility. For the first time since the *Suffolk*, *Norfolk*, and *Prince of Wales* had lost contact, one-and-a-half days ago, a ship had visual contact with the *Bismarck*. The *Sheffield* did everything she could to avoid being seen by us. Her mission was only to help the second wave of carrier planes find the target and to maintain contact.

In the *Ark Royal*, hasty preparations for a second attack were being made. For one thing, the torpedoes' magnetic detonators were replaced by contact detonators. There was so much to be done that the originally intended launching time of 1830 slipped. It was 1915 when, under low cloud cover and in varying visibility, fifteen Swordfish were launched, one after the other, into the wind. Around 2000 they appeared over the *Sheffield*. She directed them, but wrongly at first, because in thirty minutes they were back, without having sighted their target. Directed anew, they flew off again, and the sound of the German antiair-craft fire that soon followed told the *Sheffield* that this time they had gone in the right direction.

27

The Mortal Hit

Daytime on the twenty-sixth passed into early evening. Twilight fell and, as far as we in the *Bismarck* were concerned, the dark of night could not come too soon. In spite of our experience as the object of the enemy's unerring means of reconnaissance, we were still inclined to feel night-time brought some protection. Of course, ever since a Catalina rediscovered us that morning, a wheeled aircraft had maintained almost uninterrupted contact. Its presence indicated that a carrier was nearby, but eight hours had now passed and, to our surprise, we had not been attacked. Not having any means of knowing that her Swordfish had lost time by mistakenly attacking the *Sheffield* instead of us, we began to speculate. Could the wheeled aircraft be a reconnaissance plane with extraordinarily long range? Was the carrier too far away to launch an attack? Might we be spared one today, 26 May?

Below, the men's good spirits had returned and morale was high throughout the ship. Word had spread that an enemy force was about 100 nautical miles astern of us, but unless it was much faster than we were, how could it possibly overtake us? Some men pored over charts and calculated that the next morning we would be 200 nautical miles off the coast, within range of the Luftwaffe's protection. A report circulated that a tanker was on her way to meet us, so our worries about fuel would be over. Hope sprouted anew. I could not help remembering my conversation with Mihatsch: didn't we still have a good chance of making St Nazaire? What was to stop us from outrunning the enemy?

We got the answer to that question around 2030 – 'Aircraft alarm!'

No sooner had the report that sixteen planes were approaching run through the ship than they were flying over us at high altitude. Then they were out of sight, and the order was given, 'Off-duty watch dismissed, antiaircraft watch at ease at the guns.' At ease, but not for long. In a few minutes another aircraft alarm was sounded, and this time it was a different picture. The planes dived out of low clouds, individually and in pairs, and flew towards us. They approached even more recklessly than the planes from the *Victorious* had done two days earlier. Every pilot seemed to know what this attack meant to Tovey. It was the last chance to cripple the *Bismarck* so that the battleships could have at her. And they took it.

Once more, the *Bismarck* became a fire-spitting mountain. The racket of her antiaircraft guns was joined by the roar from her main and secondary turrets as they fired into the bubbling paths of oncoming torpedoes, creating splashes ahead of the attackers. Once more, the restricted field of my director and the dense smoke allowed me to see only a small slice of the action. The antique-looking Swordfish, fifteen of them, seemed to hang in the air, near enough to touch. The high cloud layer, which was especially thick directly over us, probably did not permit a synchronized attack from all directions, but the Swordfish came so quickly after one another that our defence did not have it any easier than it would have had against such an attack. They flew low, the spray of the heaving seas masking their landing gear. Nearer and still nearer they came, into the midst of our fire. It was as though their orders were, 'Get hits or don't come back!'

The heeling of the ship first one way and then the other told me that we were trying to evade torpedoes. The rudder indicator never came to rest and the speed indicator

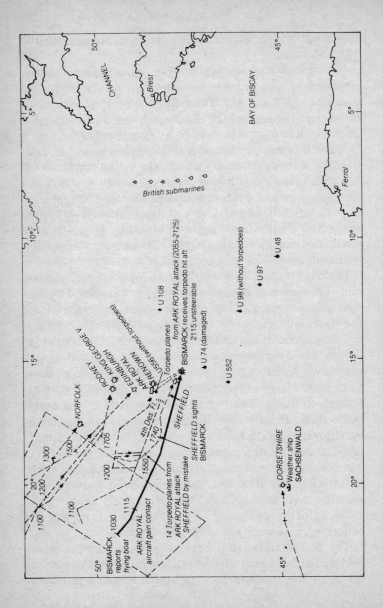

revealed a significant loss of speed. The men on the control platforms in the engine rooms had to keep their wits about them. 'All ahead full!' – 'All stop!' – 'All back full!' – 'Ahead!' – 'All stop!' were the ever-changing orders by which Lindemann sought to escape the malevolent 'eels'.

As though hypnotized, I listened for the sound of an exploding torpedo mixing with the roar of our guns. It could be much worse than it was two days earlier. A hit forward of my station could be tolerated, but what about a hit aft? There was not much distance between me and our sensitive propellers and rudders, and it seemed as though these were our attackers' favourite targets. We had been under attack for perhaps fifteen minutes when I heard that sickening sound. Two torpedoes exploded in quick succession, but somewhere forward of where I was. Good fortune in misfortune, I thought. They could not have done much damage. My confidence in our armoured belt was unbounded. Let's hope that's the end of it!

Soon after the alarm, Matrosengefreiter Herzog, at his port third 3.7-centimetre antiaircraft gun, saw three planes approaching from astern at an oblique angle, while the talker at his station was reporting other planes coming from various directions. Then, through the powder smoke, Herzog saw two planes approach on the port beam and turn to the right. In no time they were only twenty metres off our stern, coming in too low for Herzog's or any other guns to bear on them. Two torpedoes splashed into the water and ran towards our stern just as we were making an evasive turn to port.

Opposite page: From 1030, German Summer Time, to 2115, German Summer Time, on 26 May. Movements of opposing forces until the fatal rudder hit on the *Bismarck*. (Diagram courtesy of Jürgen Rohwer.)

The attack must have been almost over when it came, an explosion aft.[1] My heart sank. I glanced at the rudder indicator. It showed 'left 12 degrees'. Did that just happen to be the correct reading at that moment? No. It did not change. It stayed at 'left 12 degrees'. Our increasing list to starboard soon told us that we were in a continuous turn. The aircraft attack ended as abruptly as it had begun.

I heard Schneider on the gunnery-control telephone give targeting information on a cruiser. She was the *Sheffield*, which had come back into view after a long interval. Schneider fired a few salvoes, the second of which was straddling. The *Sheffield* promptly turned away at full speed and laid down smoke. The guns of the *Bismarck* fell silent.

Our speed indicator still showed a significant loss of speed because of the turn we were in. Our rudder indicator, which drew my gaze like a magnet, still stood at 'left 12 degrees'. At one stroke, the world seemed to be irrevocably altered. Or was it? Perhaps the damage could be repaired. I broke the anxious silence that enveloped my station, by remarking: 'We'll just have to wait. The men below will do everything they can.'

Hadn't we at least shot down some planes? I had not seen us do so, but we must have. Word that we had shot down seven began to make the rounds. How could anyone be so specific, I wondered? Not until years later did I learn that all the Swordfish returned to their carrier.

The torpedo hit shook the ship so violently that the safety valve in the starboard engine room closed and the engines shut down. Slowly the vibration of the ship

---

[1] My account of the number and sequence of torpedo hits differs from that given by the Fleet Commander in his subsequent radio reports. It is, however, my firm recollection that there were two explosions forward of my station before the one aft. The sequence and content of Lütjens's reports are, of course, important as evidence of what happened, but they are not incontrovertible proof.

ceased, accentuating individual vibrations. Above, the control station reopened the safety valve and we had steam again. The floor plates of the centre engine room buckled upwards about half a metre, and water rushed in through the port shaft well. It did not take long, however, to seal off the room and pump it out.

Casualties in the area of Damage-Control Team No. 1 were kept to a minimum by the foresight of Stabsober-maschinist Wilhelm Schmidt who, when the attack began, ordered his men to cushion themselves against shocks by sitting on hammocks. After the blow that lifted her stern, the ship rocked up and down several times before coming to rest and Schmidt reported to the damage-control centre, 'Presumed torpedo hit aft.' Inspection by his damage-control parties revealed that the hole blown in the ship's hull was so big that all the steering rooms were flooded and their occupants had been forced to abandon their stations. The water in those rooms was sloshing up and down in rhythm with the motion of the ship. In order to keep it contained, the armoured hatch above the steering mechanism, which had been opened to survey the damage, was closed. But then the after depth-finder tube broke and water rushed through to the main deck. Apparently because cable stuffing tubes through the bulk-heads were no longer watertight and the after transverse bulkheads had sprung leaks, the upper and lower passage-ways on the port side of Compartment III and the central shaft well were making water. An attempt to pump out the after steering room was delayed by an electrical failure that necessitated switching to a substitute circuit. As soon as that repair had been made, however, it was discovered that the water in the passageway to the steering mechan-ism had got into the pumps' self-starters and the pumps were unusable.

Under the supervision of two engineering officers,

Kapitänleutnant Gerhard Junack and Oberleutnant Hermann Giese, the damage-control parties, assisted by a master carpenter's team, went to work. They shored up the transverse bulkhead on the approaches to the steering gear and sealed the broken depth-finder tube. They forced their way through an emergency exit on the battery deck that led to the armoured hatch over the steering gear below. A master carpenter and a master's mate hoped that, with the help of underwater-escape apparatus, they would be able to reach the upper platform deck and there disengage the rudder-motor coupling. Very carefully, they opened the hatch. Seawater shot up past them, as high as the emergency exit, then was sucked down and disappeared the next time the stern rose in a seaway. Like a falling stone, the stern plunged into the next trough. Once again the water shot up, threatened to overflow the emergency exit, was sucked down on the next wave crest, and disappeared. It was pointless. There was nothing to do but close the hatch. No one could force his way into the steering plant, much less work there. The attempt had failed.

Hours later, we managed to get a hand rudder coupled to the rudder yoke, and the crew of the starboard third 15-centimetre turret were ordered to man it. But they weren't able to get to it. Inside the room, they were confronted with swirling and tossing seawater and oil. They returned to their stations and reported to the bridge. The crews of the starboard second and third 15-centimetre turrets were then directed to go to the quarterdeck and place a collision mat over the hole in the ship's hull. But high seas frustrated their efforts and they, too, had to return to their stations without accomplishing anything.

Above, in the after fire-control station, all we could do was sympathize with the hard work of the men struggling to repair our damage. From time to time we asked what they were trying to do and what success they were having. Most of the answers we got were brief and not very informative. For example, we were told that some water had been pumped out of the ship. There was never any intimation as to whether they were having success or were on the verge of it. I had to suppress an urge to go and see for myself. Anyone who was not involved in making repairs obviously had to remain at his station because, although that air attack was over, there might be another, and enemy ships might appear. We were still at general quarters. We could not let down our guard even for a minute.

The circle we involuntarily made after our rudder was damaged had turned us around from our southeasterly course towards St Nazaire, and we were moving to the northwest, into the wind and towards the enemy. The *Bismarck*'s hull shook noticeably as Lindemann tried various speeds and combinations of propellers in an attempt to bring us back on course. His orders from the bridge came in rapid succession: 'Port engines half ahead, centre and starboard engines stop' – 'Port and centre engines half ahead, starboard engines back slow' – 'Port engines full ahead, starboard engines stop.'

Below, the men did their best to regulate the turbines precisely and, instead of two of them standing on the control platforms, as was normally the case, there were three: one at the forward throttle, one at the backing throttle, and one ready to jump in and do whatever was needed. The minimum time prescribed for waiting between 'Stop' and 'Full power' was ignored. Boiler pressure was now the only thing the men turning the hand cranks had to go by and, inevitably, the safe maximum was sometimes overshot. Because we were in the cleared-for-action state of readiness, no doors or ventilators were open and the temperature in the engine rooms climbed to

50 degrees centigrade – this, with the men in leather clothing.

Lindemann desperately tried other combinations of speeds and propellers. Nothing did any good. When he did succeed in deflecting the ship from her course to the northwest, her jammed rudders brought her back into the wind. Increasing winds and rising seas made our useless rudders an even more critical factor. Nevertheless, we had to regard it as fortunate that, despite their proximity to the explosion, our propellers had not been damaged and we could still do a little manoeuvring.

About an hour after the torpedo hit, we in the after station got word of the suggestion that we either send down divers to cut off our rudders or set charges to sever them. Getting rid of our rudders would have the same effect as having them jammed in the midships position, which would greatly facilitate steering with our propellers. The chief engineer and his staff assembled on the quarter-deck to investigate this possibility. It has been said that Lindemann took some part in these deliberations, but I cannot be certain that he did. In any case, both ideas were rejected.

Although there certainly would have been no lack of volunteers, approaching the rudders from outside the ship was not even considered. The seas were too high and the suction under the stern was too strong for free-swimming divers or for men to work their way down safety lines rigged under the stern. Before men were asked to risk their lives there had to be a reasonable chance of success. There was not. Blowing the rudders off from inside was rejected because it would be next to impossible to measure the explosive charge so exactly that it would have neither less nor more than the intended effect. In the latter case, it might damage the nearby propellers as well as other parts of the ship.

One working party volunteered to take off the hangar door and weld it to the starboard side of the stern at a 15-degree angle, which would correspond to a rudder position of 12 degrees. The thought was that this would counteract the effect of the rudders jammed in the port position and make it easier to steer with the propellers. But this plan, too, was rejected because of the bad weather.

High above the scene of the damage, in the after station, we could do no more than witness from afar the attempts at repair, one after the other of which appeared to fail. We could only worry and try to give one another hope and confidence. Serious as the jammed rudder was, I knew it was not the worst thing. But what was the use of adding to the worries of the men around me by telling them what really doomed us? It was that the *Bismarck*, reverting inexorably to a generally northwesterly course, was travelling back over a stretch of our passage towards St Nazaire, on which our progress had seemed so promising. And more than that. The course we were on was leading us towards the overwhelming British forces that had been pursuing us. We were relieving Tovey of the job of pursuit. Naturally, there was no point in using the full power of which our engines were still capable. High speed would have only led the more quickly to the unwelcome encounter with the enemy. Therefore we maintained only enough speed to keep us from being blown about, between 5 and 7 knots.

The wind! Throughout this operation, its direction had been of varying degrees of importance. From the time we left the cliffs of Norway to the bitter end, no matter what course we were on, it blew from astern. On 22 May it did us the favour of providing us with a shield from hostile observation by driving rain clouds with us. But this evening, 26 May, the northwester, which developed into a real storm overnight, sealed our fate.

Our spirits were given a new lift when we heard that someone had succeeded in uncoupling the starboard rudder – Maschinengefreiter Gerhard Böhnel in the stern reported it through Maschinengefreiter Hermann Budich, the talker in action station 'E', to Obermaschinist Oskar Barho. Reports that this was not so dampened all our hopes. It was true that several times men managed to force their way into the port rudder room also, but they could not reach the coupling. Seawater gurgled in and out through the hole in the hull. When, after indescribable exertions, a diver did succeed in reaching the coupling, he found it so badly jammed he couldn't budge it. Several divers collapsed when they were pulled out of the rudder rooms.

A moonless, gloomy night had long since fallen over us. Incapable of manoeuvring, we crept towards the superior forces coming to destroy us – a virtual journey to Golgotha. As the hours passed, our dying hope that somehow we would still find a way to escape was supplanted by the growing certainty that there was no escape. Sometime after midnight, the word spread that work on the rudder had ceased, and certainty became absolute.

28

Destroyers Ordered to Tovey's Support

When on the afternoon of 25 May Tovey realized that the *Bismarck* was making for a port in western France, he became concerned about his shortage of destroyers. As his battleships neared the coast, they would face an increasingly grave threat from German U-boats, and it disturbed him that his destroyer escort had had to turn back for lack of fuel and the *King George V* had been unprotected since morning. He knew that the *Rodney*, which had been placed under his command but had yet to join him, had three destroyers with her but he had no idea about the status of their fuel.

That evening, therefore, Tovey asked the Admiralty to provide the *King George V* and *Rodney* with a new destroyer escort. By the time it received this request, the Admiralty had already recognized the problem and decided how to handle it. The solution, which had not been easy to find because destroyers were in short supply in general, was to recall the 4th Destroyer Flotilla – the *Cossack*, *Maori*, *Zulu*, *Sikh*, and *Piorun*[1] – from convoy duty. On the evening of 25 May, this flotilla, under the command of Captain Philip Vian, was some 300 nautical miles ahead of the *King George V*, which meant it would be able to join Tovey's battleships early the next afternoon. At 0200 on 26 May Vian in the *Cossack* received orders to close with the *King George V*, taking with him

---

[1] The destroyer *Piorun* left the building ways in Great Britain in May 1940 and was later transferred to the Polish government-in-exile in London. She served in the British fleet, but under the Polish flag and with a Polish crew.

the *Sikh* and *Zulu*. He was to send the *Maori* and *Piorun* to join the *Rodney*. Under way, Vian read the Catalina's report of the rediscovery of the *Bismarck*, which fixed her position to the southeast of his, and saw that the question before him was should he obey the letter of the Admiralty's order or simply make for the enemy? Thinking his destroyers might help to intercept the *Bismarck* on her way to France, he decided to do the latter. He turned onto a pursuing course at maximum speed but a storm astern and heavy seas prevented him from maintaining it. Around 2200 on the twenty-sixth he sighted the *Sheffield*, which had been taken under fire by the *Bismarck* only shortly before and was now steaming north, and from her he learned the *Bismarck*'s exact bearing. By 2230 both the *Piorun* and the *Zulu* had found the *Bismarck*. His destroyers could begin operating against the German battleship.

29

The Last Night Aboard the Bismarck

For about an hour and a half after the air attack, the battle zone close around the *Bismarck* was deserted. Then, somewhere before 2300 we saw destroyers. Alarm bells sounded and, as usual, our 38-centimetre and 15-centimetre turrets were ready for action in seconds. 'Permission to fire'. Salvoes of both calibres went off towards the nearest of the destroyers – the *Piorun*, as I learned later. Our guns must have been very well laid at the start, for the enemy turned away and got out of range.

We did not know how many destroyers there were around us. The pitch-blackness of the night and frequent rain squalls made it impossible for us to make out silhouettes, so we couldn't tell whether we were seeing a few destroyers over and over again or whether there was a great number of them. The only thing clear to us was that we could expect endless torpedo attacks. Everything was going to depend on extreme vigilance and the flawless functioning of our range finders. Fortunately for us, however, the attacks were not synchronized, that is, they did not come from different directions at the same time, which would have made our defence much more difficult. The wind and seas, which gave even the *Bismarck* trouble, probably handicapped the destroyers even more. With seas breaking over them and sprays as high as the bridge – conditions that I experienced many times in German destroyers – they would often be compelled to reduce speed just when for tactical reasons they wanted to run at high speed.

Our range finders worked to perfection. From 8,000 metres down to 3,000 we tracked the destroyers. Tension in my station rose as the incoming ranges went down, 7,000 metres . . . 6,500 . . . 4,000 . . . In spite of the darkness, I could see through my director our shadowy attackers coming nearer and nearer, twisting to attack – each time, I thought, 'Now the torpedoes are hissing out of the tubes' – then drawing off. They dared not stay near us for long because of the speed with which our gunnery found its targets. This, in spite of the fact that our fire control had to contend with occasional heavy rolling of the ship caused by seas coming in off our beam and with the even greater disadvantage of our inability to manoeuvre. Her jammed rudders made the *Bismarck* swing some eighty points between northwest and northeast. Changes in target bearing, always rapid at short range, were accelerated, not only by the swinging of the ship but also by the use of our propellers for steering, so that an oncoming destroyer might change from one side of the ship to the other during the same attack. This meant that Albrecht in the forward station had to keep switching between the port and starboard 15-centimetre turrets. The darkness, made worse by drifting rain squalls and clouds of undissipated powder smoke, made observation difficult for him as well as for Schneider in the foretop. As I waited at the ready in case I was needed on any battery, I saw shells bursting over enemy ships but I could never be sure that the flames indicated a hit. At times like this there is always the danger of 'seeing' what one wants to see.

If the men in the engine rooms thought their turbines had reached peak performance during the two air attacks, they now learned better. They found out how those turbines could really perform. They went without pause from 'Full speed ahead' to 'Full speed astern'. Scarcely was the forward throttle closed when two men wrenched

Günther Lütjens as a Kapitän zur See and commanding officer of the light cruiser *Karlsruhe*. He is seen here with Chilean naval officers in Valparaiso in January 1935. The author was serving in the *Karlsruhe* at this time. (Photograph from the author's collection)

From left to right: Dr. Hans-Günther Busch, Dr. Hans-Joachim Krüger, and Dr. Rolf Hinrichsen, the ship's dental officer, on the bridge of the *Bismarck*. (Photograph courtesy of Frau Erika Busch)

Dr. Rolf Hinrichsen treating a dental patient on board. (Photograph courtesy of Frau Erika Busch)

In the *Bismarck*'s dispensary, bars kept the bottles of medicines and drugs from falling off the shelves in heavy seas or when the big guns fired. (Photograph courtesy of Frau Erika Busch)

Kapitänleutnant Emil Jahreis, turbine engineer and, during Exercise Rhine, first damage-control officer. Known to his friends as Seppel, he frequently accompanied the author on liberty ashore. (Photograph courtesy of Frau Marlies Hiltermann)

Some of the *Bismarck*'s complement relax. (Photograph from Bundesarchiv, Koblenz)

The *Bismarck* at anchor in Grimstadfjord on 21 May 1941. During the day, her camouflage was painted over with standard 'outboard grey.' (Photograph courtesy of Württembergische Landesbibliothek, Stuttgart)

This photograph of the *Bismarck* in Grimstadfjord, taken by Flying Officer Michael Suckling of RAF Coastal Command, confirmed the British Admiralty's suspicions that German heavy ships were preparing to break out into the Atlantic. (Photograph from the Imperial War Museum, London)

Kapitänleutnant Gerhard Junack, whose station was in the after turbine room, was close to the attempts to free the *Bismarck*'s jammed rudders. He was one of the few who survived her sinking. After the war, he served in the Federal German Navy, eventually attaining the rank of Kapitän zur See, which he held at the time this picture was taken. (Photograph courtesy of Bodo Herzog)

The Fleet Commander, Admiral Günther Lütjens, a man not given to confiding his reasoning or intentions. (Photograph from Bundesarchiv, Koblenz)

The County-class heavy cruiser *Suffolk*, the ship that shadowed the *Bismarck* by maintaining radar contact from the evening of 23 May until the early morning of 25 May. She is shown here wearing camouflage and patrolling the North Atlantic in the spring of 1941. (Photograph from the Imperial War Museum, London)

With her guns trained abeam, the *Bismarck* releases a salvo in the battle off Iceland. (Photograph courtesy of Paul Schmalenbach)

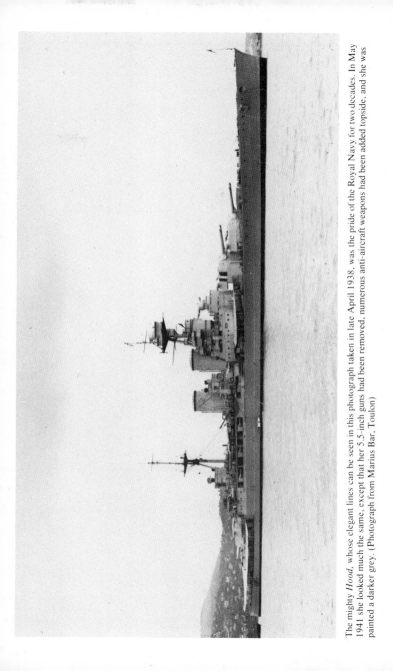

The mighty *Hood*, whose elegant lines can be seen in this photograph taken in late April 1938, was the pride of the Royal Navy for two decades. In May 1941 she looked much the same, except that her 5.5-inch guns had been removed, numerous anti-aircraft weapons had been added topside, and she was painted a darker grey. (Photograph from Marius Bar, Toulon)

Korvettenkapitän Adalbert Schneider, first gunnery officer of the *Bismarck,* who, from the foretop fire-control station, directed the gunfire that sank the *Hood* and damaged the *Prince of Wales.* (Photograph courtesy of Frau Ilse Schneider)

The *Bismarck,* running at high speed, has just fired a salvo at Admiral Holland's force. The large bow wave and the thin stream of smoke forced high out of her stack attest to her speed. Note that she is on the starboard quarter of the *Prinz Eugen.* (Photograph courtesy of Paul Schmalenbach)

Turrets Caesar and Dora fire on the *Prince of Wales*. The *Bismarck* has pulled to port of the *Prinz Eugen* and her guns now point at a bearing of about 310 degrees. Note the position of the foretop range-finder cupola. (Photograph courtesy of Paul Schmalenbach)

The *Hood* blows up. A giant column of black smoke marks the spot where the battle cruiser had been. The smoke at left is from the guns of the *Prince of Wales*. (Photograph courtesy of Paul Schmalenbach)

The *Bismarck* has turned to starboard of her cruiser consort. Her guns trained astern, she has just fired a salvo. To the right, is the smoke from a previous salvo and a column of water from one of the *Prince of Wales's* 14-inch shells. The splash of a major-calibre projectile could easily reach seventy metres in height. (Photograph courtesy of Paul Schmalenbach)

To the left, the wreckage of the *Hood* still burns as the *Prince of Wales* comes under fire by the *Bismarck*. Between the *Prince of Wales* and the burning remains of the *Hood* are splashes from the *Prince of Wales's* shells, which fell hundreds of metres short. (Photograph courtesy of Paul Schmalenbach)

After the battle off Iceland, the *Bismarck* pulls into line astern of the *Prinz Eugen.* Her guns, now silent, are again trained fore and aft. (Photograph courtesy of Paul Schmalenbach)

The *Bismarck* passing the *Prinz Eugen* during a change of station. She is down by the bow and pitching heavily as a result of a hit forward. When the *Prinz Eugen* had taken station astern, she tried to determine how much oil was leaking into the *Bismarck's* wake. This photograph, shot on the morning of 24 May, is the last one of the *Bismarck* taken from the German side. (Photograph courtesy of Paul Schmalenbach)

Korvettenkapitän Walter Lehmann, chief engineer of the *Bismarck*. (Photograph courtesy of Frau Ursula Trüdinger)

Flying Officer Dennis Briggs, pilot and aircraft commander of the Catalina flying boat that sighted the *Bismarck* on 26 May 1941. This sighting re-established the contact that had been lost for thirty-one hours. (Photograph from the Imperial War Museum, London)

Splinter damage in the light cruiser *Sheffield*. She was shadowing the *Bismarck* at the time of the *Ark Royal's* last air attack on the evening of 26 May. Just after the attack, the German battleship sighted her coming out of the mist and fired on her, straddling her on the second salvo. Splinters from the exploding 38-centimetre projectiles wounded twelve men, three of whom later died. The *Sheffield's* radar was also put out of action, preventing her from continuing to shadow that night. (Photograph from the Imperial War Museum, London)

A Swordfish torpedo-spotter-reconnaissance aircraft returning to the *Ark Royal* after making an attack on the *Bismarck*. The Swordfish carried one 1,600-pound, 18-inch torpedo. In order to deliver an attack, it had to fly at a speed of about 75 knots and an altitude of 50 feet or less. (Photograph from the Imperial War Museum, London)

The battleship *Rodney* looses a salvo on the *Bismarck* during the action on 27 May. (Photograph from the Imperial War Museum, London)

The battleships *Rodney* and *Bismarck* in action on 27 May. (Photograph from the Imperial War Museum, London)

The interior of one of the *Bismarck*'s armoured fire-control stations, such as the author occupied at general quarters. The light-coloured instrument mounted in the overhead is an observation periscope-telescope for the range-finder officer. Behind it, the darker, tall instrument is a gun director. (Photograph from Bundesarchiv, Koblenz)

This exterior view of the *Bismarck*'s after fire-control station shows the optical range finder in its revolving cupola. Its lenses are pointing downward and have protective covers in place. Attached to the front of the cupola is a 'mattress' radar antenna. To the left and behind the cupola base is the lens housing for one of the two directors in this station. (Photograph from Bundesarchiv, Koblenz)

Salvos falling near the *Bismarck* during her final action with the Home Fleet. (Photograph from the Imperial War Museum, London)

Swordfish torpedo planes flying over the *King George V* on the morning of 27 May. Twelve aircraft were launched from the *Ark Royal* to make another strike on the *Bismarck* but, when they reached the area, they decided to stay clear lest they be hit by the gunfire being directed at the German battleship. (Photograph from the Imperial War Museum, London)

Survivors from the *Bismarck* are pulled aboard the *Dorsetshire*. With the admiral's staff, prize crews, and war correspondents, the *Bismarck's* complement numbered more than 2,200 men. Only 115 were saved. (Photograph from the Imperial War Museum, London)

open the reverse throttle. Looking back, it doesn't seem possible that our engines survived the strain.

The men, sweat oozing from every pore, had hardly a dry stitch on their bodies. A sweatband around the head, a slice of lemon in the right corner of the mouth, a cigar or pipe in the left – they looked comical and their mood matched their appearance.

At around 0100, a destroyer attack having just ended, the starboard turbine was ordered to 'Stop', while the centre and port turbines were ordered 'Ahead'. Therefore, the throttle of the starboard turbine was closed, shutting off the propelling steam. Even so, the turbine should have been turning at idling speed, but it was not. The order came to start it just to see if it would turn. The second mate opened the throttle to supply steam for 'Forward': first two, then three, four, and five times atmospheric pressure. Nothing happened! The turbine remained frozen in position. Even at ten, twenty, and thirty atmospheres of pressure it refused to budge. The engine control station was advised of the situation. 'Try everything!' was the reply, which meant 'Get steam to it, by hook or crook.' Steam pressure was increased to forty, fifty, fifty-eight atmospheres. One nozzle opened and injected steam against the rotors, stressing the turbine unevenly and dangerously – with steam pressure at fifty-eight times atmospheric pressure at 400 degrees centigrade. More steam! Then, the nozzle on the other side also began to register pressure: five, ten, twenty atmospheres. When it reached thirty, the turbine suddenly began to rotate: it did not break and it did not turn into 'blade salad'. From that time until the moment the ship went down the next morning, it kept on turning.

The seas were so heavy that we were not surprised by the long lulls between attacks. We supposed the destroyers were either trying to get in position to attack or were satisfied just to keep contact with us. In any case, we welcomed the lulls as moments in which, for however short a time, we could rest. Then, we would have totally illogical flashes of hope that despite everything we were going to escape. To St Nazaire? On our enforced course to the northwest? But the destroyers always came back, and the noise of our guns brought us back to the immutable present. And so the cycle went, hour after hour: we sighted the enemy; he attacked; our guns went into action; awareness of our inability to manoeuvre made us afraid that we'd be hit; once again, we had been lucky; the enemy was lost to sight; hope returned.

Around 0100 something new was added. A star shell fired by a destroyer suddenly burst in the sky – the thought flashed through my mind that it was the handwriting on the wall. It exploded high in the air and a flare suspended from a parachute slowly floated down, illuminating a wide expanse of water. We thought it was too far off to do the enemy much good in calculating our exact position. But gradually, as more shells were fired at long intervals, the range closed, until one of them came very near and seemed to be saying, 'There's no escape!' Although others followed and lit up the scene for attacks, in the darkness between them, contact was lost – or did I imagine that? After one particularly long lull, we saw a flare coming down almost directly onto us. 'Fire on the bow!' and men hurried to put it out.[1] For a moment, as it burned furiously, we were certain that it was revealing our position.

After the sinking of the *Bismarck*, I learned from

[1] Russell Grenfell, *The Bismarck Episode*, may have been describing this incident when, on page 168, he wrote: 'As the *Maori* retreated those on board her were sure they saw a torpedo hit [on the *Bismarck*]. A bright glow seemed to illuminate the enemy's waterline and shortly afterwards another vivid glare appeared to betoken a second explosion.'

Captain Benjamin C. S. Martin, commanding officer of
the heavy cruiser *Dorsetshire*, that the periodic firing of
star shells after 0230 was ordered by Tovey, who was
worried that the positions worked out in his battleships
might differ greatly from those plotted in the destroyers.
Tovey's hope was that this means of reconnaissance would
provide continuous information on the *Bismarck*'s position.

Nevertheless, the firing of the shells died out around
0300. The destroyers that were firing them had to come
within fairly close range of the *Bismarck* for the shells to
be of any help, and when they did so they were promptly
taken under fire. Captain Vian later wrote Tovey that, as
he saw it, his duty was, 'Firstly to deliver to you at all costs
the enemy, at the time you wished. Secondly to try to sink
or stop the enemy with torpedoes in the night if I thought
the attack should not involve the destroyers in heavy
losses.'[2] In view of the *Bismarck*'s obviously hopeless
situation, he certainly must have considered that to continue firing star shells would unnecessarily endanger his
destroyers.

We were happy that darkness again prevailed and
contact was broken. Or so it seemed, because when I
looked through my director I did not see any destroyers.
The coming of dawn seemed like a succession of curtains
being opened, each of which instantaneously disclosed a
more distant view. A little before 0600 it was light enough
for me to see that the destroyers were back in position
around us. Seeming quite suddenly to discover that they
were dangerously near the *Bismarck* they withdrew at
high speed to a more salubrious distance. The last we saw
of them, they were disappearing into the still numerous
rain squalls.

[2] Ludovic Kennedy, *Pursuit*, p. 184.

It was announced over the loudspeakers that we had sunk one destroyer and set two on fire, but this turned out to be understandable wishful thinking, a phenomenon common to all sides in time of war. No one on either side knew it at the time, but the truth of the matter is that, as of about 0700, we had not taken any torpedo hits nor, despite numerous straddling salvoes, had we made any direct hits on the destroyers.[3]

I was no longer concerned with the destroyers. They had managed to keep us under surveillance throughout the night, fired a lot of torpedoes at us, and surely reported our position to Tovey that morning. Our thoughts and our attention were now concentrated on the British battleships. Their hour had come, and I expected them to appear at any moment.

At 1954 on the twenty-sixth Group West radioed Lütjens that the *U-48* was near him and had been ordered to proceed at full speed to operate against the *Sheffield*. Lütjens sent the following sequence of radio signals to Group West:

2054: 'Attack by carrier aircraft.'
2105: 'Have torpedo hit aft.'
2115: 'Torpedo hit amidships.'
2115: 'Ship no longer steerable.'
2140: To the Oberkommando der Kriegsmarine and Group West: 'Ship unable to manoeuvre. We will fight to the last round. Long live the Führer.'

That last signal was sent only about half an hour after

[3] In his book, *The Loss of the Bismarck*, Vice-Admiral B. B. Schofield remarks on page 59 that the *Maori* observed one certain torpedo hit on the *Bismarck* during the night. On page 60, he writes, 'The question of how many torpedo hits were obtained during these attacks will never be known with absolute certainty.' I can certify that the *Bismarck* was not hit by a single torpedo from a destroyer that night.

the hit that jammed our rudder and long before we had tried every means of repairing the damage. Of course, the content of the message proved correct, but I cannot help wondering what made Lütjens send such a premature and certainly, for the fleet staff and the radiomen, depressing message.

At 2205 Group West informed Lütjens that the eight U-boats in the area had been ordered to close the *Bismarck*. Half an hour later he signalled, 'Am surrounded by *Renown* and light forces.'

In fact, the *Renown* did not participate in the destroyer action, and I do not remember seeing a ship of her size that night. Either Lütjens was labouring under an optical illusion or his B-Dienst team misidentified the *Renown*.

During the night the ship's command tried to keep the crew informed on the most important things that were going on. Information was relayed by loudspeaker and telephone as often as possible. The preceding signals were read out shortly after midnight, and later the following exchange of messages was announced:

2303 Group West to Fleet: 'Complete aerial reconnaissance on 27 May between 46° and 48°30′ north and sector from Brest northwest. Earliest possible start 0430, bombers 0630.'

2358 Fleet Commander to Führer of the German Reich, Adolf Hitler: 'We will fight to the last in belief in you, my Führer, and in unshakable confidence in Germany's victory.'

2359 Fleet to Group West: 'Ship is able to defend herself and propulsion plant intact. Does not respond to steering with engines, however.'

0004 Commander in Chief, Group West, to Fleet Commander: 'Our thoughts and good wishes are with our victorious comrades.'

0014 Commander in Chief, Kriegsmarine, to Fleet Commander: 'All our thoughts are with you and your ship. We wish you success in your hard fight.'

0113 Group West to Fleet: 'Tugs have been dispatched. Three Focke-Wulf 200 near the *Bismarck* at dawn. Three bomber groups start between 0500 and 0600.'

Soon after the signal of 0113 had been read out, a report circulated that at daybreak eighty-one Junkers-88 bombers would take off from France to attack the British fleet. Where this precise figure originated, I have never been able to discover, but it may be that the Luftwaffe officer on his staff, Hauptmann[4] Fritz Grohé, told Lütjens that a bomber group consisted of twenty-seven aircraft. If he did, Grohé did not say and probably did not know how many of them were operational. In any case, the news gave the crew a big lift.

Radio signals continued:

0147 Group West to Fleet: '*Ermland*[5] leaves La Pallice 0500 to assist.'

0153 Adolf Hitler to Fleet Commander: 'I thank you in the name of the entire German people.'

0153 Adolf Hitler to crew of *Bismarck*: 'All Germany is with you. What can be done, will be done. Your performance of duty will strengthen our people in the struggle for its destiny.'

0217 Fleet Commander to Commander in Chief, Kriegsmarine: 'Recommend bestowal of the Knight's Cross on Korvettenkapitän Schneider for sinking *Hood*.'

0221 Group West to Fleet: 'Send directional signals on

[4] Captain (Army and Luftwaffe)
[5] A supply ship

852 metres wavelength for five minutes at 0 and 30 minutes every hour for U-boats.'

0235 Commander in Chief, Group North, to Fleet Commander and *Bismarck*: 'We think of you all with loyalty and pride.'

0351 Commander in Chief, Kriegsmarine, to Korvettenkapitän Schneider, Fleet Commander to be informed: 'The Führer has bestowed Knight's Cross on you for sinking battle cruiser *Hood*. Hearty congratulations.'[6]

0419 Group West to Fleet: 'For Luftwaffe, weather reports every two hours with cloud ceiling. First report needed immediately.'

0443 Group West to Fleet: 'For bombers send directional signals on 443 kHz. for five minutes at 15 and 45 minutes every hour. Begin at 0615.'

0500 Fleet to Group West: 'Partly overcast, ceiling 600 metres, [wind] northwest 7.'

0542 Group West to Fleet: 'Two Focke-Wulf 200 took off 0330. Reconnaissance 0445 to 0515. Three bomber groups 0530.'

0652 Fleet to Group West: 'Situation unchanged. Wind strength 8 to 9.'

0745 Group West to Fleet: 'Fifty-one bombers took off 0520 to 0645, appearance from 0900.'

0835 Group West to Fleet: 'Today, around 1100, Spanish cruiser *Canarias* and two destroyers leave El Ferrol [for the position of the *Bismarck*] as a precaution to render assistance. Speed 20 to 22 knots.'

I do not recall the signal of 0835 being announced to the ship. When it arrived the *Bismarck* must have been in her

---

[6] Korvettenkapitän Adalbert Schneider was posthumously promoted to Fregattenkapitän.

battle with the *King George V* and the *Rodney*, which began at 0847. The cooperation of the neutral Spanish was the result of a request that the chief of staff of the Seekriegsleitung, Admiral Otto Schniewind, had transmitted to the Spanish Navy through the German naval attaché in Madrid, Kapitän zur See Kurt Meyer-Döhner.

0900 Group West to Fleet: 'Important for Luftwaffe. What is in sight where?'

This signal was not answered.

The destroyers' attacks, their manoeuvres, and their firing of star shells naturally meant tension-filled, exciting minutes for us. They claimed our attention and all our actions were concentrated on defence. The news the Fleet Commander and the ship's command gave us over the loudspeakers took our minds off the hopeless situation, raised morale, and revived sinking hopes. However, defending ourselves and listening to reports of the radio traffic were only brief episodes and were interspersed with long, indeed endless-seeming, periods of inactivity, which gave us time to talk or think.

Most of the time during the lulls between destroyer attacks we proceeded at very low speed, but occasionally we stopped. At such times the *Bismarck* lay athwart the seas and rolled quite heavily. Of course, except for helping us to defend ourselves, it did not matter whether we made headway or not, because when daylight came on 27 May, Tovey's battleships would find us one way or another.

Besides the assigned midshipman, the fire-control petty officers, and an ordnanceman, there were at my station two prize-crew officers and one of the reporters assigned to cover Exercise Rhine. Fate had decreed that the prize officers would never take a captured enemy merchantman with a valuable cargo into a German port. And the journalist, who in his eight days at sea had collected a wealth of dramatic material for publication at home, would never be able to write his story. Naturally, we chatted about the prospects of our situation changing for the better. The men were full of hope and seemed convinced that somehow we would reach France. They lived in the expectation that the promises from home would be fulfilled and were sure that 'our bombers will mop up in the morning.' For the sake of the crew in my station, I had to show optimism, so I agreed. Actually, I assessed our situation quite differently, but could not share my deep uneasiness with anyone.

Finding it rather close in the station, when a lull in the battle allowed I walked out to the open, searchlight-control station. In the darkness I could discern the out-lines of our superstructure, but the sea was empty. It happened to be a moment when we were lying athwart the seas and rolling heavily. Some distance below me on the upper deck a heavy door was making a metallic clang as it swung open and shut in rhythm with the movement of the ship. It was enough to get on one's nerves. A symptom of slackening discipline? Of course not. A death knell for us? That was more like it. Thank goodness, someone finally closed it tight.

Thoughts rushed in on me. There we were, in the Atlantic 400 nautical miles west of Brest, in the most modern and most powerful German battleship of the time. A highly refined work of technology, she was virtually without equal, yet one small part of her, the rudder, was the cause of the situation we were in. It was amazing that our principle of carrying replacements for all important components apparently did not apply to the rudder. That omission proved to be a real Achilles' heel.

There was nothing wrong with our propulsion plant and our hull was in good enough condition to get us to port. If only we had some sort of replacement rudder, a bow rudder or a rudder that could be lowered from the keel in deep water. Yes, if only we had! Then perhaps on this moonless night we could slip away from the enemy. But what use were those hypothetical reflections? They were only wishful thinking, illusions born of the abundance of time and the impossibility of doing anything.

The northwest wind increased steadily throughout the night and chased low rain clouds ever faster across the water. I thought the likelihood that tankers and tugs would be able to bring us relief in the morning was nil. What about the eighty-one Junkers-88s? In weather like this and at the limit of their range? They would never find us. These doubts, too, I kept to myself. Suddenly it began to blow more violently. In a matter of seconds the wind strength seemed to increase by two or three numbers. It must now be Force 9. That would have to happen, I thought, to create still another complication. The wind howled through the signal halyards. Before I went back to my station, I glanced up at Leutnant zur See Hans-Joachim Ritter's flak-control station 'C,' where a lookout was on duty. How draughty it must be up there! A strange thought flashed through my mind – you up there, unknown shipmate, it will be over for both of us on 27 May. In the grey of morning the British battleships will arrive long before help can get anywhere near us.

The minutes crept past. It didn't seem to want to pass, this sinister night of waiting, and waiting for nothing but the end. Enforced inactivity and the certainty of approaching defeat made it doubly depressing. The end must and indeed would come, but it was coming in agonizingly slow motion. Action was the only thing that could relieve the most unbearable tension.

What did the men think about the situation they were in? For days they, too, had been at their action stations, cut off in their compartments and turrets from all but a few of their comrades, often without an officer near. They did have in common the experience of listening to what Lütjens had to say two days earlier about the predicament their ship was in, but his sombre way of presenting things had created an atmosphere of depression. Lindemann's ensuing words gave some comfort and the intervening time had quieted many of their fears – but with the news of the jammed rudder, their dejection returned. They were told about all the efforts that were being made to repair the damage, but not in detail and only at long intervals. They could not have heard much that was encouraging, and so they had once again to prepare themselves to face the fate they had drawn. When, after midnight, it was announced that work on the rudders had ceased, hope evaporated. The older men took the news as a sentence of death for ship and crew. Everyone had to find his own way of dealing with the inevitable. Some fell into a mood of total indifference, in which nothing more could have any effect on them.

Later in the night permission was given for everyone to help himself to anything he wanted. This was a clear sign that the ship's command knew the end had come. And the men, above all the young ones, clung more than ever to the radio signals from home, to the promised help, the planes, the U-boats, the tanker, and the ocean tugs. Repeatedly, the word came over the loudspeaker, 'Watch for our planes' – 'Watch for our U-boats'. Over and over again new hope was built.

Hope, so useful and so fragile, how often it had come and gone in these days and nights.

Down in the engine rooms, where endurance had been strained to the utmost during the destroyer attacks, things were calmer that morning. The tension and stress of the last hours gave way to irresistible fatigue. Four days without sleep were too much, and they had been followed by this frenzied night. Men, hardly able to stay on their feet, lay down where they were and slept the sleep of exhaustion. Some of them were aroused only by the firing of our guns and the explosion of enemy shells.

30

Attempts to Save the Fleet War Diary

So sure was Lütjens that the *Bismarck* would not survive the approaching battle that early on the morning of 27 May he decided to have the Fleet War Diary taken to safety in France. He realized that it would be of inestimable value not only for the Seekriegsleitung but for any analyst of Exercise Rhine to know:

Why he, an experienced and successful leader of Atlantic operations, did not take the B-Dienst's radio signal of 21 May, which told him that the British had been alerted, as a warning that they would intensify their surveillance of the Denmark Strait as well as to the south of it, and adjust his plans accordingly. Did Group North's signals of 22 May, telling him that his departure from Norway had apparently not been noticed and that the British were searching too far to the south, remove any concern he may have had about being detected as he went north? Did he unquestioningly accept what these messages said?

Why he did not postpone Exercise Rhine and turn away when he first encountered the *Suffolk* and *Norfolk*, as he did during the corresponding phase of his operation with the *Scharnhorst* and *Gneisenau* three months earlier.

Why, when he held his course, he did not make an all-out attempt to sink his shadowers.

Why he abandoned the pursuit of the obviously

hard-hit *Prince of Wales*, thereby renouncing the possibility of achieving another apparently easy and important victory.

Why he interrupted Exercise Rhine so soon after the battle off Iceland and tried to reach port.

Why, on the evening of 24 May, he suddenly viewed the *Bismarck*'s fuel situation as so critical that he had to steer for St Nazaire by the shortest route instead of making a detour into the Atlantic, which might have been our salvation.

Why, on the morning of 25 May, he thought the enemy still knew our position.

The diary would also show exactly when on the night of 24–25 May and at what intervals the *Bismarck* made the gradual change of course to starboard that led to the breaking of contact.

Between 0500 and 0600 one of our planes was put on the catapult and made ready to carry the War Diary to safety. With full power, we manoeuvred to turn the starboard end of the catapult into the wind so that the plane could fly off. Nothing happened. The compressed-air line to the catapult was bent. Another effort to launch was made, but again nothing happened. The track was unusable. We had no means of making the necessary repair and, after some discussion, the launching was cancelled. Obviously, the Arado could not be left on the catapult, where in battle it would be a fire hazard. So, with its wings folded and holes made in its floats, it was pushed to the end of the track and tipped overboard. I watched it drift by and disappear.[1]

---

[1] The Bismarck's reconstructed War Diary states that, while we were trying to launch the Arado, waves were washing over the upper deck of the ship and some of the men of the 10.5-centimetre flak crews were washed overboard. Also, we were listing so far to port that our

I don't know what damaged the catapult, but I suspect it was the hit that shattered one of our service boats during the battle off Iceland.

In another effort to get the War Diary to safety in the short time remaining before the final action, at 0710 Lütjens radioed Group West, 'Send a U-boat to save War Diary.' That was his last radio signal home.

Send a U-boat! That was the last hope, the vague possibility of saving the War Diary. With the failure to launch the Arado, the *Bismarck* had exhausted her own means of carrying out that mission. And, with the dispatch of the message to Group West, there was nothing Lütjens could do towards the fulfilment of his wish but wait for the outside world to respond. Wait and wait.

At first, of course, Lütjens had reason to suppose that a U-boat would be sent. In fact, at 0801, Group West informed him, '*U-556* will pick up War Diary.' But as the morning wore on, no U-boat appeared. Presumably, so I thought then, there was none near enough or none that had enough fuel to detour to us.

In order to understand why we never saw the *U-556* it is necessary to go back a day.

On 26 May, when dispositions were being made to support the *Bismarck* in her increasingly critical situation, new instructions were sent to the U-boats in the Bay of

---

15-centimetre turrets on that side were under water. I cannot reconcile this entry with reality. There being no action in progress or, as it appeared, in immediate prospect between 0500 and 0600, I went to watch the aircraft being launched. It is true that the ship was listing to port, but our 15-centimetre turrets were certainly not under water at the time. Furthermore, our beamy ship was doing so little rolling that it would not have been possible for any members of the flak crews to be washed overboard from the still-elevated superstructure deck. I did not observe conditions such as those described in the diary until about twenty minutes before the ship sank.

Biscay. One of those boats was the *U-556*, whose commanding officer, Kapitänleutnant Herbert Wohlfarth, was ordered to reconnoitre and operate in the area of the *Bismarck*'s most recently reported position. When Wohlfarth received those orders, he was on his way home from a patrol that began on 1 May. Therefore, he was low on fuel and, on his way to the *Bismarck*, he would have to be extremely economical with what he had left. Furthermore, he had expended all his torpedoes against British convoys.

Wohlfarth reached the immediate area around the *Bismarck* on the evening of 26 May. Around 1950 he saw the *Renown* and the *Ark Royal* coming out of the mist at high speed – the big ships of Force H. Nothing for it but to submerge. 'Enemy bows on, ten degrees to starboard, without destroyers, without zigzagging,' as Wohlfarth later described it. He would not even have had to run to launch torpedoes. All he would have had to do was position himself between the *Renown* and the *Ark Royal* and fire, at both almost simultaneously. If only he had some torpedoes! He had seen activity on the carrier's flight deck. Perhaps he could have helped us. Yes, perhaps – that is what he thought at the time. But what he saw was the activity after the launching of the second and decisive attack on the *Bismarck*. So, even if he had had torpedoes, he would not have been able to save us from the rudder hit. The Swordfish had long since banked over the *Sheffield* and were just about to attack us.

Fifty minutes later, at 2039, Wohlfarth surfaced and made a radio report: 'Enemy in view, a battleship, an aircraft carrier, course 115°, enemy is proceeding at high speed. Position 48°20′ north, 16°20′ west.' Wohlfarth intended his report to be picked up by any of his comrades who might be in the vicinity and able to manoeuvre to attack. Then he proceeded on the surface at full speed behind the *Renown* and the *Ark Royal*. Their course to the *Bismarck* coincided almost exactly with his own. Every now and again, he submerged and took sound bearings to both ships, but after 2200 he could no longer hear them. The race between his little boat and the two big ships was an unequal contest.

At 2330 Wohlfarth, then 420 nautical miles west of Brest, gave the alarm again. A destroyer came out of the mist at high speed. Once more, he quickly dived. He had reached a depth of thirty metres when the enemy passed him, her propellers making a devilish row. Relieved, he noted in his War Diary: 'Fingers crossed again, no depth charges!'

It was probably one of Vian's destroyers, but at that moment she was not interested in a U-boat. She was too busy trying to shadow and torpedo the *Bismarck*.

Another entry in Wohlfarth's War Diary reads: '27.5.0000, [wind] northwest 5, seaway 5, rain squalls, moderate visibility, very dark night. Surfaced. What can I do for the *Bismarck*? I can see star shells being fired and flashes from the *Bismarck*'s guns. It is a terrible feeling to be near and not to be able to do anything. All I can do is reconnoitre and lead in boats that have torpedoes. I am keeping contact at the limit of visibility, reporting the position, and sending directional signals to call up the other boats.'

At 0352: 'I am moving around on the east side to the south, in order to be in the direction of the activity. I soon reach the limit of what I can do in view of my fuel supply. Otherwise I won't get home.'

0400: 'The seas are rising ever higher. *Bismarck* still fighting. Reported weather for the Luftwaffe.'

Around 0630 Wohlfarth sighted the *U-74*, one of the other boats that had been in the Bay of Biscay. Optically and by megaphone, he transferred the mission of maintaining contact with the *Bismarck* to her commanding officer, Kapitänleutnant Eitel-Friedrich Kentrat. He gave Kentrat the *Bismarck*'s position, which he based on his observations of the star shells fired during the night, adding: 'I have not seen her directly. You assume contact. I have no more fuel.' And after blinking a greeting to Kentrat, he turned away.

In his War Diary Wohlfarth wrote: 'Around 0630 gave last contact report, sighted *U-74*, by visual means gave *U-74* the mission of maintaining contact. I can stay on the scene only by using my electric motors at slow speeds. Above water I need fuel and would have to retire.'

After transferring his mission, Wohlfarth promptly submerged and did not surface again until 1200, a time at which radio signals were routinely repeated. That was when he heard for the first time the order radioed to him between 0700 and 0800 to pick up the *Bismarck*'s War Diary. Having no more idea than had the headquarters ashore that in the meantime the *Bismarck* had sunk, he immediately asked Commander in Chief, U-Boats, to transfer this mission to Kentrat.[2] In the course of the

---

[2] Wondering why on 27 May the *U-556*, which had been at sea for almost four weeks and was therefore presumably in a precarious fuel situation, was assigned to pick up the War Diary, in 1978 I wrote to ask Wohlfarth. He replied: 'The U-boat operational command had only a general idea of my fuel situation from a report I sent when I was off Greenland that I was returning because of a shortage of fuel and did not know that, after I had been en route home for a day, I spent half a day operating at high speed against a convoy in a northwesterly direction, which used up my last reserves.

'Admiral Dönitz selected me for the pick-up because I had given running contact reports throughout the night. The *U-74*, to which I gave the mission of maintaining contact around 0600 that morning, would have automatically assumed responsibility for carrying out the order. But I don't think the order was radioed until around 1000, so that Kentrat could not have performed the mission with the *U-74*, either.

'I was submerged from 0600 to 1200 and did not receive the radio signal until 1200, at which time radio signals were regularly repeated.'

morning Wohlfarth did hear a series of explosions, but had no way of interpreting their significance.

By the time Kentrat received the radio order issued in response to Wohlfarth's signal, 'U-boat Kentrat pick up *Bismarck* War Diary,' he could only search in vain.

I still see it as something more than a coincidence that the *U-556* was the boat ordered to pick up the *Bismarck*'s War Diary because, to us on board, the *U-556* was no ordinary U-boat. There was a very special bond between the little boat and the giant battleship. Both were built at Blohm & Voss and in the summer of 1940 they were often neighbours on the ways. When the *U-556* was commissioned, the mighty bow of the *Bismarck* towered over her. Wohlfarth, who was known in naval circles as 'Sir Parsifal', decided that the commissioning ceremony would not be complete without a band and, since a U-boat certainly did not carry one, he would ask the big neighbour to provide the music. Accordingly, he went to see Lindemann, but he did not go empty-handed. In exchange, he offered the *Bismarck* the Patenschaft[3] of his boat. Lindemann readily accepted. Wohlfarth got his band and thereafter his artistically designed Patenschaftsurkunde[4] hung in the *Bismarck*.

Lindemann and Wohlfarth became friends. At the beginning of 1941 the *Bismarck* and the *U-556* were together during gunnery exercises in the Baltic, and once even used the same target. The *U-556*, which Lindemann had allowed to precede him, damaged the target so badly with ten hits that the *Bismarck* could not use it that day. Lindemann, however, did not take it amiss and soon dispelled Wohlfarth's fear that he would be greeted with an ill-humoured reaction, 'I do not begrudge you that in the least. I wish that you may have as much and rapid

[3] Sponsorship
[4] Certificate of Sponsorship

Patenschafts Urkunde

Wir U 556 (500 t) erklären hiermit vor Neptun, dem
Herrscher über Ozeane, Meere, Seen, Flüsse, Bäche, Teiche und Rinnsale
daß wir unserem grossen Bruder, dem Schlachtschiff
Bismarck (42 000 t) in jeder Lage zu Wasser, unter Wasser,
zu Lande wie in der Luft beistehen wollen

Hamburg, den 28. Januar 1941

Kommandant u.
Besatzung U 556

The Patenschafturkunde of the *U-556* for the *Bismarck*. (Courtesy of Herbert Wohlfarth.)

success in the Atlantic and win the Knight's Cross for it.'
Relieved, Wohlfarth replied, 'I hope we both receive the
Knight's Cross in the common struggle in the Atlantic.'[5]

Wohlfarth heard over the radio about the sinking of the
Hood during the operation he had just ended against
convoys. At first he could not believe it. Now, only two

---

[5] Wohlfarth was, in fact, awarded the Knight's Cross on 15 May 1941.

days later, the situation of the *Bismarck* was drastically different, almost hopeless. What did his Patenschaftsurkunde say? 'We, the *U-556* (500 tons), hereby declare before Neptune, the ruler of the oceans, lakes, seas, rivers, brooks, ponds, and rills, that we will stand beside our big brother, the battleship *Bismarck* (42,000 tons), whatever may befall her on water, under water, on land, or in the air. Hamburg, 28 January 1941. The captain and crew of the *U-556*.' One of the two sketches on the certificate shows 'Sir Parsifal' warding off aircraft attacking the *Bismarck* with a sword in his right hand and stopping torpedoes coming towards her with his left thumb. The other sketch shows the *Bismarck* being towed by the *U-556*. It almost seemed as though Wohlfarth had the gift of prophecy when he prepared that certificate.

Help against aircraft and torpedoes, and then a tow. That was exactly what the *Bismarck* needed, and he, of all people, Godfather Wohlfarth, was near her. But he was powerless to help her.

31

A Last Visit to the Bridge

The clock was crawling towards 0800. It had been bright daylight for a long time. I could not understand why there was still nothing to be seen of the enemy battleships. Hadn't they had time to catch up with us during the night? Where were they?

At the moment there was no specific order from the ship's command that I had to carry out and nothing important demanded my presence in the after fire-control station, so I decided to circulate a little and started with the wardroom. As I went in, for the first time I became strongly aware that we were listing to port. It was strange how much more pronounced the effect was in this closed room than elsewhere. A handful of officers, the senior of whom was Korvettenkapitän Wilhelm Freytag, were sitting round a table. The names of the others escape me. On the opposite side of the room was a large tureen, its dippers hanging in a sweet gruel that sloshed back and forth with the rolling of the ship. The silence at the table was broken from time to time by a laconic, hopeless remark. How could it have been otherwise? After all, we were by ourselves – why continue to play games? We all knew what was to come. Finally, someone said, 'Today my wife will become a widow, but she doesn't know it.' After that, the atmosphere was so heavy that if anyone else had wanted to say anything, the words would have stuck in his throat. It was depressing. Too depressing to stay there.

Next I went to the bridge, which struck me as pretty deserted. That was an illusion, because there were men stretched out in the corners. Lindemann was standing in the forward command post. He was wearing an open life jacket. I had to look twice to believe it.[1] His steward, Arthur Meier, was just handing him his breakfast and, while he ate it, he seemed strangely detached from his surroundings. He saw me coming, but he did not return my salute, which I held as I looked at him intently in the hope that he would say something. He did not say a word. He did not even glance at me. I was greatly disturbed and puzzled. After all, I had been his personal adjutant and the situation we were in seemed to me unusual enough to merit some remark. I would have given a great deal for a word from him, one that would have told me how he felt about what had happened. But there was only silence, and I had to try to interpret it for myself.

That was not the Lindemann we all knew. I thought back. In private conversations in the past year he told me how much he had always wanted to have command of a great battleship, and how happy he was to be appointed commanding officer of the *Bismarck*. He did say, however, that command of a flagship was not exactly what he had hoped for. Having an admiral embarked could, at critical moments, lead to differences that did not arise in a 'brown' ship.[2] Naturally, the personalities involved would have a lot to do with that. Early in 1941 a classmate asked him, 'How goes it with Lütjens?' His terse reply was, 'Not

[1] Jochen Brennecke, *Schlachtschiff Bismarck*, note 329, quotes statements I allegedly made to the Zurich *Weltwoche* in 1959 on the subject of this meeting with Lindemann. I have never made any statement, either oral or written, to that newspaper. I disavow both the content and the form of the remarks ascribed to me there. My impression of Lindemann on this last morning and the thoughts I had about my meeting with him are described in this book.

[2] In the Kriegsmarine a 'brown' ship was one in which no force commander (usually from the rank of Konteradmiral upwards) was embarked, and consequently the captain was the highest-ranking officer on board.

easy.' His only consolation, Lindemann also told me, was that if his ship, the flagship of the Fleet Commander, were ever to be put in unnecessary danger, the blame would be on the admiral and not on him. These words came back to me, loud and clear, as I watched him standing there: was that the way he felt about what had happened? Was his demeanour intended to show that he accepted none of the responsibility for the situation into which his ship had been led? When command decisions were called for in the course of Exercise Rhine, wouldn't at least some of those he made have been different from those made by Lütjens, and wouldn't he have chosen differently from among the alternatives available? After the B-Dienst centre's report about the alerting of the enemy on 21 May, for example, or when the *Suffolk* and the *Norfolk* were first sighted? And what decision would he have made on the question of continuing the action against the *Prince of Wales* on the morning of 24 May? If just one question had been decided differently early in the game, the subsequent course of the operation could have been different in so many ways. There would have been no guarantee against defeats and losses, but the *Bismarck* might not have suffered such a lingering death.

The personalities of the two officers certainly played a role in what took place. Lütjens was deeply impressed with what he took to be the superiority of British radar and his mood varied between optimism and despondency. Lindemann judged matters more realistically and resisted the depression of the Fleet Commander until finally, in military submission, he capitulated.

Junack's impression of Lindemann was much like mine. Towards morning, he later said, 'full power' orders to the engines gradually stopped coming and the atmosphere in the ship became somewhat calmer. Lehmann called him to the engine-control station to take over the watch for a little while. Just then the order came from the bridge, 'All engines stop'. When some time passed and no other order came, Junack began to fear that, after the strains of the past hours, the turbines might be warped by heat expansion. He therefore picked up the telephone and asked for the captain. Having reported his concern to Lindemann, he requested an order for 'ahead slow', and was greeted with the reply, 'Ach, do as you like.' That was not the Lindemann Junack knew.

Only four hours earlier Lindemann was a completely different person. Around 0400 he was standing silently beside Schneider in a corner of the bridge. Then he moved away, but a moment later returned, beaming with delight, and went over to Schneider. A radio signal announcing that Schneider had been awarded the Knight's Cross had just arrived, and Lindemann offered congratulations to his first gunnery officer. Cool and collected as ever – nothing about him betrayed his awesome worries. But, when I saw him at about eight o'clock, he had been on the bridge of his helpless ship for eleven hours straight. The rudder hit, the destroyer attacks, it was all too much.

Was this really, as it was to all appearances, the way Lindemann felt? The answer to that question was lost when he died two hours later.

Before I left to continue my tour of the ship, I threw a glance at Lindemann and at Meier, who was still standing in front of him. The good Arthur Meier, who managed a pub in Hanover. When I was serving as Lindemann's adjutant I saw him every day as he looked after the needs of his captain and brought him his Three Castles cigarettes. Arthur Meier was always ready for a little chat. He could imagine much nicer things than war and being in the navy, but, as he said resignedly, one had to serve somewhere, and being in the *Bismarck* was quite all right with him. Such a big ship and such heavy armour! It would be hard for anything to happen to him there. How often he said that. And now his last dawn had broken.

From the bridge I went down the small ladder to the charthouse. The atmosphere in there was ghostly. A lamp lit up the lonely chart on which no more courses would be plotted. The rest of the room was dark; apparently no one was there. Our position when we received the rudder hit the previous evening was marked on the chart. I could see where our course towards St Nazaire ended. From there on, a serpentine line showed our swerving course to the northwest, into the wind. Where the line stopped must be where we were at the moment. Navigationally, everything was up to date. Was there really no one in there? Then, in a corner I saw two men stretched out on the deck. Well, they had nothing better to do. I quickly left the room.

As I passed the heavy flak guns on my way back to my station, I suddenly saw Lütjens. I had not seen him since Exercise Rhine began on 19 May. And now, in this situation! What would he say to me? Accompanied by his Second Staff Officer, Fregattenkapitän Paul Ascher, he came straight towards me, obviously on his way to the admiral's bridge. There was not much room to pass, so I stood aside and saluted. Lütjens looked at me, briefly, attentively, and returned my salute. But not a word came from him, either. He gave no sign of acknowledgement that we were in an extraordinary predicament – although we almost brushed together as he passed. I knew that I would never see the two gentlemen again and watched them until they disappeared behind the superstructure.

Günther Lütjens, Fleet Commander and my command-ing officer in the *Karlsruhe* during her cruise to North and South America from 1934 to 1935. What memories he brought back!

As a Leutnant zur See in the *Karlsruhe* I was the range-finding officer and a divisional section officer. Lütjens attended divisional instruction more often than any other commanding officer I ever served with, and paid closer attention. Having been chief of the Office of Naval Personnel in the Defence Ministry from 1931 to 1934, he took special interest in how his junior officers performed in the training of their men and wanted to see for himself.

Other images came before me. The tall, slim figure and the dignified bearing of the *Karlsruhe*'s commanding officer when he was representing his country on ceremonial occasions in foreign ports. He was not the kind of superior whom we junior officers would seek out for ourselves. He was too reserved for that; he seemed almost melancholy. Yet we were conscious of the integrity and reliability that he exuded.

And now as Fleet Commander? I had no firsthand knowledge. I had never served directly under him. But we in the officer corps were aware that Raeder had a very high degree of confidence in him.

Lütjens and Ascher had long since disappeared out of sight. I looked at the clock. It was past 0830. Where were the Britons? They should have been here at daybreak at the latest. I still could not understand their delay. Hardly had I formulated that thought than the alarm bells began to ring shrilly. It seemed as though they would never stop.

The *Bismarck*'s last battle had begun.

32

Tovey Sets the Time of the Final Action

At about 2130, after the second air attack on the *Bismarck*, its leader, Lieutenant Commander Tim Coode, reported to Admiral Tovey in the *King George V*, 'Estimate no hits.' It was bitter news, for it buried Tovey's last hope of being able to stop the German battleship. However, he found it strange that shortly before this the *Sheffield* had reported the *Bismarck* on course 340 degrees. A northwesterly course? Towards his own formation? Highly improbable, not to say unbelievable. For, after Coode's negative report, reason argued against the *Bismarck* making such a drastic course change, and Tovey sarcastically remarked to his staff, 'I fear Larcom has joined the Reciprocal Club.'[1] Scarcely had he said this than a message came in from one of the aircraft shadowing the battleship, '*Bismarck* steering northerly course.' Really? Was Larcom right? Nine minutes later, a second aerial signal told him that the *Bismarck* was on a northerly course. Then a second report from the *Sheffield* confirmed the news.

If the *Bismarck* had not been damaged, why in the world would she steer this suicidal course towards the main body of his fleet? She must have been hit; indeed, she must be seriously damaged. No other explanation was possible. Now the opposing sides were coming towards

[1] An expression used in the Royal Navy when a 180-degree error is made in reporting a ship's course or bearing. It is easy to make such a mistake because, when a warship is lying almost bow-on or stern-on to the observer, her stern and bow are sometimes indistinguishable. Captain Charles Larcom was commanding officer of the *Sheffield*.

one another at a relative speed of almost 40 knots. This meant Tovey could force an action before it got dark. The *King George V* and the *Rodney* turned on a southerly course, towards the *Bismarck*.

It was somewhere about 2230 by the time the *Ark Royal* had recovered all her aircraft from the second attack. Captain Maund's debriefing of their crews revealed that a hit amidships on the *Bismarck* had been observed. Tovey was so advised but he was still mystified. If she really had been hit amidships, how could that have anything to do with her present course?

It being completely dark by this time, Tovey realized that the last reconnaissance planes would have returned to the *Ark Royal* and no more reports would be forthcoming from them. He consoled himself with the knowledge that Vian's destroyers would still be in contact with the *Bismarck* and, indeed, their subsequent reports convinced him that she was so seriously damaged that she could not change materially the course she was on. She was obviously compelled to run into the wind and, fortunately, towards Tovey's position.

His German opponent would not escape him now. But, not being absolutely certain of the positions of either Force H, to the south of him, or the *Bismarck*, he decided to delay any action until dawn rather than risk collisions on this pitch-black night. Around 2230 he and the *Rodney* turned to a north-northeasterly and, later, a northerly and westerly course. What he wanted to do was come out of the northwest the next morning, so that the *Bismarck* would be silhouetted against the glowing, eastern horizon and he would have the most favourable conditions possible for directing his guns.

Tovey had no sooner made his first change in course than a report from Somerville, in the *Renown*, informed him that the *Bismarck* had probably received a second

hit – this one on her starboard quarter. That was what
Tovey had been hoping for. It told him that the *Bismarck*'s rudders or propellers must have been damaged
and she was therefore as good as incapable of manoeuvring. Now nothing could prevent a fight in the morning. He
dashed off a handwritten note to the commanding officer
of his flagship, Captain W. R. Patterson: 'To K.G.V. The
sinking of the *Bismarck* may have an effect on the war as a
whole out of all proportion to the loss to the enemy of one
battleship. May God be with you and grant you victory.
JT 26/5/41.'

Tovey received the *Ark Royal*'s last reconnaissance
report shortly before 0100 on 27 May. According to this
message, immediately after the air attack the *Bismarck*
turned two complete circles and came to rest on a
northerly heading. If there was any lingering doubt about
her inability to manoeuvre, it was now dispelled. After
days and nights of almost unbearable tension, Tovey and
his staff felt immeasurable relief. Only seven hours earlier
hope of stopping the *Bismarck* had been virtually abandoned. The odds against it were a thousand to one. Only a
miracle could help, and a miracle had happened, one that
allowed him not only to determine almost to the minute
the time of the action but to choose his tactics against the
crippled enemy.

Tovey was not the only one who, on 26 May, was
making calculations that seemed to have only the slightest
chance of being correct. His almost vanished hope corres-
ponded with our remote fear that the *Bismarck*'s steering
gear would be hit. How likely was it that that would
happen? During our training period, we occasionally
practised the battle problem 'hit in the steering gear'. The
drill was that two or three compartments were 'flooded'
and the men in them had to stay where they were. 'How
would it work in reality,' they asked their training officer,

'if a hit penetrated, would we all be dead?' 'Well, yes,' the officer replied, 'and you should pretend to be dead. Put your caps on backwards and you'll be counted as dead.' Then after a pause, he added, 'But the chances of such a hit are a hundred thousand to one, practically nil.'

Within a matter of seconds, a half-buried British hope became a miracle, and a piece of almost impossible German bad luck became a catastrophe!

Soon after he heard that the *Bismarck* had turned two complete circles, Tovey, wanting to be sure he didn't get too far away from the enemy, returned to a somewhat southerly course. He ordered Somerville to keep his task force at least 20 nautical miles away from the *Bismarck*, which would be close enough for air operations by the *Ark Royal* yet far enough to keep the *Renown* from being exposed to the *Bismarck*'s superior gunnery. About 0230 Tovey, as previously mentioned, instructed Vian to have his destroyers fire star shells periodically so that a better continuous watch could be kept over the position of the *Bismarck*. However, Tovey was not particularly chagrined when Vian decided some half-hour later that the firing of the shells was endangering his destroyers and ordered it to cease. Numerous rain squalls were reducing visibility to the point where hardly anyone in the *King George V* could see the flares, anyway.

At daybreak, still not sure of the exact position of the *Bismarck* and visibility being poor, Tovey decided to wait an hour or two after it had become completely light before beginning to fight. Thus, the *King George V* and the *Rodney* did not sight their enemy until 0843 – 0843 on 27 May.

It might be said that this was Tovey's fourth effort to bring about this encounter. The first, 0900 on 25 May, was missed because the *Suffolk*'s radar contact with the *Bismarck* had been broken a few hours earlier. The second, on the evening of 26 May, was missed because, by the time he knew the *Bismarck* had been hit, night had fallen. The third, dawn on 27 May, had had to be passed up because he did not have the *Bismarck*'s precise position and the weather was not favourable. It wasn't really a very long time since the evening of 26 May, but it seemed to me then like eternity.

Besides the *King George V*, the *Rodney*, and Force H, two other British ships were trying to reach the scene of the coming battle on the morning of 27 May.

From the north came the *Norfolk*, our old 'friend' from the Denmark Strait. Although she was running low on fuel, she had kept up the chase all day long on 26 May and, naturally, wanted to be in on the kill. As early as 0753 she sighted us to the southeast, at a distance of nine nautical miles. Assuming that we were the *Rodney*, Captain A. J. L. Phillips, the skipper of the *Norfolk*, ordered visual recognition signals to be made. He had no sooner done so than he realized that he was heading straight for the *Bismarck* at a speed of 20 knots. As he made an immediate, sharp turn to get his ship out of danger, he saw the *King George V* and the *Rodney* coming over the horizon and signalled Tovey, '*Bismarck* bearing 130°, range 16 nautical miles.' Thereupon, recognizing that he was a bit too far to the north, Tovey turned southward.

From the west came the *Dorsetshire*, which had been escorting a northbound convoy. When, at about 1100 on 26 May, Captain Martin received the Admiralty's radio signal reporting that a Catalina had found the *Bismarck* again he calculated that she was 360 nautical miles north of him. He immediately recognized that he had a good chance of intercepting her if it was true that she was making for the coast of France. On his own initiative, he decided to intervene and proceeded towards the *Bismarck* on an easterly course at high speed and with a following sea. When he appeared, unannounced and unexpected, at the scene of action, Tovey's forces took him to be the *Prinz Eugen*, and he narrowly missed being fired on by the Home Fleet.

When Tovey, with the *King George V* and the *Rodney*, finally steered towards the *Bismarck*, he did so in the hope that the sight of his two battleships heading straight for them would unnerve the German range-finding and fire-control officers. After all, the four anxious days and nights through which they had lived must have taken their toll.[2]

[2] 'Sinking of the German Battleship *Bismarck* on 27th May 1941.' Dispatch by Admiral Sir John Tovey, Supplement to the *London Gazette*, 14 October 1947, Item No. 80.

33

The Last Battle

The alarm bells were still ringing when, returning from the bridge, I entered my action station. I picked up the control telephone and heard, 'Two battleships port bow.' I turned my director and saw two bulky silhouettes, unmistakably the *King George V* and *Rodney*, at a range of approximately 24,000 metres. As imperturbable as though they were on their way to an execution, they were coming directly towards us in line abreast, a good way apart, their course straight as a die. The seconds ticked by. Tension and anticipation mounted. But the effect was not what Tovey hoped for. The nerves of our gun directors, gun captains, and range-finding personnel were steady. After the utterly hopeless night they had just spent, any action could only be a release. The very first salvo would bring it. How many ships were approaching no longer meant anything; we could be shot to pieces only once.

Our eight 38-centimetre guns were now opposed to nine 40.6-centimetre and ten 35.6-centimetre guns; our twelve 15-centimetre guns by twenty-eight 15.2-centimetre and 13.3-centimetre guns. A single British broadside weighed 18,448 kilogrammes (20,306 kilogrammes, including the sixteen 20.3-centimetre guns on the heavy cruisers *Norfolk* and *Dorsetshire*) against 6,904 kilogrammes for a German broadside.[1] In our foretop Schneider was giving orders in his usual, calm voice. He announced that our

---

[1] The *Bismarck*'s main battery fired one round per barrel every twenty-five seconds; her secondary battery fired ten rounds per barrel per minute.

target was the *Rodney*, which was off our port bow and heading straight for us. Then, to the ship's command, 'Main and secondary batteries ready, request permission to fire.' But it was the *Rodney* that got off the first salvo, at 0847. The *King George V*'s first salvo followed one minute later.

The range had closed to less than 20,000 metres, at which distance the time of flight of the shells was less than one minute, but it seemed many times that long. Finally, white mushrooms, tons of water thrown up by heavy shells, rose 70 metres into the air. But they were still quite far from us. At 0849 the *Bismarck*'s fore turrets replied with a partial salvo at the *Rodney*. At this time, our after turrets could not be brought to bear on the target. Schneider observed his first three salvoes as successively 'short', 'straddling', and 'over', an extremely promising start that I only knew about from what I heard on the telephone because the swinging back and forth of the *Bismarck* allowed me only intermittent glimpses of the enemy. Obviously not considering dividing our fire, he continued to concentrate on the *Rodney*.

As the shells hurtled past one another in the air, I tried to distinguish incoming ones from those being discharged from our own guns. Suddenly I remembered wardroom conversations that I had had with British naval officers regarding range-finding techniques. They had high praise for their prismatic instruments while I praised our stereoscopic ones. Did we have the better principle? The *Rodney* seemed to need a lot of time to find our range.

I spent the first few minutes of the battle wondering why no enemy shells were landing on us, but that soon changed and there were more than enough of them. At 0854 the *Norfolk*, which was off the *Bismarck*'s starboard bow, began firing her 20.3-centimetre battery at a range of 20,000 metres. A few minutes later, the *Rodney* opened

From 0800, German Summer Time, to 1039, German Summer Time, on 27 May. The last battle. (Diagram courtesy of Jürgen Rohwer.)

up with her secondary battery and, around 0902, she observed a spectacular hit on the forward part of the *Bismarck*. At 0940 the *Dorsetshire* began firing on us at a range of 18,000 metres. The *Bismarck* was under fire from all directions, and the British were having what amounted to undisturbed target practice.

Not long after the action began the *King George V* and, a little later, the *Rodney* gradually turned to starboard on to a southerly course, where they manoeuvred so as to stay on our port side. This tactic caused the range to diminish with extraordinary rapidity, which seemed to be exactly what Tovey wanted. Lindemann could no longer manoeuvre so as to direct, or at least influence, the tactical course of the battle. He could neither choose his course nor evade the enemy's fire. Tovey, on the other hand, could base his tactical decisions on the sure knowledge that our course would continue to be into the wind. We could not steer even this course to the best advantage of our gunners, who were faced with great difficulty in correcting direction. Though I could not see what was going on around me from my completely enclosed, armoured control station, it was not hard to picture how the scene outside was changing. As the range decreased, the more frequent became the *harrumphs* of incoming shells and the louder grew the noise of battle. Our secondary battery, as well as those of the enemy, had gone into action. Only our antiaircraft guns, which had no targets of their own and were useless in a close engagement between battleships, were silent. At first, their crews were held as replacements for casualties at other guns, and were stationed in protected rooms set aside for them. These 'protected rooms', however, being on the upper deck and not armoured, provided little protection even against shell splinters, let alone direct hits.

When perhaps twenty minutes had passed since the

firing of the first salvoes, I searched the horizon through my starboard director for other hostile ships. Off our bow, I made out a cruiser, the *Norfolk*, which by chance had just stopped firing. We had not fired on her because Schneider and Albrecht were still concentrating on the battleships, which were off our port bow and at that moment not visible from aft. No sooner had I begun to wonder whether, with so many enemies around us, our ship's command would decide to divide our fire, than I received an indirect answer. Cardinal came on the control telephone and said that the main fire-control station in the foretop was out of action or, at any rate, could not be contacted, that turrets Anton and Bruno were out of action, and that I was to take over control of turrets Caesar and Dora from aft. He said nothing about the forward fire-control station. I supposed that it would continue to direct the secondary battery, unless it had been disabled, which seemed not unlikely in view of the number of times the forward section of the ship had been hit. There was not time to ask long questions and, since I was not given a target, I had a completely free hand.

An observer in the *Norfolk* saw both barrels of turret Anton fall to maximum depression as though its elevating mechanism had been hit. The barrels of turret Bruno, he commented, were trained to the side and pointing high into the air.

'Action circuit aft,'[2] I announced and, beginning forward,

[2] 'Action circuit aft' meant that the turrets were being directed by the after fire-control station through the after computer room. Then on duty in that computer room were the following men: Leutnant zur See Heinz Aengeneyndt and Stabsoberbootsmann (Chief Warrant Officer) Friedrich Adams, order-transmission officers for the main and secondary battery, respectively; Bootsmaat (Boatswain Petty Officer) Paul Rudek,

scanned the horizon through my port director. Strangely enough, there was no trace of the *Rodney*, which I had not seen to starboard, either. She must have been in the dead space forward of my station. But there, steaming on a reciprocal course and now a bit abaft our beam, was the *King George V*. She was about 11,000 metres distant – near enough to touch, almost like a drill in the Baltic. 'Passing fight to port, target is the battleship at 250°,' I told the after computer room and, upon receiving the 'ready' report from below, 'One salvo.' *Boom!* It went off and during the approximately twenty seconds that it was in the air, I added, 'Battleship bow left, one point off, enemy speed 20 knots.'

The excellent visibility would be a great help in finding the range quickly, I thought, which was particularly important because the target was rapidly passing astern of us. 'Attention, fall,' announced the computer room. 'Two questionably right, two right wide, questionably over,' I observed, then ordered, 'Ten more left, down four, a salvo.' *Boom!* . . . 'Attention, fall' . . . 'Middle over' . . . 'Down four, a salvo' . . . 'Attention, fall' . . . 'Middle short' . . . and, full of anticipation, 'Up two, good rapid!' Then again our shot fell and the four columns of water began to rise . . . quarter, half, three-quarters of the way, at which point they were useful for observation 'Three over, one short.' I never did see the splashes reach their full height. Lieutenant Commander Hugh Guernsey, in the *King George V*, heard my fourth salvo whistle over and, wondering if the next one would be a hit, involuntarily took a step back behind a splinter shield.

The director gave a violent shudder and my two petty

---

range-averager; Matrosenhauptgefreiter Herbert Langer, firing data compiler; Matrosengefreiter Adolf Eich, direction and elevation transmitter; and Matrosengefreiter Hans Halke, firing signal transmitter.

officers and I had our heads bounced hard against the
eyepieces. What did that? When I tried to get my target in
view again, it wasn't there; all I could see was blue. I was
looking at something one didn't normally see, the 'blue
layer' baked on the surface of the lenses and mirrors to
make the picture clearer. My director had been shattered.
Damn! I had just found the range of my target and now I
was out of the battle. Though no one in the station was
hurt, our instruments were ruined. Obviously, a heavy
shell had passed low over our station and carried away
anything that protruded. We tested all our optics and
couldn't see our targets through any of them. I walked
under the ladder to the cupola and looked up towards our
large range-finder and its operators. There was nothing
there. Nothing at all. What only a moment before was a
complete array had vanished without a trace. A heavy
shell had ripped through the middle of the cupola, whose
jagged ruin allowed a clear view of the cloudy sky. From
the *Rodney*? The *King George V*? Who knows? It made
no difference. My God, we said to ourselves, that was
close. Two metres lower and it could have been the end of
us. The armour of our station would not have been
enough protection against a direct hit at that range.

Nothing could have been more devastating to me than
being put out of action just when I had every hope of
hitting the *King George V*. For our ship, that was the end
of all central fire control. I called both computer rooms,
but neither of them could get through to the forward
fire-control station. The only thing to do was let turrets
Caesar and Dora fire independently. My station being
blind, I told their commanders that they were free to
choose their targets.

At 0916, shortly after loosing six torpedoes from a
distance of about 10,000 metres, all of which missed us,
the *Rodney* turned to a northerly course and became the

target chosen by our turret commanders. This choice was made apparently because the range to the *Rodney*, which did not go as far to the south as the *King George V*, had closed to 7,500 metres.[3] The last shots of our after turrets were not badly aimed; a few shells fell very near the *Rodney*. At 0927, one of our fore turrets, either Anton or Bruno, fired one more salvo, but the firing became irregular and finally petered out.[4] Shell damage brought the end nearer and nearer. First turret Caesar and then Dora fell silent. At 0931 the *Bismarck*'s main battery fired its last salvo.

Our list to port had increased a bit while the firing was going on. Around 0930, gas and smoke began to drift through our station, causing us to put on gas masks from time to time. But it wasn't too bad.

Unable to leave our station because an inferno was raging outside, we knew little about what was going on elsewhere. Was the ship's command still in the forward command post? Was Lindemann still in charge there? No reports came down to us nor were we asked what was happening in our area. We had not heard a single word from the forward part of the ship since the action began but, considering the large numbers of hits we had felt, there must have been some drastic changes. Suddenly I heard Albrecht's voice on the control telephone. 'The forward fire-control station has to be evacuated because of gas and smoke,' he said, and immediately rang off,

[3] After the turn to the north, the *Rodney*, which had been astern of the *King George V*, became the lead ship. Russell Grenfell in *The Bismarck Episode*, pp. 181–82, suggests that this was perhaps the reason for the Bismarck shifting her fire to the *Rodney*, but such was not the case.

[4] Russell Grenfell, *op. cit.*, p. 182, says that at 0927 our forward turrets fired a salvo together, which I consider extremely improbable. It would have been an extraordinary coincidence if the serious damage done to both turrets by hits they received shortly after 0900 had been repaired at so much the same pace that they were able to fire a last, joint salvo.

precluding any questions. I was surprised. I had assumed that the reason for the fire control being turned over to me was that the forward station was out of action. Had Albrecht been directing the secondary battery from there? Was his own station serving only as a place of refuge? Those questions were never answered.

I was using all the telephone circuits and calling all over the place in an effort to find out as much as possible about the condition of the ship. I got only one answer. I reached the messenger in the damage-control centre, and asked: 'Who has and where is the command of the ship? Are there new orders in effect?' The man was in a great hurry and said only that both the First Officer and the Damage-Control Engineer had had to abandon the damage-control centre, adding that he was the last one in the room and had to get out. Then he hung up. That was my last contact with the forward part of the ship.

Before 1000, men who had had to abandon their own stations or protected rooms began arriving to take refuge in my station. Most of them came through the narrow emergency exit where a perpendicular companionway led down to the after gunnery reserve circuit space. They clambered up its iron rungs, the uninjured, the slightly wounded, and many so badly wounded that one could only marvel that they did it. We were lucky that my station was not hit. Shortly before the firing ceased, I had its two small hatches cranked open, explaining to the men that it was better to take a chance on a few splinters than risk having the opening mechanism jammed by a hit. In fact, we were spared both shell splinters and fragments.

Around this time, the order was given to scuttle and abandon the ship, although I did not know it then. In fact, no such order ever reached me, but the situation on board compelled me to conclude that it must have been given.

Nevertheless, I did not allow the men in my station to leave while shells were exploding all over the super-structure and upper decks, and ready ammunition was blowing up. To do so would have been nothing less than suicide. I did not give the order to leave until long after our guns had fallen silent, the enemy stopped firing and, presumably, the shooting had come to an end.

By this time our list to port was heavier than ever and starboard was the lee side. I called to the men to look for a place aft and to starboard on the upper deck. Forward, there was too much destruction and the smoke was unbearable. The quarterdeck was out of the question: the sinking ship was too far down by her stern and heavy breakers were rolling over her from her port quarter. Those who made the mistake of jumping from that side or who were washed overboard in that direction were thrown back against the ship by the sea, in most cases with fatal consequences.

The last one to leave the station, I went forward, towards the searchlight-control station or, rather, towards where it had been. The scene that lay before me was too much to take in at a glance and is very difficult to describe. It was chaos and desolation. The antiaircraft guns and searchlights that once surrounded the after station had disappeared without a trace. Where there had been guns, shields, and instruments, there was empty space. The superstructure decks were littered with scrap metal. There were holes in the stack, but it was still standing. Whitish smoke, like a ground fog, extended from the after fire-control station all the way to the tower mast, indicating where fires must be raging below. It obscured anything that was left on the superstructure. Out of the smoke rose the tower mast, seemingly undamaged. How good it looks in its grey paint, I thought, almost as if it had not been in the battle. The foretop and the upper antiaircraft station also looked intact, but I well knew that such was not the case. Men were running around up there – I wondered whether they would be able to save themselves, to find a way down inside the mast. The wreckage all around made it impossible for me to go any farther forward and I returned to my station, only to leave it again immediately and go aft. I had to clamber over all manner of debris and jump over holes in the deck. I saw the body of a fleet staff officer, lying there peacefully, without any sign of injury. He must have left his action station when the order was given to abandon ship, without waiting for the enemy fire to cease. Turret Caesar, apparently not damaged, even its paint not chipped, had its guns trained aft. Its commander, Kapitänleutnant Karl Knappe, was forced to stop firing when his left gun barrel was disabled. From the upper deck I saw turret Dora, blackened by smoke, trained aft. Its right barrel had exploded when one of its shells detonated prematurely, after which the gun captain, Oberbootsmannsmaat Friedrich Helms, fired two more rounds from the left barrel. When Mechanikersmaat Ernst Moog came from the interior of the turret shouting 'Turret D is on fire!' the crew, which was still intact, evacuated it, and the turret fell silent. Later a shell exploded, probably on the armoured deck, and blew the lid off the shell hoist in the handling room. Helms and others had their faces and hands burned by the jet of flame that shot up.

Moving on, I glanced across the water off our starboard quarter, and couldn't believe what I saw. There, only around 2,500 metres away, was the *Rodney*, her nine guns still pointing mistrustfully at us. I could look down their muzzles. If that was her range at the end of the battle, I thought, not a single round could have missed. But her guns were silent now and I didn't expect that they would go into action again.

In the words of an observer in the *Rodney*: 'From about 0936 until cease firing at 1016 the *Rodney* steamed back and forth by the *Bismarck* at ranges between 2,750 and about 4,500 yards firing salvo after salvo of 16″ and 6″ during this entire period.' The trajectories of the shells were nearly flat and the devastation of the *Bismarck* was readily visible to her enemies. Several fires were raging and the rear wall of turret Bruno was missing. The superstructure had been destroyed, men were running back and forth on deck, vainly seeking shelter, their only escape from the hail of fire being over the side.

Around 1000 the *Bismarck* appeared to the British to be a wreck. Her gun barrels pointed every which way into the sky, and the wind drew black smoke out of her interior. The glow of fires on her lower decks shone through the holes in her upper deck and citadel armour.

To Tovey it appeared almost incredible that the *Bismarck* was still afloat. The knowledge that German long-range bombers or German U-boats might appear at any moment made the urgency of sinking her ever more pressing. Moreover, his flagship and the *Rodney* were running alarmingly low on fuel. Repeatedly he urged Patterson, 'Get closer, get closer – I can't see enough hits.' In order to hasten the end of the *Bismarck*, the *Rodney* fired full salvoes with her 40.6-centimetre battery scoring three or four hits per salvo. At a range of 2,700 metres, she released her last two torpedoes and the *Norfolk*, at a range of 3,600 metres, fired her last four torpedoes – the *Bismarck* remained afloat.

The *Ark Royal*'s aircraft were anxious to get into the fight. Twelve Swordfish were launched at 0926 but, when they reached the scene of the action, they realized the risk they would be taking if they attacked. Four ships were firing simultaneously at the German battleship from several sides at very close range. That meant flat trajectories, and the Swordfish had to fly low to launch an attack. It was much better for them to forgo it.

Meanwhile, Tovey became increasingly irritated by the *Bismarck*'s refusal to sink. She endured a hail of shells, such as he could not have imagined. How much more would it take? How much more time would her obstinacy cost him? He had no more time. His fuel supply was almost exhausted; every additional half-hour spent on the scene would make his return home that much more hazardous. Once again he examined the *Bismarck* through his binoculars. She lay deep and sluggish in the water; it now appeared certain that she could never reach port. And with that certainty he had to be content. At 1015 he ordered the *Rodney* to follow in the wake of the *King George V* on a northeasterly course at 19 knots. It was the course home.

At 1022, Admiral Somerville with Force H, out of sight to the south of where the action was, ordered the *Dorsetshire* to torpedo the *Bismarck*. Two minutes earlier, Captain Martin, acting on his own initiative, fired two torpedoes at the *Bismarck*'s starboard side at a range of 3,000 metres. One was observed to hit below her bridge, the other astern. Thereafter, the *Dorsetshire* went over to the battleship's port side and, at 1036, launched a third torpedo at 2,200 metres. This was the last of all the projectiles fired at the *Bismarck* on 27 May.

Suppressing a desire to retrieve a few personal belongings from my stateroom, which was not far away on the port side, I joined a little group of men assembled to starboard, forward of turret Dora, where they were waiting to jump overboard. For the moment, that seemed the best refuge. Many men were already in the water, and those with me were wondering whether this was the moment for them to jump. I told them to wait: 'There's still time. We're sinking slowly. The sea is running high and we'll have to swim a long time, so it's best we jump as late as possible. I'll tell you when.'

Before joining the group, I had seen the *King George V* and the *Rodney* steaming away to the north in line ahead and concluded that they would not take part in rescuing our survivors. But that other ships would do so, I was firmly convinced. 'Some ship will surely come along and pick us up,' I told my companions, but I had no idea which it would be. Had I given them false hope? Looking around us far and wide, I saw only empty ocean.

Although we all must have heard many of the same terrifying sounds and must have shared a sense of incredible desolation that morning, we did not all have the same experiences or see the same things. Here, then, are accounts, in more or less their own words, of the events that stand out most vividly in the memories of some of the other survivors.

Soon after the battle started water began pouring through the ventilator shafts into Junack's action station, the central turbine room, below the armoured deck in Compartment VIII. It was clear that the enemy's shots were striking close to us. After a while, red-orange fumes coming through the ventilators forced the crew to put on gas masks. The bridge issued hardly any orders over the engine telegraph but, when the din of battle was reduced to an occasional explosion, Junack received the order through the engine-control station, 'Clear ship for scuttling.' That was the last order given aboard the *Bismarck*. At this moment, the entire communications system broke down; the central turbine room was cut off from the engine-control station and the bridge. When scuttling charges had been brought to the cooling-water intakes and things became quieter above, Junack sent his best petty officer to get further orders. The petty officer did not return, and Junack had no choice but to act on his own responsibility. He had all bulkhead doors to the shaft tunnels opened, then sent his men to the main deck, and ordered the chief machinist to set the charges with a nine-minute fuse. He was the last to leave the turbine room, where the lights were still burning and the engines turning in accordance with the last order, 'slow ahead'.

Not until he reached the battery deck did Junack see the devastation of the battle. As he made his way through the wreckage, he heard the charges in the turbine room exploding. There was no getting forward and, on his way aft, he ran into a crowd of men, scared because they found their passage blocked. Telling them not to panic, he pushed his way into the midst of them and, as soon as they realized he was an officer, they calmed down. They tried to shove their way through an armoured hatch that was jammed half-open, but their gas masks and inflated life jackets made it a tight squeeze. Things went faster when, at Junack's suggestion, they took off their life jackets and jettisoned whatever other equipment they had. Junack waited until last to climb through the hatch to the upper deck. There, five junior officers and several hundred men were gathered around the after turrets, getting ready to go over the side. By this time, the enemy was doing very little firing. A curtain of flame amidships hid from view what was forward of it. All he could see were some dead and wounded scattered about the deck. Our ensign still flew from the mainmast but seawater was spilling over the quarterdeck in the brilliant sunshine and the ship was sinking ever deeper. There was no doubt that the *Bismarck* was slowly capsizing.

Far aft, the leader of Damage-Control Team No. 1,

Stabsobermaschinist Wilhelm Schmidt, could tell whenever our guns fired by the shuddering of the ship. Five enemy shells penetrated the upper deck in the area of his responsibility and exploded on the battery and the main decks. One landed in Compartment I and another in Compartment II, where it produced a huge flash. Nitrogen gas seeped through the closed armoured hatch to the vicinity of the damage-control command post in Compartment III. Shell splinters from the third hit put the lighting and ventilator for the main deck out of action. All that was left was emergency lighting. Hits four and five were in Compartment IV where, among other things, they demolished the companionways. Fumes from fires penetrated everywhere. A messenger arrived from the damage-control centre with an order to Schmidt to send some men to put out a fire on a superstructure deck aft. A party went, but none returned. Schmidt had already lost some of his people to shell splinters. A chief gunner rushed up with the news that there was fire in turret Dora, and Schmidt, reversing pump No. 2, flooded the ammunition chambers near the turret. Schmidt continued to receive reports of fires, some of them on the superstructure decks and in compartments on the battery and main decks.

Finally the order came from the bridge to all areas, 'Scuttle ship'. Schmidt reversed whatever pumps were still in operation in his area and flooded the compartments. He heard the condenser intakes and the seacocks blowing up in the engine and boiler rooms. A messenger brought another order, 'All hands on the upper deck.' All the armoured hatches on the main and battery decks were jammed and the companionways gone. The only way they could get to the upper deck was by using a narrow shell hoist. When they reached topside, Schmidt and his men joined the life-jacketed men waiting on the quarterdeck. The *Bismarck* was lying in heavy seas, fire and dark columns of smoke belching from her superstructure There was no sign of the enemy near or far, only a few wheeled aircraft circling overhead.

Very soon after the firing started, most of the shells were landing forward in the ship, where fires raged and huge pieces of iron and steel flew through the air. The *Bismarck* was jolted particularly hard when, shortly after 0900, her fore turrets, forward fire-control station, and tower mast were hit. A little later, somewhat aft, a heavy shell went right through the deck under the aircraft catapult. The protected space it landed in was used for storing ready ammunition, which blew up, killing the crews of the heavy antiaircraft guns who were taking shelter there. Around 0940 the rear shield of turret Bruno, which had jammed pointing athwartships, was blown off and the turret was on fire. Shortly before the British ships stopped firing, bright flames burned briefly on the gun platform of turret Anton.

As a member of the ammunition-handling group assigned to the after antiaircraft control station for the heavy flak, Musikmaat[5] Josef Mahlberg was stationed in a powder chamber in Compartment IX. When the fight had been going on for some time, the door to the chamber opened and in stepped Bootsmaat[6] Rolf Franke of the after antiaircraft computer room. He had a strange expression on his face. Mahlberg knew him well; the two of them always went most of the way to their stations together. Franke cried out, 'The word's just come through, abandon ship, the ship's going to be scuttled!' Dropping everything, Mahlberg and his men scrambled to go through the auxiliary shell hoists to the superstructure.

[5] Petty Officer (Bandsman)
[6] Petty Officer

When that proved impossible, they turned back and went through the bulkhead door to the decks, where, in contrast to their well-lighted chamber, they were in darkness and soon lost sight of one another. Only flashlights made pools of light here and there.

Mahlberg's first stop was the battery deck in Compartment X, where hundreds of men were jostling one another in an effort to get to the upper deck. Suddenly, he heard the familiar voice of the First Officer, sharp and incisive: 'What's all this? Go forward and help put out the fires. We aren't lost, not by a long shot. Is there no officer here who can take command?' But none came forward. Whatever happened, Mahlberg somehow reached the starboard upper deck in the neighbourhood of the aircraft crane. Only then did he fully grasp our plight. All that was left of the once-proud ship was ruin. He tried to get to the forecastle, but water flowing over the deck near the middle 15-centimetre turret blocked his way. He turned back towards the quarterdeck and when he passed turret Dora, he saw some of its badly burned crew sitting or lying on the upper deck. Because the quarter-deck was already partly under water, Mahlberg climbed on top of the turret. 'Just look at what's happened to my turret!' exclaimed one of the burned men who was sitting up there, Oberstückmeister[7] Friedrich Alfred Schubert. Mahlberg turned and went back to the upper deck.

In the starboard turbine room Maschinenmaat[8] Wilhelm Generotzky was aware that our own guns were firing very irregularly and that we were being hit again and again, but not a single shell penetrated his area or anywhere else below the armoured deck. He felt very proud of German naval architecture and German workmanship. He and his

[7] Chief Petty Officer (Ordnance)
[8] Petty Officer (Machinist)

men had no idea what the upper decks looked like, but they could not fail to think that the end was at hand. The *Bismarck* seemed to have been transformed into a practice target for the enemy. The second mate of his watch, his face chalk-white, called to him in passing, 'It's over, it's all over!' He knew the young mate well, knew he was happily married.

From the ventilator shafts that led to the diesel engines there came a sound like peas dancing on a drum. It was shell splinters falling on the upper deck. A highly excited stoker came in and yelled, 'Herr Maschinenmaat, transformer room No. 1 is on fire. You must go below!' Generotzky put on his respirator, grabbed a fire extinguisher, and tumbled down the companionway. Below, he carefully opened the door to the transformer room – nothing, neither fire nor smoke greeted him. He went on to the door to the diesel room, but all was clear here, too. Still, while he was climbing down, he thought he smelled smoke. Where was it coming from? He checked all the spaces near the companionway and, as he opened the door to a 10.5-centimetre shell and powder chamber, acrid yellow fumes assailed him and he saw a reddish glare. Quick as a flash he closed the door and rushed back up on deck to where the flood-control valves were mounted on a bulkhead. Oh, God, how long it took, half a turn one way, half the other – and beneath him the burning ammunition! At last, open. Quickly, open the seacocks, start the pumps. Open the flood-control valve more. Hold it, that won't work. Too much water pressure on the valve. Shut off the pumps, open the valve, let the pumps run again. Water was beginning to cover the burning ammunition! His hands were shaking, his knees trembling, and sweat was pouring down his face. Just as he was making his report to his leader, his division officer came from the engine-control station and gave orders to flood the rooms in flood group No. 4. But at the same moment, a petty officer from Damage-Control Team No. 4 reported that the rooms in flood groups Nos. 4 and 5 were already flooded. There had been fires in several ammunition chambers. Generotzky and his men did not know that all the 10.5-centimetre guns had been demolished or that all the 15-centimetre turrets had been hit and most of their barrels shot off.

When 'abandon ship' was ordered, Generotzky climbed to Compartment X of the battery deck, where some sixty men were already waiting to use the companionway to the upper deck. Hits landing above were clearly audible. In the passageway stood the First Officer and the commander of Division 11, Kapitänleutnant (Ingenieurwesen) Albert Hasselmeyer. Fregattenkapitän Oels said: 'Don't go up there. It would be certain death. Better go to the forecastle and help put out the fires!' But that didn't make any sense. Fuses had been set and the scuttling charges would go off at any moment.

Generotzky was standing about five metres from the companionway, with a wall of waiting comrades ahead of him. Suddenly there was a flash of light, a rumbling roar, and he was thrown into the air, landing hard on his back. A shell had hit the companionway. Men stumbled over him, one helped him up, and they both ran aft to Compartment VIII, where the companionway to the upper deck was a mass of men. Maschinenmaat Heinrich König unloaded the ammunition hoist from the shaft in the adjacent 10.5-centimetre shell and powder chamber, the one that Generotzky had flooded a few minutes earlier, so that it could be used to escape. Forty men, one behind the other, began to climb up the narrow shaft, only fifty centimetres wide. The lights had gone out and some of them held their flashlights in their mouths. Everyone waited his turn patiently. There was no pushing, no

jostling. Each man was lifted by the ones behind so that he
could grab the first rung of the ladder. Muffled explosions
below encouraged them to make the greatest possible
haste. Finally Generotzky's turn came. He was pushed up
into the duct and, rung by rung, he pulled himself up.
When he got a hold on the upper deck, his hands were in a
pool of blood. He stood up inside the demolished superstructure and found himself surrounded by dead bodies,
three and four deep, lying where they had fallen. But he
was out, out of the frightening coffin the *Bismarck* had
become. At least, there was light up there and the
whitecaps on the water showed that there was life. The
enemy was still firing, adding to the chaos, as corpses piled
on top of one another. He made for the hangar, where,
although it had a huge hole in one side, he hoped to find
shelter, but when he got there he shrank back. Too many
had already tried to find shelter there, in vain. He jumped
down to the upper deck and ran aft, but so much water
was already washing over it that he clambered back up. At
last, the firing ceased.

On his way up from below deck, Maschinengefreiter
Bruno Zickelbein of Damage-Control Team No. 6 saw the
First Officer in Compartment XIII on the battery deck.
'Comrades,' Oels was shouting, 'we can no longer fire our
guns and anyway we have no more ammunition. Our hour
has come. We must abandon ship. She will be scuttled. All
hands to the upper deck.' Oels then led Zickelbein and
seven other men aft to Compartment IX and told them to
carry four wounded men, who were waiting there, to the
upper deck. Carrying their burdens, the men went to
the only companionway they could get up, the one near the
catapult, amidships. When Zickelbein and his partner
were halfway up with their load a shell struck and hurled
them back to the battery deck. Another hit killed the

wounded and a number of other men. Now, the companionway was wrecked and, through a huge hole in the battery deck, Zickelbein could see all the way down to the main deck. 'Everyone here is dead,' Maschinenmaat Erich Vogel told him, 'we are the only ones alive.' They gave up trying to get to the upper deck and went to Compartment X. Then came the order, 'Petty Officer Silberling and his party report to the engine-control station immediately.' Hans Silberling gave Zickelbein his hand and said: 'We won't see each other again, this is the end! Say hello at home for me.' They clasped hands for a moment and tears ran down their cheeks. Zickelbein was barely nineteen years old and the twenty-five-year-old Silberling had been a kind of fatherly friend to him. But there was nothing for it, and Silberling carried out his last order.

There were more hits and the lights went out. Holding handkerchiefs over their mouths and noses to protect themselves from the dense smoke, Zickelbein and his companions tried to get to the upper deck by way of the companionway near the enlisted men's mess. While they were waiting for wounded men to be carried up, they heard Marinestabsarzt[9] Arvid Thiele say, 'Leave them, they'll sleep better here.' Everyone knew what he meant. Hardly had the doctor spoken when a shell smashed the mess companionway, killing those closest to it. Fearing that none of the companionways forward was usable, the surviving men tried to climb the shattered one. So much water was pouring in from above that by the time Zickelbein reached it he was standing in water higher than his waist. Eventually he, too, escaped.

In power plant No. 2 in Compartment VIII of the lower

---

[9] Lieutenant Medical Corps

platform deck Maschinenobergefreiter[10] Hans Springborn gave the generators and the diesel engines a final inspection shortly before the scuttling charges went off. He wanted to ensure that there would be light right up to the end, and there was.

Topside, the *Bismarck* looked like a heap of scrap metal, all on fire. Men were running back and forth, trying to find a way of saving themselves. But the service boats, life rafts, and floats had all been long since destroyed. Amid all the devastation on the upper deck, he saw wounded men lying on stretchers. They were supposed to have been carried to the dressing station below but, because the continuing fall of shells made that impossible, the doctors were scurrying around giving them sedatives.

Maschinengefreiter Hermann Budich, the talker in action station 'E' in Compartment IX of the lower platform deck, who around midnight had taken Maschinengefreiter Gerhard Böhnel's telephone report that the starboard rudder had at last been uncoupled, was wounded and brought to the action dressing station aft. Since he was not seriously hurt, he was laid on the deck outside. He had just heard one of the doctors say, 'Only serious cases inside,' when there was a frightful crash. A direct hit on the dressing station. Inside it nothing stirred.

The order to prepare to scuttle the ship must have arrived shortly before Oels and Jahreis left the command and damage-control centre in Compartment XIV on the upper platform deck. Their mission had ended. There was no longer any point in tallying hits and trying to confine and counter damage. The opposite had to be done: everything had to be destroyed. Now the two officers had to supervise

[10] Seaman (Machinist)

preparations for the scuttling and devise ways for the men to get through the chaos of the main and battery decks to safety.

None of the survivors saw what happened to Jahreis; perhaps he went forward, where most of the fires were. Oels and some of his men reached the battery deck in Compartment VIII, where they found a surging mass of some 300 men pushing and shoving towards the ladders. Acrid, yellow-green smoke swirled across the deck, and the men who didn't have gas masks were racked by choking coughs. The hatch at the top of one ladder was jammed halfway open. 'Get out, get out,' called Oels in an emotional, cracking voice, 'everyone off the ship. She's being scuttled. You can't get through forward. Everything up there is burning!' The words were barely out of his mouth when a green flash whizzed by, burst into a fireball, and exploded with a deafening crash. Men reeled, were hurled through the air, and fell hard on the deck; more than one hundred were killed, Oels among them. He was standing between the mess and the companionway when the shell struck.

Some men were trapped below. The hatches leading to the upper deck were either jammed shut or there was heavy wreckage lying on top of them. In Compartment XV near the forward mess on the battery deck, two hundred men were imprisoned behind jammed hatches. They were all killed by shell fire. Flames cut off the whole forward part of the ship. One of the starboard 15-centimetre turrets had been hit and its access hatch was jammed. No amount of effort from inside or out could pry it open. The turret became a coffin for its crew. Farther aft, two men who had managed to reach the upper deck were blinded by the dense smoke and fell through holes in the deck back into the fire below. There were young sailors, petty officers, even men of the prize crews, experienced seamen, who decided it would be pointless to try to climb out.

With the silencing of our guns, one after the other, the doctor's and corpsmen's hour had come – and in what dimensions! Hundreds of wounded lay where they had been hit, in the foretop, on the bridge, in the control stations, at the guns, on the upper deck, and on the battery and main decks. Stretcher-bearers, including civilians, carried them from the upper deck amid a hail of shells, but the only thing that could be done for such numbers was relieve their pain by giving them morphine. None of those who really knew what feats were accomplished in the dressing stations and at the collection points lived to tell the story.

The task of the doctors and corpsmen became overwhelming as one action station after another was knocked out and the men who were no longer able to take part in the fight crowded the battle dressing stations. As the minutes passed and ever greater numbers of wounded requiring ever more attention pressed into the stations, the possibility that our medical people would have a chance to save themselves became slimmer and slimmer. The armour of the battery and main decks within the citadel offered them no protection as they laboured amid a stream of heavy hits, every casualty providing them with a preview of what lay in store for them. What they suffered was the epitome of what observers in two British ships preferred not to imagine: 'What that ship was like inside did not bear thinking of; her guns smashed, the ship full of fire, her people hurt; and surely all men are much the same when hurt.' 'Pray God I may never know what those shells did as they exploded inside the hull.'[11]

Referring to the forty-five minutes of relentless can-

---

[11] Ludovic Kennedy, *Pursuit*, pp. 206, 208.

nonading that followed the silencing of our guns, the commanding officer of the *Rodney*, Captain F. H. G. Dalrymple-Hamilton, said, 'I can't say I enjoyed this part of the business much, but didn't see what else I could do.'[12] Captain W. R. Patterson of the *King George V* would have stopped firing earlier had he been able to see what was happening on the *Bismarck*, but the wall of splashes from near misses obscured his view of her port side.[13]

The doctors and the corpsmen endured the horror and helped the wounded until they themselves fell victim to a hit. When and where they died, I do not know. Only the direct hit in the action dressing station aft has been recorded. Marineoberstabsarzt[14] Hans-Günther Busch, Marinestabsarzt Hans-Joachim Krüger, Marinestabsarzt Arvid Thiele, Marineassistenarzt der Reserve[15] Rolf Hinrichsen, and their corpsmen and assistants are here remembered with special respect.

This is as far as I can reconstruct the *Bismarck*'s last battle from my own experiences and from the testimony of others. The concentration of hits on the forward section of the ship in the opening stage of the battle explains why the *Bismarck*'s command system was crippled so early. Only afterwards did I understand why, once the battle had started, not one order or message from the bridge reached me in the after station. To us participants, each phase of the action seemed much, much longer than it actually was. By 0902, fifteen minutes after the first salvo was fired, the

---

[12] Ludovic Kennedy, *op. cit.*, p. 207.
[13] Russell Grenfell, *op. cit.*, p. 184.
[14] Lieutenant Commander, Medical Corps. Dr Busch was posthumously promoted to Geschwaderarzt (Squadron Surgeon); Dr Krüger, to Marineoberstabsarzt.
[15] Assistant Surgeon (Reserve)

foretop, the forward fire-control station, and turrets Anton and Bruno had been disabled, which meant we had lost more than fifty per cent of our firepower. No one who was in those forward action stations survived, and my report, from the perspective of a position aft, can only be a fragment.

No survivor saw the Fleet Commander during the last battle. I assume that Admiral Lütjens and his staff fell at their action stations.

34

The Bismarck *Sinks*

While the little group I was with was waiting to starboard, forward of turret Dora, the *Bismarck* sank still deeper by her stern and her list to port increased. The gradual emergence of more and more of her hull on the starboard side told me that the moment to jump was approaching. 'It's that time,' I said, 'inflate your life jackets, prepare to jump.' Just as earlier it was vital not to go over the side too soon, now, it was vital not to delay so long that we would be sucked down with the ship when she finally sank. 'A salute to our fallen comrades,' I called. We all snapped our hands to our caps, glanced at the flag, and jumped.

In the water we were pushed together in a bunch, as we bobbed up and down like corks. At first we swam away from the sinking ship as hard as we could to escape her suction. When I got clear by some 150 metres, I stopped and turned around for one last look and to take in everything I could about her.

What I saw was that the *Bismarck* was listing still more. She had no stability left. She was also deeper down by her stern, her bow rearing steeply out of the water. The whole starboard side of her hull, all the way to the keel, was out of the water. I scrutinized it for signs of battle damage and was surprised that I saw no trace of any. Her port side had borne the brunt of the battle, and that side of her hull may have told a different story.

When swimmers close to the bow of the ship looked back, they saw Lindemann standing on the forecastle in front of turret Anton. His messenger, a seaman, was with him. Soon, both men went forward and began climbing a steadily increasing slope. Lindemann's gestures showed that he was urging his companion to go overboard and save himself. The man refused and stayed with his commanding officer until they reached the jackstaff. Then Lindemann walked out on the starboard side of the stem which, though rising ever higher, was becoming more level as the ship lay over. There he stopped and raised his hand to his white cap.

The *Bismarck* now lay completely on her side. Then, slowly, slowly, she and the saluting Lindemann went down. Who among us knew at that moment that here was being fulfilled the boyhood dream of a man who developed a passion for the navy at the age of thirteen and told his brother and his friends that his 'greatest hope' was someday to command his own ship and to go down with it 'with flags flying'? Later a machinist wrote, 'I always thought such things happened only in books, but I saw it with my own eyes.' The time was 1039 and the battleship's position was approximately 48°10' north and 16°12' west.

At 1322 Group West radioed to Lütjens, 'Reuter reports *Bismarck* sunk. Report situation immediately.' But at the place where such messages had previously been received and answered there was now only empty sea.

The sight of the sinking *Bismarck* and the thought of my many comrades who had gone down with her cut deep into my heart.

Another thought that came to me was that a Lenbach[1] portrait of Prince Bismarck had sunk with the ship. It hung where the guard outside the commanding officer's stateroom was posted. Lindemann did not want to take this picture on an Atlantic operation and, before our departure, he recommended that it be taken ashore. But this recommendation was rejected and he was ordered to

---

[1] Franz von Lenbach was the leading German portraitist of the Imperial era.

keep the painting in the *Bismarck*. Just three weeks earlier, during Hitler's visit to the ship, Lindemann had pointed it out to him and expressed concern that something might happen to it in the war. Hitler shook his head. 'If anything happens to the ship,' he said, 'the picture might as well be lost, too.' Now it had come to pass.

For us in the water the scene changed quickly. We found ourselves being continuously swept from one cluster of men to another. In the distance I saw the familiar faces of Kapitänleutnant Werner Schock, commander of Division 12 and second damage-control officer, and Oberleutnant Gerhard Hinz, commander of Division 8 and the ship's technical gunnery officer. I saw them briefly, then they were lost to sight, forever. All of a sudden, I found myself next to the ordnanceman from my action station. 'Careful, careful,' he called out, 'don't get too close to me, I've lost a foot.' 'Listen,' I replied, 'we'll soon be aboard a Briton, and they'll take care of you.' Shortly thereafter he, too, disappeared in the swells.

Like toys, we floated on the heaving Atlantic. Only when we topped the crests of the waves did we catch glimpses of the horizon. Were there any British ships around? Would they come to our rescue? Although there were none in sight, I was quite sure they would come. Repeatedly, I called to the men near me, 'Stay together, as soon as a ship comes we'll swim over and get aboard.' It wasn't much encouragement but, I thought, better than none.

Even today, when I think about being out there in the Atlantic, it strikes me as remarkable that I was not conscious of the temperature of the water. It was 13 degrees centigrade. Cool enough. But I was fully dressed, which helped keep me warm. And, still more important, the tension and excitement were such that external circumstances didn't matter. In our helplessness, all we thought about was what's going to happen, what's coming next. The minutes flew past, and the water temperature meant nothing to me.

One thing that was really horrible was the fuel oil from our sunken ship that was floating on the surface of the water in a wide, thick sheet. The odour stung our noses. It blackened our faces and forced its way into our eyes, noses, and ears. What luck it's not burning, I thought, although I knew that was not much of a danger with heavy oil. My Tissot wristwatch stopped at 1031 – salt water and fuel oil, the combination was too much for it. We continued to float in high swells. There were still no British ships to be seen.

When almost an hour had passed, from the crest of a wave I sighted a three-stack cruiser, her ensign stiff in the wind: the *Dorsetshire*. I urged my companions to hold on, 'Cheer up, we'll soon be aboard her.' The *Dorsetshire* steered for the thickest concentration of survivors and stopped shortly before reaching it. Soon she lay athwart the waves, drifting and rolling rather heavily. I had quite a long way to go to get to her. I told the men in my vicinity to be sure to head for the port, or lee, side of the ship and stay there.

The *Dorsetshire* threw lines over, a few of which had bowlines on the end. Lines and bowlines became so slippery from the oil in which they dangled that it was difficult to handle them, but it was that or nothing. I had a vision of a wide net up which a lot of men could climb at the same time, as they would up ratlines. But it was only a vision. At last, the *Dorsetshire* lowered a rectangular wooden raft for us to hold onto so that we could catch our breath.

Getting up those lines was not easy even for an experienced seaman. Not only were they slippery as eels but, because of the rolling of the ship, they were in the water

one second and the next they were too far above our
outstretched hands for us to grab. It was quite a trick to
catch one at the right moment. Most of the men I saw
were technicians, who had probably not had to use lines
since they were in basic training, so I advised them to
choose those that had bowlines. That, too, was easier said
than done. I soon found that there was a limit to what the
best-intentioned advice could accomplish. At some points
men bunched up, all trying to grasp the same line, while
lines nearby were ignored. Feeling that I was strong
enough to do so, I decided to wait a while. Then I noticed
that certain lines were almost always free. I called attention to this fact and swam to one with a bowline. I don't
remember how many times I was within a few feet of the
line for a fraction of a second only to have it jerk far out of
reach. I almost gave up, but then I was lucky. Just as the
ship was about to roll back up, I got one foot firmly in the
bowline, closed both hands round the line, and gave
the two British seamen above the signal to hoist. They did,
and slowly, slowly, I went up the grey hull, past the
portholes – how high can a ship be? – to the upper deck. I
reached one hand out to grab the lifeline, intending to
hold on to it as I climbed out of the bowline. But my reach
was longer than my grasp was strong. One hand was not
enough to hold the line, and I fell back into the water.
Fortunately, I didn't land on anyone's head, nor did I hurt
myself, but it was very disheartening. Had I so greatly
overestimated my reserve of strength? I wouldn't wait
long before I tried again. After getting my breath I looked
for and found another line with a bowline. I glanced up
and there were the same two seamen. Unwittingly, I had
returned to the same line! They hoisted me up again. This
time I kept both hands on the line and said, 'Please, pull
me on board.' They did, and there I was standing on the
upper deck, aft of the second port life boat, a prisoner of

war, in an oil-stained uniform. The first thing I did was take a look over the side at my comrades still in the water. There were hundreds of them, hundreds of yellow life jackets. Perhaps eight hundred, I estimated. It would take a good while to get them all on board. That they would all be saved, I had no doubt, but I was not allowed to stay on deck for long. Others were now the masters of my time. Also, my two rescuers had to carry on with their humanitarian work.

One of them, Tom Wharam, a young telegraphist, obeyed an officer's order to take me below, to the midshipmen's quarters. Little did I know that barely a year later he would be among the survivors of the *Dorsetshire* when she was sunk in the Indian Ocean by Japanese dive-bombers. After the war he became a good friend of mine, in that unique brotherhood that, as he once wrote me, binds men who once fought on opposite sides.

Below I saw some of my shipmates in various stages of undress. They were being given dry, warm clothing. My allotment was the civilian suit of an obviously very large officer.

Stabsobermaschinist Wilhelm Schmidt went over the stern into the water, and found himself surrounded by three or four hundred men. From a distance of 100 metres he watched the *Bismarck* roll over, saw her keel uppermost and air bubbles rising from under her – then she sank. After he'd been in the water a long time, he spied mast tips on the horizon. They belonged to the *Dorsetshire* and, together with many others, Schmidt soon found himself on her port side, the lee side. Amidships he found a stout manila line with an eye at the end of it. Some of his companions had already been hoisted up when he succeeded in getting a grip on the line and was pulled up.

*

Musikmaat Josef Mahlberg was also 100 metres away from the *Bismarck* when she capsized. Just as I did, he looked for signs of torpedo hits or other damage to the starboard side of her hull and saw none.

Maschinenmaat Wilhelm Generotzky, who was standing on the superstructure deck, saw men jumping into the water, among them his best friend. He also saw Luftwaffe sergeants shoot themselves and heard a chief engineer say, 'If I had a pistol, I'd do the same thing.' Then there were shouts, 'She's sinking!' and 'Turret Dora's blowing up!' The deck was trying to slide out from under him. He and several others leapt down and went into the water from the starboard side of the upper deck. At almost the same moment that side of the ship rose completely out of the water. The jump must have brought a quick end to many of those men. Generotzky's leap took him to a considerable depth and, as he fought his way to the surface, he kept telling himself, 'It'll get light any minute now.' When that finally happened, he shot halfway out of the water and sucked precious air into his empty lungs. He saw the *Bismarck* some 100 metres away, floating keel-up. Hissing jets of water escaping from various apertures in her hull were soaring into the air. While he watched, her stern sank, her bow rose, as if in a last farewell, and, with a gurgling sound, the *Bismarck* slid below the waves.

All that was left were the men in the water, hundreds of them, fighting a desperate battle with the elements. Generotzky did not expect to be rescued. He had lost his socks and cold pressed ever deeper into his body. His legs became numb. Floating oil burned his face and hands and forced its repulsive way into his mouth. It took him about forty minutes to reach the *Dorsetshire* and the many lines that had been thrown over. He let himself be lifted up by a wave and grabbed hold of one of the lines. But in the trough of the wave he lost his hold and fell helplessly back into the cold bath. Several other times he tried, in vain. As more and more men reached the ship, a struggle for survival broke out. When two or three men would try to hang on the same line, none of them made it. In the scramble someone stepped on Generotzky's head and while he was under water a wave threw him against the ship's hull, injuring his leg. Noticing that the British seamen aft were tying eyes in more lines, he floated in that direction, managed to get his foot through one of them, and clamped both hands on the line. Seamen pulled him on board.

Maschinenobergefreiter Hans Springborn saw many men dive overboard headfirst, hit the bilge keel, and fall into the water with broken necks. He wasn't going to let that happen to him, so he slid down the hull from the upper deck to the bilge keel and jumped into the water from there. When the *Bismarck* rolled over on her side, strong currents pulled him under and he was violently whirled around before he managed to regain the surface. That experience told him to get away from the ship as fast as he could.

After some time he saw the British destroyer *Maori* and had the luck to drift over to her. After several tries he got hold of a line, and was hoisted to safety by two seamen.

35
Survival

I was still changing my clothes when the *Dorsetshire*
suddenly began to vibrate violently. What was happening?
Was she leaving the area, and at full power? Now, in the
midst of the rescue? Was there some sudden danger?
From what? There weren't any U-boats around, as we
knew all too well. Only that morning, we had asked for
one to pick up the War Diary and none had appeared.
That was a sure sign that there were no U-boats in the
vicinity. Also, neither during the night nor at dawn had
any boat come to the aid of the *Bismarck*. No rumour
even of any intended U-boat action had reached me in the
after station. It couldn't be a U-boat that had caused this
precipitate withdrawal. What could have? German
planes? If that was it, the aircraft alarm would have been
sounded. I racked my brain, but the only thing that
registered was horror that our men in the water, hundreds
of them, before whose eyes the *Dorsetshire* was moving
away, were being sentenced to death just when safety
seemed within reach. My God, what a narrow escape I
had. There was nothing that I, a prisoner of war, could do.

After a while, we survivors were led to the wardroom,
where we sat around a big table and were given hot tea.
We were still numb and not very talkative, but the tea
helped. When we had finished, Kapitänleutnant Junack,
Oberfähnrich zur See[1] Hans-Georg Stiegler, Nautischer
Assistent[2] Lothar Balzer, and I – just four of the *Bismarck*'s ninety officers – were taken aft to our allotted

[1] Midshipman in fleet service
[2] Nautical Assistant

quarters. The eighty-one petty officers and men were taken forward.

That afternoon we rested. I lay on my bunk in a strange state between sleep and wakefulness. I could not take in all the terrible things that had happened in the last few hours. Did they really happen? Somehow, my mind rejected the thought; no one could have survived that devastating storm of steel. So many good men had been lost. Why they and not I?

As the senior-ranking survivor aboard, I received the next morning a hand-written note from Captain B. C. S. Martin, the commanding officer of the *Dorsetshire*:

I will be glad if you will visit your men this morning with my commander and then come to the bridge with him to see me.

If there is anything you require for your personal needs please let me know.

I hope you slept well and feel none the worse for your swim.

Escorted by the First Officer, Commander C. W. Byas, I went to see how our men were getting along. Everything was satisfactory; the ship's surgeon was taking care of the sick and injured, and they all felt they were being treated very well. They were getting five meals a day and eating the same excellent food as the crew. The smokers among them were being issued twenty cigarettes a day. I learned later that it was no different in the *Maori*, which picked up twenty-five men, bringing the number rescued by British ships to 110, about 5 per cent of the more than 2,200 on board.

When Byas took me to the bridge, Captain Martin greeted me in a friendly enough manner and gave me a Scotch. The gesture was well meant but I was still too horrified at his leaving all those men in the water the day before to really appreciate it. 'Why,' I burst out, 'did you suddenly break off the rescue and leave hundreds of our men to drown?' Martin replied that a U-boat had been sighted, or at least reported, and he obviously could not endanger his ship by staying stopped any longer. The *Bismarck*'s experiences on the night of 26 May and the morning of the 27th, I told him, indicated that there were no U-boats in the vicinity. Farther away, perhaps, but certainly not within firing range of the *Dorsetshire*. I added that in war one often sees what one expects to see. We argued the point back and forth until Martin said abruptly: 'Just leave that to me. I'm older than you are and have been at sea longer. I'm a better judge.' What more could I say? He was the captain and was responsible for his ship.[3]

[3] In the first edition of his *Schlachtschiff Bismarck*, Brennecke writes on page 392: 'In this connection [the *Dorsetshire*'s departure from the rescue scene], we have learned that it was one of the German survivors who, on the basis of his knowledge of the last radio signals, warned the British cruiser's captain of German U-boats. Did he do this out of nervousness? Out of fear? Or was it his intention to leave the rescue of the rest of the survivors to German U-boats?'

In his fourth edition, instead of saying 'one of the German survivors' warned the captain of the *Dorsetshire*, Brennecke says 'one of the ranking survivors,' to which statement he attaches Note 361a, 'It was not the now-retired Kapitän zur See Junack.' I cannot imagine to what radio signals he refers. Furthermore, when we got aboard the *Dorsetshire*, none of us could have warned the captain, who was high up on the bridge, about anything. Upon coming on board, every survivor was immediately taken below. That applied to me also and, as I have recounted, I did not see Captain Martin until the morning of 28 May, twenty-four hours after the rescue operation. My repeated requests for documentation on the alleged warning have not been answered by Herr Brennecke. Needless to say, I flatly reject the insinuation that, since 'it was not Kapitän Junack,' it could have been I, the senior-ranking survivor.

Captain Martin's official report leaves no doubt as to who warned him: 'When about 80 survivors had been picked up and I was on the port wing of the bridge directing operations in that vicinity, I received a report from LtCdr. Durant that a suspicious smoking discharge was seen to starboard, or leeward beam about two miles away. I went to the compass platform and saw this myself. It appeared to me that it could have been caused by a submarine, and in view of this and other indications that

H.M.S. DORSETSHIRE

Dear von Mullenheim,

I will be glad if you will visit your men This morning with my commander and Then Come To The bridge with him to See me.

If There is any Thing you require for your personal needs please Let me Know.

I hope you Slept well and feel none The worse for your swim.

Yours Sincerely

28/5.

Apparently some floating object had been mistaken for a periscope or a strip of foam on the water for the wake of a torpedo. No matter what it was, I am now convinced that, under the circumstances, Martin had to act as he did.[4]

At 1100 on 27 May Churchill informed the House of Commons of the final action against the *Bismarck*. 'This morning,' he said, 'shortly after daylight the *Bismarck*, virtually at a standstill, far from help, was attacked by the British pursuing battleships. I do not know what were the results of the bombardment. It appears, however, that the *Bismarck* was not sunk by gunfire, and she will now be dispatched by torpedo. It is thought that this is now proceeding, and it is also thought that there cannot be any lengthy delay in disposing of this vessel. Great as is our loss in the *Hood*, the *Bismarck* must be regarded as the most powerful, as she is the newest, battleship in the world.' Scarcely had Churchill sat down when a note was passed to him. He rose again and announced to the members that the *Bismarck* had been sunk. 'They seemed content,' he wrote.[5]

A day later he telegraphed Roosevelt: 'I will send you

---

enemy aircraft and submarines were most likely operating at the scene of the action I was reluctantly compelled to leave some hundreds of the enemy personnel to their fate.'

[4] The presence of a U-boat in range to attack the *Dorsetshire* at around noon on 27 May has never been proved. I did not know it at the time, but the *U-556* (Wohlfarth) and the *U-74* (Kentrat) may have been *relatively* near the *Bismarck*. However, Wohlfarth, who did not see even the *Bismarck* on 26 or 27 May, wrote me in February 1978, 'I don't believe that a German U-boat was in the vicinity of the *Dorsetshire*, for, as all the boats [those in the ocean area around the *Bismarck*] were on the way home, it would have been reported somehow and be known today.' Kentrat, having received the radio order, 'Search for survivors, the sinking of the *Bismarck* is to be expected,' spent the whole day in a fruitless search.

[5] Winston Churchill, *The Second World War*, Vol. III, p. 283.

later the inside story of the fighting with the *Bismarck*. She was a terrific ship, and a masterpiece of naval construction. Her removal eases our battleship situation, as we should have had to keep *King George V*, *Prince of Wales*, and the two *Nelsons* practically tied to Scapa Flow to guard against a sortie of *Bismarck* and *Tirpitz*, as they could choose their moment and we should have to allow for one of our ships refitting. Now it is a different story.'[6]

After my talk with Captain Martin I remained on the bridge of the *Dorsetshire* for a while.[7] When I asked if I could see the chart in the navigation room, permission was readily granted. Alone with my thoughts, I gazed for a moment at the mark showing where the *Bismarck* had gone down. Then I asked and was given Martin's permission to visit our men in their quarters once every day and to concern myself with their wishes.

Among the survivors was Maschinengefreiter Gerhard Lüttich. He had lost an arm and was so badly burned that none of us could understand how he managed to get aboard. He was being cared for in the ship's sick bay, but he died on 28 May. The following day the ship's chaplain officiated at the military rites accorded him and, after the firing of three salvoes by an honour guard, his body was solemnly committed to the deep. In the late sixties, when I was consul general of the Federal Republic of Germany in Toronto, an extraordinary thing happened. I was

[6] Winston Churchill, *op. cit.*, p. 286
[7] Russell Grenfell, *The Bismarck Episode*, mentions in a footnote on page 180 that a survivor is alleged to have told Captain Martin that it was a shell from the *Dorsetshire* that disabled the *Bismarck*'s fire-control station. He supposes that the survivor did this because he wanted to ingratiate himself with his captor. Grenfell is referring to me, but how this theory could have arisen is a mystery to me. I did not even know that the *Dorsetshire* was present. A shell that came in shortly after 0910 left my station blind. Therefore, I could not have said anything to Captain Martin about it.

approached at a social gathering by Philip Mathias, assistant editor of the *Financial Post*. Conveying friendly greetings from his father, Arthur, who, as master-at-arms in the *Dorsetshire*, was in charge of the prisoners of war, he handed me the identity tag that Arthur Mathias had removed from Lüttich's dead body.

While the *Dorsetshire* and the *Maori* were steaming north, far to the south of us a dinghy was floating in the Atlantic. Its occupants were three seamen, Herbert Manthey, Otto Höntzsch, and Georg Herzog, who, towards the end of the firing, took cover behind turret Dora. Nearby they saw a rubber dinghy and, with the help of shipmates, dragged it behind the turret. Soon thereafter, as they stated later, they and the dinghy were washed overboard by the splash of a near miss. Although the dinghy floated away from them, they were able to reach it in about fifteen minutes and climb in. Very close by they saw a rubber raft with two men on it, one of them wounded, but they could not bring their drifting dinghy alongside and it was soon lost to sight. About the time the sun reached its zenith, they sighted a Focke-Wulf 200 Condor and tried to attract its attention by waving at it. Exhausted as they were, their hope of being rescued sank lower and lower as the day wore on until, around 1930, they became aware that there was a U-boat nearby.

As already recounted, Kapitänleutnant Kentrat in the *U-74* was alerted on the evening of 26 May to go to the assistance of the *Bismarck*. Between 0000 and 0400 the next day, he saw gunfire and star shells on the horizon. He tried to approach the *Bismarck* but, with a freshening wind and rising seas, it was very difficult for him to make any headway and waves constantly washing over his bridge made it virtually impossible for him to see what was

going on. Around 0430, however, on the opposite side of
the *Bismarck*, he saw the end-on silhouette of what he
took to be a heavy cruiser or a battleship at a range of
approximately 10,000 metres. He turned towards it, but
visibility was so poor that he promptly lost sight of it. In
his War Diary, he remarked: 'It's an abominable night.
No torpedo could run through these swells.'

At about the same time as he sighted the silhouette, he
heard three explosions, one of them particularly loud.
Some two hours later, he made visual contact with Wohlfarth's *U-556* and, as we already know, Wohlfarth transferred to him the mission of maintaining contact with the
Bismarck. Around 0730, a cruiser and a destroyer suddenly emerged from a rain squall directly ahead of him at
a range of 50,000 metres and he was forced to submerge.
From 0900 on, Kentrat heard one explosion after another,
but when he surfaced at 0922 there was nothing to be
seen. At first, he assumed that what he was hearing was
the scheduled Luftwaffe bomber attack. However, he
wrote in his War Diary, 'It must have been the *Bismarck*'s
last battle.'

For 1200, the *U-74*'s War Diary contains the entry, 'The
pick-up of the *Bismarck*'s War Diary could not be carried
out.' Thereafter, in accordance with a radio directive from
Commander in Chief, U-Boats, Kentrat began looking for
survivors from the *Bismarck*. After about seven hours of
searching, the *U-74* sighted three men in a rubber dinghy.
With considerable difficulty because of high seas, Kentrat
took them aboard. Scarcely had Herzog, Höntzsch, and
Manthey gone down the hatch of the conning tower when
an aircraft was seen to starboard. Kentrat waited until it
had disappeared astern, before resuming his search. His
objective was the spot where the *Bismarck* had gone down
and, in order to be there àt dawn on 28 May, he
maintained a northerly course and travelled at low speed.

At about 0100 Kentrat's men became aware of a strong smell of oil, and a couple of hours later the watch officer saw a red star below the horizon to the southeast. In the War Diary, Kentrat noted: 'I was so exhausted I did not take in this report. A pity, perhaps we could still have saved a few comrades.' The *U-48* and the *U-72* joined the *U-74* to form a line of search but, other than oil fumes in the air, they found no trace of the *Bismarck*'s sinking. Kentrat thought he had missed the position where she sank. In the afternoon, however, he saw floating corpses and debris. He kept up his search for survivors until 2400, then headed for Lorient. His War Diary entry for 2400 on 28 May states:

The weather has abated, the seas are getting progressively calmer. As though nature were content with her work of destruction.

The 27 and 28 May will always be bitter memories for me. There we were, powerless, our hands tied, against the unleashed forces of nature. We could not help our brave *Bismarck*.

At Lorient, representatives of Group West awaited Herzog, Höntzsch, and Manthey. They were taken to Paris and there gave the first eyewitness account of the end of the *Bismarck*.

While the *U-74* was looking for survivors, the German weather ship *Sachsenwald* was doing the same thing to the south of her. On 27 May this ship, under the command of Leutnant zur See Wilhelm Schütte, was en route home after fifty days at sea. At 0200 that day she received a radio signal ordering her to proceed immediately to the *Bismarck*'s position. That meant steaming directly into the seas against a north-northwest wind of Force 6 or 7. At 0600, she was ordered to stay where she was. Between 1100 and 1200 she sighted German planes and shortly after 1400 an order came to steer for another position. The weather was deteriorating. At 2010 a Bristol Blenheim that suddenly appeared to starboard fired at the *Sachsenwald* with her machine guns at a range of 11,000 metres, but did not hit her.

Schütte spent the morning of 28 May in a fruitless search for survivors. Around 1300 he picked up some thin streaks of oil and followed them to the north. Before long the lead case of a German gas mask was seen on the water and, minutes later, numerous corpses in life jackets, empty life jackets, and wreckage came into view. The *Sachsenwald* cruised back and forth through the debris, but saw nobody. After darkness fell, around 2230, three red flares suddenly shot up into the sky nearby. The *Sachsenwald* turned towards them and, through his night glasses, Schütte made out a rubber raft with two men on board. When he was close enough, he yelled, 'Are you German?' and got the resounding reply, 'Ja, hurrah!' By 2245 the ship and the raft were alongside one another and two exhausted men were hauled up a Jacob's ladder. They were Matrosengefreiter Otto Maus and Maschinengefreiter Walter Lorenzen.

The men told Schütte that there was another raft in the vicinity, so he searched the area throughout the twenty-ninth. He made wide swings to the east and west, every turn taking him five nautical miles to the south, following the wind and seas. An empty rubber dinghy that Maus recognized as belonging to the *Bismarck* was taken on board that evening.

Around 0100 on 30 May Schütte, still in the search area, saw the *Canarias*, the Spanish cruiser that Group West had asked to go to the *Bismarck*'s assistance, and the two ships exchanged recognition signals. Immediately thereafter Schütte, his provisions almost spent and his search being unproductive, headed for home. When, on 1 June,

the *Sachsenwald* entered the Gironde, Maus and Lorenzen disembarked and were taken to Paris where they
reported to Group West.

After her encounter with the *Sachsenwald*, the *Canarias*
picked up two dead bodies which, through their tags and
uniforms, were identified as Musikgefreiter[8] Walter
Grasczak and Marinesignalgast[9] Heinrich Neuschwander.
At 1000 the next day, covered with the German flag and
accorded full military honours, both bodies were buried at
43°46' north and 08°34' west.

The time in the *Dorsetshire* passed quickly and on our
fourth day, 30 May, she arrived at Newcastle. The *Maori*
had separated from her at sea and gone into the Clyde.

The last time I talked with Commander Byas, he
warned me that the army, which would take us into
custody at Newcastle, would not treat us as well as the
Dorsetshire had. Naturally, he was right. From many
peacetime associations, I was aware of the bond between
our two navies. Although we were then at war, this feeling
came to the surface under certain circumstances. The fight
that the *Bismarck* put up to the bitter end earned the
admiration of British seamen, which probably accounts
for the good accommodations we were given and the way
we were treated on board ship. The fact that Captain
Martin was well treated as a prisoner of war in Germany
in World War One may also have had something to do
with this. When he made his rounds among our men he
always told them, 'As long as you are here with me, you'll
have it just as good.' And the attitude of his crew was the
same. The British seamen were always pleasant and
helpful. 'You today, us tomorrow,' they said. Their
tomorrow was not long in coming. On 4 April 1942 the

[8] Seaman Apprentice (Bandsman)
[9] Signalman

Dorsetshire, under a new commanding officer, Captain A. W. S. Agar, was sunk by Japanese bombs southeast of Ceylon.

On the morning of 31 May, the petty officers and men were the first to disembark. We officers followed and were piped over the side as the ship's watch presented arms, a ceremony usually reserved for peacetime.

Our journey to the prisoner-of-war camp had begun.

36

Exercise Rhine in Retrospect

The battleship *Bismarck* owes her place in naval history primarily to the gunnery actions in which she engaged on 24 and 27 May 1941.

On 24 May she demonstrated her exceptional striking power. At an average range of 16,000 metres, it took her only six minutes and the expenditure of only ninety-three heavy shells to sink the largest and most famous British battle cruiser of the day. This lightning success exceeded the most sanguine expectations and showed the *Bismarck* to represent a high point in German naval gunnery.

On 27 May the *Bismarck* displayed an almost unbelievable staying power. She was also a high point in German shipbuilding. It required the collective efforts of a British fleet of five battleships, three battle cruisers, two aircraft carriers, four heavy and seven light cruisers, and twenty-one destroyers to find and destroy her. In addition, more than fifty aircraft of the RAF's Coastal Command participated in her destruction.

At ranges that diminished to 2,500 metres and brought a proportionately high rate of hits, the following ordnance was fired at the *Bismarck* after the action off Iceland:

Shells
    380 40.6-centimetre (16-inch), *Rodney*, 27 May
    716 15.2-centimetre (6-inch), *Rodney*, 27 May
    339 35.6-centimetre (14-inch), *King George V*, 27 May
    660 13.3-centimetre (5.25-inch), *King George V*, 27 May
    527 20.3-centimetre (8-inch), *Norfolk*, 27 May
    254 20.3-centimetre (8-inch), *Dorsetshire*, 27 May

*

A total, therefore, of 2,876 shells in the course of an action that lasted ninety minutes.

Torpedoes
   8, aircraft from the *Victorious*, 1 hit, 24-25 May
   13, aircraft from the *Ark Royal*, 2 hits and possibly a third, 26 May
   3, *Cossack*, no hits, 0140, 27 May
   1, *Cossack*, no hit, 0335, 27 May
   2, *Maori*, no hits, 0137, 27 May
   2, *Maori*, no hits, 0656, 27 May
   4, *Zulu*, no hits, 0121, 27 May
   4, *Sikh*, no hits, 0128, 27 May
   12, *Rodney*, 1 hit claimed, 27 May
   8, *Norfolk*, 1 possible hit, 27 May
   3, *Dorsetshire*, 2 hits and possibly a third, 27 May

On 27 May not one shell from the *Rodney* or the *King George V* penetrated the armoured belt or armoured deck to reach the *Bismarck*'s vital spaces[1] and, as his force left the scene of the action, Tovey signalled Somerville, 'Cannot get her to sink with guns.'

There has been a great deal of discussion as to whether the *Bismarck* sank as a result of the three torpedoes fired by the *Dorsetshire* in the concluding phase of the action or whether she was scuttled. Although I was still on board when the *Dorsetshire* fired her first two torpedoes, around 1020, I was not aware of the explosions they produced. That fact, however, has no bearing on the question of what damage, if any, they did. I certainly was aware, as I left the after fire-control station at about 1020, that the *Bismarck* was very, very slowly sinking. Heavily down by

---

[1] The single exception to this invulnerability is the shell from the *Prince of Wales* that penetrated beneath our armour belt in Compartment XIV and exploded against the torpedo bulkhead on 24 May.

her stern, she was behaving as though one compartment after the other was flooding, gradually but irresistibly. She showed all the effects to be expected after the scuttling charges had been fired and the seacocks opened somewhere about 1000. The settling, the sinking by the stern, and the heel to port increased more rapidly after 1030, so it may be that, with the battleship already extremely unstable, the *Dorsetshire*'s third torpedo hastened her end, but it was not responsible for it. I am morally certain that the *Bismarck* would have sunk without this torpedo hit, only perhaps somewhat more slowly.[2]

In his final report on Exercise Rhine, Tovey wrote: 'She [the *Bismarck*] put up a most gallant fight against impossible odds, worthy of the old days of the Imperial German Navy, and she went down with her colours flying.'

How effective was German gunnery, at least at the beginning of the *Bismarck*'s last battle? 'No casualties or damage to any of our ships during the action on 27 May,' wrote Tovey in the above-mentioned report. This outcome may seem surprising in view of Schneider's incredibly accurate straddling fire in the first few minutes of the action, between 0850 and 0900. But it must be remembered that the crippled *Bismarck* could not steer a straight course. She kept on heeling to port and turning unpredictably, whereas the *Rodney*, being maneuvrable, could take action to avoid the *Bismarck*'s registering salvos while the latter was adjusting her fire. And than at 0902, less than

[2] Patrick Beesly, *Very Special Intelligence*, says in a note on page 85: 'There seems little doubt that scuttling charges were fired but whether they actually caused *Bismarck* to sink is doubtful. It would have been a remarkable coincidence if they [the charges] had taken effect at exactly the same moment as *Dorsetshire*'s torpedoes.' I do not see that any meaningful coincidence would have been involved even if steps to scuttle the ship had been taken at the same moment the *Dorsetshire*'s torpedoes arrived. After all, the scuttling actions did not produce instantaneous results, and by the time the torpedoes arrived, some twenty minutes later, the *Bismarck* was irretrievably sinking.

fifteen minutes after we opened fire, Schneider's control station in the foretop and our two forward main turrets, Anton and Bruno, were put out of action. Apparently Albrecht's forward fire-control station was also put out of action, at least temporarily, at about the same time. This meant that we had been in the fight only a quarter of an hour when two of our four main batteries and, with the foretop, the 'brain' of our gunnery were knocked out. The *Bismarck*'s main fire-control station was not well enough protected, a defect common to foretop control stations on all battleships of the time: in the interest of stability, heavy armour could not be installed at that height.

After 0902 I was able to fire only four salvoes from the after turrets, Caesar and Dora, before my own control station was put out of action. That happened just as I had registered on my target, the *King George V*. Thereafter Caesar and Dora went on firing under local control, lay well on target, but without the help of a fire-control apparatus could not score any hits.

There is no doubt that the *Bismarck* had an outstanding gunnery system, and it was very efficiently directed by Schneider and Albrecht. But, because of the number of ships she was up against, their threefold superiority in weight of shells, and the constantly closing range, the decisive blows she suffered were delivered quickly and almost simultaneously.

If a question remains pressing on our conscience, it must be why Lütjens did not attempt to end the increasingly frightful and, finally, hopeless slaughter of the last battle by capitulating – for example, by sending a message to Tovey: 'Cease fire, we will scuttle the *Bismarck*, rescue our survivors.' How Tovey would have reacted to this, I cannot say. The conduct of a German ship's captain or force commander in action must be gauged in the light of Raeder's decree of 22 December

1939, which stated: 'Every German warship will fight with everything she's got until she is victorious or goes down with flags flying.' This decree, which was echoed almost word for word by Lütjens's radio signal of 2140 on 21 May, made it difficult to show a white flag, as the light cruiser *Emden* did in the final phase of her action with the Australian cruiser *Sydney* in November 1914, without ruining her reputation. In principle, Raeder's directive was binding, but in the final analysis the personality of the commander on the scene probably determined whether or not it would be observed to the letter. I tend to the opinion that Lütjens was not the man to set himself above it, but I cannot and will not make such an assertion. In the first place, I do not know at exactly what time Lütjens was killed or perhaps wounded, and, therefore, do not know whether he was physically able to bring an end to the firing. Nor do I know whether Lindemann knew of Lütjens's incapacitation in time to act on his own. So much is uncertain that I have no choice but to let the matter drop.

The enemy's detection of the beginning of Exercise Rhine and his almost continuous contact with our task force thereafter resulted in all our encounters being with heavy British warships, in the *Bismarck*'s spectacular sea fights, her lightning victory over the *Hood* on 24 May, and her lonely, tormented death on 27 May. Given the drama of what took place, it is easy to lose sight of the fact that the destruction of enemy warships was not the primary aim of German surface forces in the Atlantic, and that, viewed strategically, Exercise Rhine was a failure from the moment we left Norway. The *Bismarck* did not even come close on one single occasion to carrying out her principal mission of commerce warfare.

It is worth taking a look at the overall risk the See-kriegsleitung took in sending the *Bismarck* out and the individual risks Lütjens took in the course of the operation.

Concerning the former, the best source is the highest professional witness, Grossadmiral Raeder, commander in chief of the Kriegsmarine, who wrote:

Whether or not to send the *Bismarck* out presented me with an extraordinarily difficult decision. Some of the conditions on which the Seekriegsleitung based its original thinking on the subject no longer pertained. The sortie of the *Bismarck* was to have been part of a broad operational plan, but now, if she went out, it would be an individual undertaking and there was the possibility that the enemy would concentrate all his forces against her. That seriously increased the risk. On the other hand, the military situation was such that we could not afford simply to conserve such a powerful combatant. Postponing the operation until the *Scharnhorst* and *Gneisenau* were again ready for sea, might mean that we would never be able to use the new battleships for offensive operations in the Atlantic. It was almost impossible to predict when the *Scharnhorst* and *Gneisenau*, which were in port in northern France and constantly exposed to attacks by the Royal Air Force, would be combat-ready. In fact, neither ship got to sea until they both escaped in February 1942. Postponing the operation still further, until the *Tirpitz* was operational, would result in at least half a year of inactivity – a period during which the enemy would not be inactive and the situation in the Atlantic would probably deteriorate because of the attitude of the United States, if for no other reason.

An extremely strong psychological ground for my decision was the confidence I had in the leadership of Admiral Lütjens, an officer who understood sea warfare and its tactics inside and out. Even as a young officer in the First World War he commanded a half-flotilla of torpedo boats off Flanders. He later became a flotilla chief, cruiser commander, and Commander in Chief, Torpedo Boats, and was for a long time engaged in staff work. It was when he served as my chief of personnel that he won my special confidence. At one time during the Norwegian campaign he replaced the ailing Fleet Commander in command of the heavy striking forces, and finally demonstrated his great ability during the Atlantic sortie of the *Scharnhorst* and *Gneisenau*.

The decision to give the final order to execute the operation was made very much more difficult for me by Hitler's attitude. When I informed him of my plans, he did not reject them, but it was evident that he was not in complete agreement with them. However, he left the decision up to me. At the beginning of May he had a long conversation in Gotenhafen with Admiral Lütjens, who described his experiences during the Atlantic cruises of the *Scharnhorst* and *Gneisenau* and explained his intentions regarding the tactical deployment of the *Bismarck*. The Fleet Commander also pointed out that enemy aircraft carriers could be a serious danger for the battleship.

After carefully weighing all the circumstances, I gave the order to execute.[3]

It was undoubtedly his awareness that the risks would be far greater if the *Bismarck* were sent out alone that led Lütjens to express certain reservations to Raeder in Berlin on 26 April. At that time he suggested that it might be better to postpone the operation until the *Scharnhorst* had been restored to combat-readiness or even until the *Tirpitz* was operational. Granted, he reverted on his own to the original idea of Exercise Rhine, that the sortie of the *Bismarck* and *Prinz Eugen* should not be delayed. Both of his immediate predecessors as Fleet Commander were relieved of that command because of disagreements with the Seekriegsleitung.[4] So I think his desire to be in accord with Raeder and the Seekriegsleitung was responsible for his reversal because that was so very obviously what they were striving for. As I interpret Lütjens's conduct, he was going against his better judgement in agreeing to immediate 'teaspoon' deployment of our battleships, which could only diminish their chances of accomplishing anything in the Atlantic. Later, the British saw it just as he had. Russell Grenfell wrote: 'But happily for us, the Germans decided to expend their capital ships in penny packets.'[5]

[3] Erich Raeder, *Mein Leben*, Vol. II, p. 266 ff.
[4] Jochen Brennecke, *Schlachtschiff Bismarck*, p. 15
[5] Russell Grenfell, *The Bismarck Episode*, p. 196

Reader continued: 'I bear responsibility for the deployment of the newest German battleship, just as I do for all naval deployments made during my time as commander in chief of the Kriegsmarine. I alone bear it. No one forced me to carry out the operation. My decision was based solely on the necessity to fight the enemy in war with every available means and according to all the rules of the military art, and that entails committing one's own forces.' Although Raeder accepted full responsibility he did not regard it as a personal matter.

In chronological order, the risks that Lütjens accepted or could not avoid are detailed below.

British intelligence learned in March or April 1941 that the *Bismarck* was going to take on a new supply of charts at Gotenhafen. This news confirmed the suspicion that she was about to undertake an operation in the Atlantic, and the Home Fleet was alerted accordingly.

British intelligence got that information either from an agent in Gotenhafen or by decoding German administrative radio signals – it is still not clear which.

Evaluation of this risk raises questions concerning such matters as who served in the Gotenhafen chart centre and why orders like the one to take on new charts were transmitted by radio rather than telephone or teletype. I do not have any personal knowledge in these areas nor is it possible for me to reconstruct what happened. The handling of administrative details of that nature could hardly have entered into Lütjens's calculations at all, let alone as risks to be averted.

In the second week of May 1941 the British noticed a significant increase in German aerial reconnaissance over Scapa Flow and as far west as the Denmark Strait.

They also deduced from a few Luftwaffe radio signals that they decoded that a breakout by the *Bismarck* was imminent. Admiral Tovey directed the cruisers *Suffolk* and *Norfolk* to conduct intensive surveillance of the Denmark Strait.

This was an unavoidable risk, and the Seekriegsleitung had to live with it unless it was prepared to give up the idea of breaking out into the Atlantic. Lütjens must have been aware that our intensified aerial reconnaissance would not go unnoticed by the British, who therefore had some warning.

The Seekriegsleitung had known since at least the middle of April that by March 1941 the British naval attaché in Stockholm, Captain Henry W. Denham, had built up an organization to monitor the traffic passing through the Great Belt.

Whether Lütjens knew of this risk, I cannot say. So far as I know, nothing that might prejudice our chances of conducting war at sea happened during our passage through the Great Belt on the night of 19 May. Either we were lucky or the enemy's organization was not foolproof.

The heavy traffic in the Kattegat on 20 May made it obvious that there was a danger of enemy agents learning about the movement of our task force. That risk increased when the *Gotland* came into view.

I do not know how Lütjens evaluated the danger we faced from agents in Scandinavian waters, but we do know from his radio report that he had misgivings about having been seen by the *Gotland*. That he did not take that risk more seriously may be attributed to the response his radio report brought from Generaladmiral Carls. As it turned out, the *Gotland*'s report and its transmission to London led to the loss of the *Bismarck* on 27 May. On 28 May, the Admiralty wired Denham in Stockholm: 'Your 2058 of 20th May initiated the first of a series of operations which culminated yesterday in the sinking of the *Bismarck*. Well done.'

On the evening of 20 May Viggo Axelssen saw our task force off the coast, near Kristiansand. His ensuing radio message confirmed for the Admiralty Denham's earlier report.

Whether Lütjens took a risk of this nature into account is beyond my knowledge. Even though Axelssen's message did not tell the Admiralty anything new, it was extremely valuable confirmation.

After entering the fjords near Bergen, we spent a whole day within reach of British short-range aerial reconnaissance. Tovey wrote later: 'The *Bismarck* and the *Prinz Eugen* were contemplating a raid on the ocean trade routes, though, if this was so, it seemed unlikely that they would stop at a place so convenient for air reconnaissance.'[6]

This was a risk that Lütjens did accept. Consequently, British aerial reconnaissance identified the *Bismarck* and an *Admiral Hipper*-class cruiser around noon on 21 May. Further aerial reconnaissance on the evening of 22 May ascertained that the task force had left Norway.

[6] 'Sinking of the German Battleship *Bismarck* on the 27th May 1941'. Dispatch by Admiral Sir John Tovey, Supplement No. 3 to the *London Gazette*, 14 October 1947.

Upon leaving the fjords on the evening of 21 May Lütjens learned that a British radio message had instructed the Royal Air Force to be on the lookout for two German battleships and three destroyers that had been reported on a northerly course the day before.

Lütjens, apparently unperturbed, continued on his way. He thereby accepted the risk that the enemy, once alerted, would extend his search to the latitudes through which the task force was to pass.

On the evening of 23 May, when he first met the *Suffolk*, Lütjens did not turn away. After the subsequent appearance of the *Norfolk*, he continued to hold his course, followed by both cruisers.

During the commanders' conference in the *Bismarck* on 18 May Lütjens had indeed said that, should he encounter enemy cruisers, he would attack them if the circumstances were favourable, but that his highest priority would be to preserve the *Bismarck* and the *Prinz Eugen*, so that they could continue their operation for as long as possible. In the above instance, he applied the principle of preserving his ships by pressing on without engaging. In so doing he may have hoped, not unreasonably in the light of experience, to shake off the *Suffolk* and the *Norfolk* during the night. Yet, he thereby unavoidably accepted the risk that he would not succeed and that, instead, the cruisers would call up heavier ships.[7]

---

[7] In the corresponding phase of his operation with the *Gneisenau* and *Scharnhorst*, on 28 January 1941, Lütjens did turn away when he encountered cruisers of the British Home Fleet in the ocean area between Iceland and the Faeroes. He then postponed the operation until the beginning of February, at which time he broke out unseen through the Denmark Strait. Presumably, the Denmark Strait was his first choice for Exercise Rhine because he knew that visibility in that area was

Lütjens was poorly served by German aerial reconnaissance, misinformed about the ships at Scapa Flow in the decisive days, and encouraged by Group North to continue an apparently unendangered operation. He did not realize it, but he was in fact operating with his task force in a goldfish bowl.

The battle off Iceland deprived Lütjens of the freedom of tactical decision he had had before he encountered the *Suffolk* and the *Norfolk* the previous evening. Thereafter, the damage that the *Prince of Wales* had inflicted on the *Bismarck* determined the course of Exercise Rhine. It forced Lütjens to head for the west coast of France through an ocean area that could be covered by British long-range aerial reconnaissance. The pursuit of the *Bismarck*, which began on her 1,700-mile run for St Nazaire, was fraught with almost unbearable suspense on both sides. It led to exciting changes of fortune, hopes alternately rising and falling, and continuous fluctuations between high optimism and profound disappointment. The enemy lost contact with the *Bismarck* and regained it. We suffered from the hits scored by the *Prince of Wales* and from our failure to take on fuel in Norway or from the *Weissenburg*, which prevented us from steaming at higher speeds and thus, perhaps, saving ourselves. Then, there was the rudder hit that crippled our ship and led to her destruction – the end of a journey which, since she was discovered in Norway, had taken the *Bismarck* nearly 3,000 nautical miles.

The loss of the ship and most of her crew was a bitter, heartrending blow. But it remains to be said, and in the

---

usually poor – indeed, he had found it so before – and therefore he would minimize the chance of being discovered. Moreover, in the Denmark Strait he would not have to worry about running into British battleship squadrons as soon as would be the case in the ocean area around the Faeroes, which was much nearer to Scapa Flow.

interest of historical truth it must be said, that in view of the risks that the Seekriegsleitung and Lütjens knowingly accepted, the loss could not be ascribed to an unforeseeable fate, nor was it tragic in the classic sense, because it was not the result of a fatal flaw in the character of the Fleet Commander.

The sinking of the *Bismarck* had a decisive effect on the war at sea. Shortly thereafter, British forces sank six of the steamers belonging to the resupply organization for the conduct of the war in the Atlantic, thereby dealing that force a devastating blow. It was no longer possible for our surface forces to undertake large-scale operations of any duration in the Atlantic. Tovey's words of 26 May came true: 'The sinking of the *Bismarck* may have an effect on the war as a whole out of all proportion to the loss to the enemy of one battleship.'

It has been nearly forty years since the *Bismarck* sank at 1039 on 27 May 1941. She lies at 48°10' north and 16°12' west, not very far out in the North Atlantic, and yet the distance of an eternity from the shores of France. The end of her brief career foreshadowed the passing of the battleship era, of which she was a technological triumph and upon which she and her brave, fallen crew left an indelible mark.

APPENDIX A

The Seekriegsleitung's Operation Order for Exercise Rhine[1]

Commander-in-Chief of the Navy
and Chief of the Seekriegsleitung
B. Nr. 1. Skl. I Op. 410/41 Gkdos Chefs.[2]

Berlin, 2.IV.1941

COMMANDERS' EYES ONLY!   SECRET –
OFFICER COURIER ONLY!   COMMANDS ONLY

I.) Copies to: Group West
 Group North
 Fleet Commander
 Commander-in-Chief, U-Boats
 Subj.: Directives for Future Operations by Surface
 Forces
 No direct references
 I. During the past winter the conduct of the war was
 fundamentally in accord with the Seekriegsleitung's
 directives for the war in the winter 40/41 (Seekriegs-
 leitung I. Op. 2270/41 Chefs.) and closed with the
 first extended battleship operation in the open
 Atlantic.
 Besides achieving important tactical results, this
 battleship operation, as well as the operations of the
 cruiser *Hipper*, showed what important strategic
 effects a similar sortie could have. They would reach

---

[1] The complete original text of this document, found in the Bundesar-
chiv-Militärarchiv after this book had gone to press, differs in minor
points from the version excerpted in Chapter 5.
[2] Seekriegsleitung Operations Section, Chief Operations Officer, Order
Number 410/41, Commands Only, Commanders' Eyes Only.

beyond the immediate area of operations to other theatres of war (Mediterranean, South Atlantic).

The goal of the war at sea must be to maintain and increase these effects by repeating such operations as often as possible. To accomplish this, the experience already gained must be exploited and the operations themselves expanded.

We must not lose sight of the fact that the decisive objective in our struggle with England is to destroy her trade. This can be most effectively accomplished in the North Atlantic, where all her supply lines come together and where, even in case of interruption in more distant seas, supplies can still get through on the direct route from North America. The employment and operational area of our battleships and cruisers must take this viewpoint into account.

Gaining command of the sea in the North Atlantic is the best solution to this problem, but this is not possible with the forces that at this moment we can commit to this purpose, and given the constraint that we must preserve our numerically inferior forces. Nevertheless, we must strive for local and temporary command of the sea in this area and gradually, methodically, and systematically extend it.

During the first battleship operation in the Atlantic the enemy was able always to deploy one battleship against our two on both the main supply lines. However, it became clear that providing this defence of his convoys brought him to the limit of the possibilities open to him, and the only way he can significantly strengthen his escort forces is by weakening positions important to him (Mediterranean, home waters) or by reducing convoy traffic. (Escort by American warships or active intervention by the USA would necessitate new decisions.)

What we need to do is, on the one hand, cause the enemy to disperse his strength by continually changing both our operational methods and our area of operations, and, on the other hand, attack with concentrated forces the weak points thus created.

As soon as the two battleships of the *Bismarck* class are ready for deployment, we will be able to seek engagement with the forces escorting enemy convoys and, when they have been eliminated, destroy the convoy itself. As of now, we cannot follow that course, but it will soon be possible, as an intermediate step, for us to use the battleship *Bismarck* to distract the hostile escorting forces, in order to enable the other units engaged to operate against the convoy itself. In the beginning, we will have the advantage of surprise, because some of the ships involved will be making their first appearance and, based on his experience in the previous battleship operations, the enemy will assume that *one* battleship will be enough to defend a convoy.

II. The main features of the conduct of the war in the summer of 1941 will be determined by their connection to Operation Barbarossa.[3] The relevant general directives are set out in Seekriegsleitung I op 262/41 Chefs. of 6.3.41.

The regions of emphasis and the assignment in broad outline of forces and missions in the group command areas will be according to that directive.

The following directive, therefore, deals only with the next deployment of battleships and cruisers to the Atlantic.

[3] The invasion of the Soviet Union

III. *Directive for the Deployment of the Battleships* Bismarck *and* Gneisenau *and the Cruiser* Prinz Eugen *in the North Atlantic at the End of April*

1) At the earliest possible date, which it is hoped will be during the new-moon period of April, *Bismarck* and *Prinz Eugen*, led by the Fleet commander, are to be deployed as commerce-raiders in the Atlantic.

   At a time that will depend on the completion of the repairs she is currently undergoing, *Gneisenau* will also be sent into the Atlantic.

2) The lessons learned in the last battleship operation indicate that *Gneisenau* should join up with the *Bismarck* group, but a diversionary sweep by the *Gneisenau* in the area between Cape Verde and the Azores may be planned before this happens.

3) The heavy cruiser is to spend most of her time operating tactically with *Bismarck* or *Bismarck* and *Gneisenau*.

   The disadvantage that is accepted by bringing along the cruiser, with her lesser radius of action, will be offset by the advantages of greater search capability, availability of a ship suitable for operations against light forces and shadowers, and her powerful torpedo armament, which could be useful in attacking strongly defended convoys as well as in disengaging from superior enemy covering forces.

   The difficulties created by her lesser operational radius must be surmounted by the appropriate disposition of tankers, by periodically releasing her to fuel, or, in emergencies, by transferring fuel to her from *Bismarck*.

   The release or dispatch of the cruiser on special

missions remains the option of the operational command or, while at sea, of the Fleet Commander.

4) In contrast to previous directives to the *Gneisenau–Scharnhorst* task force, it is the mission of this task force to also attack escorted convoys. However, the objective of the battleship *Bismarck* should not be to defeat, *in an all-out engagement*, enemies of equal strength, but to tie them down in a delaying action, while preserving her own combat capability as much as possible, so as to allow the other ships to get at the merchant vessels in the convoy.

   The primary mission of this operation also is the destruction of the enemy's merchant shipping; enemy warships will be engaged only when that primary mission makes it necessary and it can be done without excessive risk.

5) The operational area will be defined as the entire North Atlantic north of the equator, with the exception of the territorial waters (3-nautical-mile limit) of neutral states.

   In all probability, respect for the American Neutrality Zone will no longer need to be taken into account at the time of the operation. Because of the danger of shadowing by US forces, however, it does not appear expedient to station supply ships or tankers in the part of the existing Neutrality Zone that lies in the sphere of the USA.

6) Previous experiences have shown that, contrary to what might be expected, we do not have enough knowledge of convoy routes and schedules to determine the time and place in the vast area involved where convoys might be intercepted.

One major difficulty is posed by the weather conditions in the Atlantic, which often restrict visibility and prevent the use of embarked aircraft.

The effectiveness of the operation must therefore be improved by every conceivable form of reconnaissance. For this, there come into question:

a) *U-Boats*

The last battleship operation showed that co-operation between surface forces and U-boats in the same area can have advantages for both. For this, there must be a means of direct communication between the surface forces and the U-boats and there will be. The U-boat short-signal book is to be enlarged and copies placed on board the ships.

In general it would not be advisable to have battleships cruise in a line of search with U-boats that are deployed as scouts for surface forces, because such positioning would make it more difficult for them to respond. It would be better to deploy the U-boats in the designated area of operations in a scout line and to charge them with reporting targets to the battleships and subsequent shadowing or attack.

Conversely, the Fleet Commander, either by shadowing reports or direct order, will be able to advise the U-boats of any sighted convoy.

As a further test of this collaboration, the following orders will – provided the discussions held in preparation for this operation do not produce more promising possibilities – apply to the proposed operation:

1) There will be at least two boats in the U-boats' Operations Area South (Freetown area) throughout the operation, and they

will be under the command of the Commander-in-Chief, U-Boats. Should the opportunity arise for direct cooperation with the fleet forces, however, the Fleet commander has the right to give the boats operational orders.

2) On the Halifax convoy route, two or more boats of the northern group will be deployed far enough to the west to support, by reconnaissance or attack, an operation of the Fleet Commander between 30° and 45° west.

   Command and control as under paragraph 1) above.

3) The supplying of these U-boats with fuel, provisions, and munitions is to be provided for by outfitting more store and escort ships. Allocation of supplies by Commander-in-Chief, U-Boats, or Fleet Commander.

b) *Scouts*

Besides the deployment of U-boats, camouflaged ships could be deployed as scouts for the fleet formation.

This deployment might be in tactical association with the task force or in specially designated, remote scouting areas. For the former type of deployment, the ships, preferably oilburners, should have adequate operational range and a cruising speed of at least 12 knots. Ships that do not have these characteristics are not suitable for tactical association with the fleet, but can be used in the latter type of deployment.

An effort will be made to deploy two suitable ships for use in the former capacity. Prizes taken during the operation may also be used for this purpose.

Moreover, Group West will be charged with examining the captured whalers and, if satisfactory, providing one of them for use in the former capacity and *Schiff 13* and *24* in the latter.

The severe shortage of shipping tonnage caused by newly arisen transport missions will make it scarcely possible to prepare other, special ships for this purpose, but the question will be examined by the Oberkommando der Kriegsmarine, as will the deployment of *Schiff 23* and *Togo* for scouting purposes.

c) *Aircraft Mother Ships*

The question of deploying such ships (catapult; two to three aircraft, landing mat) will be examined by the Oberkommando der Kriegsmarine. The existing catapult ships *Friesenland* and *Schwabenland* are not suitable.

d) *Supply Ships*

During the last operation the deployment of supply ships for tactical cooperation with the fleet formation proved extremely useful. Nevertheless, these ships should be used for this mission only if all other possibilities fail, as their loss would have critical consequences, not only for this operation but also for subsequent ones with large formations. Moreover valuable cargoes (munitions) would be in jeopardy. With this warning, however, their deployment is left up to the Fleet Commander.

The same applies to fleet oilers.

7) *Ermland* is available as a supply ship, *Heide, Weissenburg, Brehme, Esso, Ill, Spichern,* and *Lothringen* as fleet oilers.

Care is to be taken that the requisite readiness dates are not upset by modifications or the installation of equipment. If necessary, ships undergoing such work and unable to meet the schedule must be deployed as reserve tankers.

Thorn and *Egerland*, which have been prepared for other uses, will not be available at first.

Uckermark probably cannot be made available because she is deployed with the cruiser *Lützow*; other supply ships (*Dithmarschen, Kärnten, Passat*) probably will not be operational until a later date (1.7, 1.9, 1.10).

8) The group commands have operational control in their zones. The Fleet Commander has control at sea, the U-boat groups attached to him will be under his tactical command for the duration of the joint operations (the Commander-in-Chief, U-Boats, will detail a U-boat officer to the Fleet Commander's staff for the duration of the operation).

9) The groups will contact as soon as possible the Fleet command and the Commander-in-Chief, U-Boats, regarding the execution of the operation and will report the result from such contact to the Seekriegsleitung at least fourteen days before the operation begins.

IV. As already indicated under I, the objective must be to confront the enemy with new situations created by wide-ranging changes of the areas of operations.

Upon further confirmation of the manner of conduct of the war up to now, consideration may be given to extending the next-following operation as far as the South Atlantic.

When the need to respect the PanAmerican Neutrality Zone has passed, the intersection of the route from North and Central America to Freetown and

Central Africa (important military supplies) with the La Plata route, and also with the Cape–Freetown route, will offer promising operational possibilities.

The prerequisite for the execution of such a distant operation is the deployment of the greatest possible number of auxiliaries. The Seekriegsleitung will initiate appropriate measures.

Such a shift in the area of operations may prove necessary if, as a consequence of the next operation and those past, the North Atlantic routes that we have been attacking become more strongly defended by the enemy.

Until *Tirpitz* becomes operational, attacks against strongly defended convoys on the main supply lines in the North Atlantic will not have good prospects for success.

The time for extending operations to the south must remain open at the moment. The reason for announcing the intention is that it will enable Group Command West and the fleet to evaluate their experiences with regard to this new area of operations.

> /s/ RAEDER
> Commander-in-Chief of the Kriegsmarine
> /s/ SCHNIEWIND
> Chief of the Seekriegsleitung
> /s/ FRICKE
> Chief of the Seekriegsleitung Operations Section

APPENDIX B

General Orders for the Atlantic Operation

(Annex 1 to 'Operations Order of the Fleet Commander for the Atlantic Operation with *Bismarck* and *Prinz Eugen* – Exercise Rhine,' Fleet Order 100/41 A1, Secret – Commands Only, Commanders' Eyes Only, 22 April 1941.)

1. *The object of the operation* is to do the greatest possible damage to the enemy by destroying his merchant shipping, especially that proceeding *towards* England.

2. The operation conducted with the battleships *Gneisenau* and *Scharnhorst* from January until mid-March 1941 showed that, in spite of information provided by the B-Dienst regarding the sailing dates and routes of convoys, it is extremely difficult to intercept a convoy in the vast ocean spaces with the few units available for this purpose, and it depends on coincidence and luck.

   Therefore, I do not intend to restrict the deployment of the ships exclusively for attacking convoys, but also from the outset for capturing or destroying ships steaming independently. However, as far as time permits, they will be deployed in the area of operations in such a manner that there is a prospect of intercepting a convoy.

3. *Attacks on Convoys*
Some of the convoys encountered by the battleships during the operation were escorted by a battleship and, in one case, by two cruisers and two destroyers also. Escorts of comparable strength must be anticipated in the future.

The operational directives of the Seekriegsleitung and Group West allow *Bismarck* only to *tie down* a battleship escorting a convoy, insofar as that is possible without fully engaging, and that only in the event such action gives *Prinz Eugen* the possibility of success against the rest of the escort or against the convoy.

Accordingly, when *Bismarck* and *Prinz Eugen* attack a convoy, they must do so from opposite sides. In every case, tactical and attack orders will come from the Fleet Commander.

Without coming in battle contact, the exact strength of a convoy's escort can usually be determined only by shipboard aircraft. This deployment is, however, dependent upon the tactical situation and the weather and therefore rarely possible on the Halifax–England route. It must, therefore, be anticipated that, in making an attack, *Prinz Eugen* will encounter escorting cruisers even if *Bismarck* succeeds in drawing off the big ship. In this event, the cruiser's attack on the convoy is to be broken off and an immediate report made. But even when only one big ship is escorting the convoy, the enemy, if he follows good tactics, will stay in the immediate vicinity of the convoy and *protect it from all sides*. In this case there can be no question of an attack by the cruiser; that may occur only if the big ship allows the *Bismarck* to draw her so far from her charges that the cruiser has a chance of getting within effective shooting range of the convoy.

If the ships are in search sectors and *Prinz Eugen* sights a convoy, she should report it by short signal at close range and stay at the extreme edge of visibility (smokeless). With respect to the necessity for *later surprise attacks*, it cannot be the task of the cruiser to ascertain the strength of the escort. That must be left to the *Bismarck*. In an attack on a convoy, the main objective must be to sink as many steamers as possible. When a *weakly* escorted convoy is attacked, the convoy commander will certainly disperse his charges. In this case, the first objective must be to disable the largest possible number of steamers by gunfire. (They can be sunk later.) For this, all batteries are to open up with exact firing directions and at the lowest possible range appropriate to the calibre. (Main and secondary batteries with nose-fused and base-fused projectiles, heavy flak nose-fused.) Steamers that have been disabled by gunfire are not to be sunk until there is not one steamer still moving within sight of the ship concerned. *To conserve ammunition, the heavy flak is to be nose-fused and used in the following manner: close within 300–500 metres of the ship, then have the best gunners fire individual shots into the waterline. Fire only when the ship is on the up-roll. Shoot holes in all of the steamer's compartments (the largest room is the engine room). With 3.7-centimetre ammunition, shoot holes in the upper part of the steamer, so that during the flooding of the rooms, air can escape upwards.*

Prinz Eugen will also use her torpedoes in an *attack on a convoy*. Against a *strongly defended* convoy, there will be only a short time, if any, available for the cruiser's attack. This must be exploited as fully as possible. In *this case* especially, everything will depend on speedy action. The steamers are therefore to be sunk *primarily with torpedoes*.

The work of destruction may not be delayed by rescue operations.

The rescue of survivors, especially those from a convoy that has been attacked, can expose our own ships to serious danger from enemy submarines and surface forces. In such cases, concern for our ships must take precedence over the rescue of survivors. If necessary, a small steamer is to be spared for the purpose of rescuing survivors.

4. *Ships Steaming Independently*

In the absence of orders to the contrary, all lone steamers encountered will be captured or destroyed. When weather conditions permit boats to be lowered, the steamers will be searched and, if they themselves are valuable or have valuable cargoes and they can get under way, *brought home* (examine fuel supply, provisions, etc.). In principle, tankers that can make more than 10 knots, refrigerator ships and fast motor ships, if they can get under way – whether they are laden or not – are to be captured and brought by a prize crew over the designated course into the mouth of the Gironde.

Experience has shown that it is best not to bring prizes immediately into the Bay of Biscay, especially those that have transmitted radio signals, but to wait a few weeks in a remote ocean area, then to set out for the Gironde at intervals so as to prevent the enemy from capturing them as they enter the Bay of Biscay. For this, in some circumstances it will be necessary to equip the prizes with extra provisions and send them to an escort tanker so that they can replenish. The start of the prizes' return voyage is to be reported by short signal.

Prizes must not fall into enemy hands under any circumstances. In every case, therefore, as soon as it boards, the prize crew must make preparations for scuttling at short notice.

For searching steamers, a boarding party is to be organized. Each ship has three prize crews and must organize two others from its company. Equipment is to be stored within easy reach. Prize crews must be instructed on the mission they are to discharge on board the steamers. All books, code instruments, tables, and notes found on the bridge, in the charthouse, in the radio room, in the captain's pockets, and elsewhere are to be seized and examined on board the ship by officers qualified in the language.

On approaching a ship sailing independently, fly the British ensign and keep the turrets at zero degrees to avoid arousing suspicion. Signal her to stop and forbid her to use her radio. The transmission or completion of a radio warning signal must be prevented if possible. For this, the following measures are to be taken:

a. If the steamer is radioing before the ship gets within firing range, the message must be interrupted by the sending of a prepared radio message (in the English language) or a radio weather report. As soon as the steamer is in effective range, open fire. Whenever possible take the *bridge superstructure* under fire. (On most steamers the radio room is behind or below the bridge.)

b. If the steamer is radioing within the effective range of the heavy flak, open fire immediately and destroy her radio installation as in paragraph a.

So that tankers and valuable ships come into our hands as intact as possible, do not fire any longer than is necessary to prevent the transmission of signals. Establish good connections between the radio room and the bridge.

Approach a steamer so that one side is to leeward, quickly bring the ship to a stop, and lower a boat immediately.

The boarding party will take over all important points (bridge, charthouse, radio room, engine room) and have the crew of the steamer assemble immediately on the upper deck.

APPENDIX C

British Forces Deployed Against the Bismarck *During Exercise Rhine*

Note: The right-hand column shows where the ships were before the pursuit of the *Bismarck* began.

HOME FLEET AND SHIPS ATTACHED

Battleship	*King George V*	Scapa Flow
Battleship	*Prince of Wales*	Scapa Flow
Battleship	*Rodney*	En route from Clyde to Boston with the troop transport *Britannic*
Battle Cruiser	*Repulse*	Clyde, assigned to troop convoy WS-8B
Battle Cruiser	*Hood*	Scapa Flow
Aircraft Carrier	*Victorious*	Scapa Flow, assigned to troop convoy WS-8B
Cruiser	*Norfolk*	Denmark Strait, on patrol
Cruiser	*Suffolk*	Refuelling at Reykjavik, Iceland
Cruiser	*Galatea*	Scapa Flow
Cruiser	*Aurora*	Scapa Flow
Cruiser	*Kenya*	Scapa Flow
Cruiser	*Neptune*	Scapa Flow
Cruiser	*Arethusa*	En route to Reykjavik, Iceland
Cruiser	*Edinburgh*	Off the Azores, on patrol

Cruiser	*Manchester*	Faeroe Islands passage, on patrol
Cruiser	*Birmingham*	Faeroe Islands passage, on patrol
Destroyer	*Inglefield*	En route to Scapa Flow
Destroyer	*Intrepid*	En route to Scapa Flow
Destroyer	*Active*	Scapa Flow
Destroyer	*Antelope*	Scapa Flow
Destroyer	*Achates*	Scapa Flow
Destroyer	*Anthony*	Scapa Flow
Destroyer	*Electra*	Scapa Flow
Destroyer	*Echo*	Scapa Flow
Destroyer	*Somali*	At sea with *Rodney* and *Britannic*
Destroyer	*Tartar*	At sea with *Rodney* and *Britannic*
Destroyer	*Mashona*	At sea with *Rodney* and *Britannic*
Destroyer	*Eskimo*	At sea with *Rodney* and *Britannic*
Destroyer	*Punjabi*	Scapa Flow
Destroyer	*Icarus*	Scapa Flow
Destroyer	*Nestor*	Scapa Flow
Destroyer	*Jupiter*	Londonderry

WESTERN APPROACHES COMMAND

Cruiser	*Hermione*	En route to Scapa Flow
Destroyer	*Lance*	Scapa Flow
Destroyer	*Legion*	Clyde, with battle cruiser *Repulse*

Destroyer	*Saguenay*	Clyde, with battle cruiser *Repulse*
Destroyer	*Assiniboine*	Clyde, with battle cruiser *Repulse*
Destroyer	*Columbia*	Londonderry

PLYMOUTH COMMAND, 4TH DESTROYER FLOTILLA

Destroyer	*Cossack*	Clyde, assigned to troop convoy WS-8B
Destroyer	*Sikh*	Clyde, assigned to troop convoy WS-8B
Destroyer	*Zulu*	Clyde, assigned to troop convoy WS-8B
Destroyer	*Maori*	Clyde, assigned to troop convoy WS-8B
Destroyer	*Piorun*	Clyde, assigned to troop convoy WS-8B

NORE COMMAND

| Destroyer | *Windsor* | Scapa Flow |

FORCE H

Battle Cruiser	*Renown*	Gibraltar
Aircraft Carrier	*Ark Royal*	Gibraltar
Cruiser	*Sheffield*	Gibraltar
Destroyer	*Faulknor*	Gibraltar
Destroyer	*Foresight*	Gibraltar
Destroyer	*Forester*	Gibraltar
Destroyer	*Foxhound*	Gibraltar
Destroyer	*Fury*	Gibraltar
Destroyer	*Hesperus*	Gibraltar

AMERICA AND WEST INDIES STATION

| Battleship | *Ramillies* | At sea, escorting convoy HX-127 |
| Battleship | *Revenge* | Halifax, Nova Scotia |

SOUTH ATLANTIC COMMAND

| Cruiser | *Dorsetshire* | At sea, escorting convoy SL-74 |

The following submarines were also deployed:

	Minerva	On patrol off southwestern Norway
	P-31	Scapa Flow
	Sealion	English Channel
	Seawolf	English Channel
	Sturgeon	English Channel
	Pandora	En route from Gibraltar to Great Britain
	Tigris	Clyde
	H-44	Rothesay

APPENDIX D

The Rudder Damage: Were All Possibilities of Repair Exhausted?

The existing literature on the *Bismarck* poses a question that I have been asked repeatedly: whether or not everything possible was done to repair the damage to her rudder. I want to deal with this matter, anyway, but the many questions make me feel obliged to do so.

Kapitänleutnant (Ingenieurwesen) Gerhard Junack, who not only participated in some of the attempts at repair but whose station was closer to what was going on than was mine, has said: 'I cannot help wondering whether everything was really done that night, every possibility exhausted, to save the battleship *Bismarck* in spite of everything. Would it have helped if, contrary to naval custom, the officer of the watch had conned the ship from the engine-control station or the chief engineer had stood beside the captain on the bridge and been in direct contact with the turbine operators? Full-power orders relayed through the engine telegraph certainly weren't going to work. What if a charge had been set in the stern, regardless of what it might have done to the propellers? So long as the rudders were jammed, it wasn't much use having the propellers in working order, anyway. Suppose a U-boat had been taken in tow as a course stabilizer or a stern anchor had been suspended from a float and dragged behind? With three propellers capable of 28 knots still serviceable, was there really nothing she could do but head towards the enemy at low speed? Who's to say what would have been possible with an unbroken fighting spirit?' These points will be examined in sequence.

Junack did not say what good it might have done to

have the officer of the watch conn the ship from the engine-control station, and I cannot imagine. I believe that the officer of the watch must be on the bridge. If he were below, it would be impossible for him to carry out his most important task, conning the ship by the view that is available only topside. What could he have done better in the engine-control station than on the bridge?

Similarly, Junack did not say what the advantage would have been in having the chief engineer stand beside the captain on the bridge in direct contact with the turbine operators. Orders could undoubtedly have been transmitted to the engines just as quickly by telephone as by engine telegraph but, without being told more, I cannot see how this would have helped.

As for setting a charge in the stern without regard for the propellers, we have seen that after the rudder rooms flooded, attempts to enter them and do repairs were defeated by the force of the water. For the same reason, no one could work in the after steering rooms, either. If none of the spaces in the steering plant could be entered, how could a charge be attached to the rudder shafts? Such a relatively simple task as disengaging a coupling took a diver hours of exhausting work. Has Junack given any valid reason for thinking that, despite everything, it would have been possible for anyone to force his way into a rudder room and place a charge there? As a concerned investigator, he would have surely tracked down any such possibility and provided a persuasive argument to show it could have been done. But he didn't do that. The proof is lacking, even the probability.

Let us assume, for the sake of discussion, that it would have been possible to force a way into the after steering room and there set a charge, 'regardless of what it might have done to the propellers.' It seems to me that to recommend taking the risk of losing the propellers and perhaps of more flooding simply in order to get rid of jammed rudders would have been a counsel of despair. Without her propellers, the *Bismarck* would have been dead in the water and at the mercy of every vagary in the enemy-infested ocean area around her. Reduce to impotence a propulsion plant still capable of 28 knots? Would that have been a responsible course of action?

On the other hand, since the propellers were forward of and below the rudder shafts, a correctly measured charge might not have damaged them at all. Blast effects in water tend to rise towards the surface, where water pressure is less.

I do not know how precisely demolition charges could be measured on board but, assuming that a charge commensurate with the need could have been prepared, did the *Bismarck*'s command neglect to do something that might have improved her situation? Only if there were solid prospects of achieving the desired result. And what were the prospects? During our shake-down cruises in the Baltic we found that it was very difficult to steer the *Bismarck* with her propellers alone. Obviously, it would have been even more difficult to do so in the raging Atlantic on 26 May and it would have been virtually impossible to hold the giant ship on a course for St Nazaire with a following sea. Therefore, even if it was technically possible to blow the rudders away, the objective in doing so would not have been achieved.

Take a U-boat in tow to stabilize our course? First of all, a U-boat would have to have been available. We now know that none was available. And had there been, how could the *Bismarck* have taken and kept it in tow? If even the *Bismarck* was labouring heavily in the stormy seas, how much more tumultuous would it have been for a U-boat. The U-boat's men were to handle the heavy hawsers on a very small deck, while the boat itself was being manoeuvred? And, so that all this could be done at night, should Lindemann have illuminated the area of the deck where it was going on, and perhaps have turned on a searchlight as well, thereby helping the enemy to pinpoint our position and giving him precise firing data, particularly for his torpedoes?

Moreover, it would have been necessary to post a detail on the *Bismarck*'s quarterdeck to maintain continuous surveillance of the tow connection. Had the enemy suddenly appeared, which he was expected to do momentarily, the presence of these men might very well have delayed the immediate employment of our main after turrets. Anyway, we would not have been able to fire astern without endangering the U-boat there. In other words, we might have been forced partly or completely to forgo the use of our after turrets. Such a limitation could have been put on our fighting power only with the most serious reservations and could scarcely have been maintained. Even had the tow been managed, the *Bismarck*, more than 50,000 tons of her, running before a northwester that became a storm, could hardly have been held on course by a U-boat of, let us say, 500 tons. If the sea had been calm and there had been no enemy ships around, perhaps, but, given the circumstances, I consider the idea unrealistic. In any case, there was no U-boat at our disposal.

Drag a stern anchor suspended from a float? The disproportion between the two masses would have been even greater than in the case of a U-boat. A stern anchor would not have had any effect at all on the *Bismarck*.

The answer to Junack's concluding question, 'Who's to say what would have been possible with an unbroken fighting spirit?' lies in the above rebuttals to his proposals.

Not one of the options he indicates could have been carried out, either singly or in combination. Either they shatter on hard facts, such as the suction under the stern, the inaccessibility of the steering rooms, and the lack of a U-boat, or they are contradicted by logic, such as his ideas of stationing the officer of the watch in the engine-control station or the chief engineer on the bridge, towing the stern anchor, or blowing off the rudders without regard to other damage. I do not see that the ship's command or anyone else omitted anything that could have been done. And Junack has not proved, much less documented, his tacit reproaches. The fighting spirit in the *Bismarck* was not broken. The question should not be asked, even rhetorically.

Brennecke raises still other suggestions made by third parties as to how the *Bismarck*'s rudder damage might have been dealt with.[1] Among them is the idea that a hawser or heavy anchor chain put over the side might have stabilized the course of the ship before the following sea. According to this proposal, danger of the hawser or chain being drawn into the propellers might have been averted by suspending it from a spar projecting from one side of the ship aft. According to another proposal, the starboard side of the hull could have been 'roughened up', so that it would have greater resistance to the flow of water. This might have been one way of offsetting at least to some degree the effect of having the rudders jammed in the port position.

The reservations already raised in regard to the U-boat and the stern anchor also apply to these retrospective theories. On one hand, the difference between the respective masses would have been much too great in regard to the anchor chain, hawser, or any material that might have been put over the side to increase the drag on the starboard side. And on the other, security, which required

[1] Jochen Brennecke, *Schlachtschiff Bismarck*, note 454.

that the ship be darkened and her guns be ready to fire at any moment, would have argued against the illumination of the work place and the posting of working parties on the upper deck, as would have been necessary in these cases also.

The idea put forward in Brennecke's book that the *Bismarck*, by radio messages through the Seekriegsleitung, should have asked hydrodynamic experts at home what was the best way to counter the rudder damage has all the earmarks of being armchair strategy.

Retired Kapitän zur See Alfred Schulze-Hinrichs appears to me to have the most plausible ex post facto theories on what the *Bismarck* might have done.[2] This recognized expert in the field of seamanship wonders whether the *Bismarck* should not have tried, by contra-rotating her three propellers, to reach St Nazaire by backing.

This is not the place for a detailed examination of Schulze-Hinrichs's very interesting technical arguments. In retrospect, I think the explanation for not trying a manoeuvre such as he suggests must lie in the circumstances that existed that night, the presence of the enemy and the weather, as well as in our general experience of the *Bismarck*'s steering characteristics.

Given the pressure being put upon us by the enemy, it is readily understandable that the ship's command did not try such a manoeuvre, which would have required continuous, concentrated attention – and that for hours, over hundreds of nautical miles, on a pitch-black night with no horizon and not a single star by which to navigate. Finally, as we have seen, her earliest trials in the Baltic showed that the ship was extremely difficult to steer with her

[2] Alfred Schulze-Hinrichs, 'Schlachtschiff *Bismarck* und Seemannschaft,' pp. 6–7.

propellers alone. In backing she had a strong tendency, as do most ships, to turn her stern into the wind. In the Atlantic on 26 May this would have, in effect, put us on the same unwanted course to the northwest to which we were condemned in going ahead. Experience gained in her trials may have caused the ship's command to reject from the start the idea of attempting to reach St Nazaire by backing through the Atlantic swells. It is, however, possible that had such a manoeuvre been practised more frequently and practised in bad weather, it might have been tried.

In view of the *Bismarck*'s actual situation that night, Schulze-Hinrichs's otherwise interesting line of thought is too theoretical.

The question whether the *Bismarck* did everything possible to remedy the rudder damage must, therefore, even taking into account the theories subsequently advanced by third parties, be answered affirmatively. Everything that could be responsibly undertaken, everything sensible, was tried. Brennecke is of the same opinion up to this point, but when he questions the presence of a will to win, he departs from my thinking.[3] What does 'will to win' mean here?

As retired Admiral Erich Förste correctly states, Lütjens's aim could only have been to reach port and to continue the operation after undergoing repairs and refuelling.[4] If, on the way to St Nazaire, he had been forced to fight a doubly unwelcome action, he would have done so with the necessary vigour. That the fighting spirit

---

[3] Junack's words regarding morale on board after the Fleet Commander's address (*see* page 155) may have provoked Brennecke's question. Junack's actual words were: 'The high fighting spirit that permeated the battleship on Saturday [24 May, the day of the battle off Iceland] was, however, irretrievably lost.'

[4] Jochen Brennecke, *op. cit.*, note 299.

was not broken was conclusively proved by the course of the battle on 27 May. If evidence as to the spirit of the crew after the rudder hit is needed, we have only to quote Maschinengefreiter Hermann Budich: 'The ship's inability to manoeuvre did not even have a particularly negative effect on our morale. It is true that, because at the time we left Gotenhafen we were ordered by Korvettenkapitän Freytag to perform the duties of the main electric control station in our circuit room II without the benefit of extra help, we were totally exhausted. But we were full of hope and had great faith in our captain, whose personality was such that we were very devoted to him.'

The reason why, in her inability to manoeuvre, the lonely ship was helpless in the Atlantic is not to be sought in conditions on board. The only thing that could have really helped during those hours was an attack on the enemy's forces by other German units, an attack that would have prevented or interrupted the operations of the heavy British ships against the *Bismarck*.

But no such help came. The battleships *Scharnhorst* and *Gneisenau*, then lying at Brest, had suffered bomb and other damage and were consequently not seaworthy. The destroyers there could not put to sea because of the northwester. The weather was so bad that, even had they reached the battle area, they would not have been able to accomplish much – on the night of 26–27 May we saw what a difficult time the British destroyers had in the high seas. Of the eight U-boats in the Bay of Biscay that at the last moment were ordered to support the *Bismarck* – the *U-73*, *U-556*, *U-98*, *U-97*, *U-48*, *U-552*, *U-108*, and *U-74* – *U-74* and *U-556* had expended all their torpedoes in earlier operations. The *U-74* had been damaged by depth charges and had only limited manoeuvrability. The intact boats were too far away when they received the order to assemble around the *Bismarck* to reach the scene of action in time. It was too late to send a fully equipped U-boat from a base on the west coast of France. There were still the supply ship *Ermland* and the oceangoing tugs, but it would take them between twenty and forty hours to reach us from the coast. They would have arrived too late even to rescue survivors.

Our naval headquarters ashore certainly mobilized every imaginable help for the *Bismarck*. But it was too little and too late.

The only other help we might have had was from our bomber squadrons stationed in France. But, of course, they needed notification and preparation. Apparently there was neither.

Inevitably, the questions raised earlier about the timing for Exercise Rhine and the best possible composition of Lütjens's task force come to mind. Even more important, however, is the question of how good were the arrangements for cooperation between the task force and the air and submarine arms, should that become necessary. But these are considerations that exceed the bounds of a survivor's story. So this line of thought must be abandoned with the recognition that, after the torpedo hit on 26 May, the *Bismarck* was consigned to a fate that she did not have the resources to avert.

Action between the Rodney and the Bismarck on the morning of Tuesday, 27 May 1941, as recorded by the battle observer in the Rodney

0844 Green 005 degs [starboard 5° from dead ahead].
      Enemy in sight.
0847 *Rodney* fires first salvo.
0848 *King George V* fires first salvo.
0849 Enemy replies, 1000 short of *Rodney*.
0852 Enemy shell 1000 over.
0853 Enemy shell just short starboard side.
0854 Enemy shell just over port side.
0856 Enemy salvoes over.
0857 Enemy salvoes over.
0858 *Rodney* straddled.
      Enemy, firing steadily, abeam on crossing *King George V* bow.
      Rodney's secondary armament in action.
      Main and secondary armament engaging enemy port side.
0902 Hit on *Bismarck*'s upper deck.
      Enemy salvoes short.
0905 Enemy shell 1000 over.
0906 Enemy shell 300 over.
0910 Our salvoes falling well together astern of *Bismarck*.
      Enemy turning away firing at *King George V*.[1]

---

[1] The expression *enemy turning* used in this and subsequent entries should not be understood to mean that the *Bismarck* was turning of her own volition. She was reacting to the combined influences of her jammed rudders, the seaway, and the wind. The salvoes referred to in this entry are those directed by the author from the after station (*see* pages 230–31).

0913 Good straddle on *Bismarck*, which was completely obscured.

0914 *Rodney*'s shots falling well over.

0915 *Bismarck* passing down *Rodney*'s port side.

0916 *Rodney* turning hard to starboard, enemy ship passing under *Rodney*'s stern.

0917 Good straddles on *Bismarck*, one hit observed, enemy firing very intermittently and inaccurately.

0919 Salvo from *Bismarck*'s after turrets.

0921 Good straddle on *Bismarck*.

0922 *Bismarck* fires after turrets at *Rodney*. Near miss on *Rodney*'s starboard side.

0923 *Bismarck* hit.

0924 Enemy still firing after turrets.

0924 Enemy turning towards *Rodney*.

0926 *Bismarck* straddled.

0927 Salvo from enemy's forward guns.

0928 Enemy turning towards *Rodney*.
     Enemy hit abaft funnel.

0929 *Bismarck* on parallel course hit again.

0930 Another hit.

0931 Enemy fired after turrets.[2]

0932 Enemy still on parallel course to *Rodney*, range 2 miles.

0937 Green 040 degs [starboard 40°]. Ship, probably *Dorsetshire* in sight opens fire.

---

[2] Parallel to this, Lieutenant Commander J. M. Wellings, USN, who was in the *Rodney*, reported: 'At 0902 a hit was observed on *Bismarck*'s forecastle. *Bismarck* continued to fire regularly until between 0902 and 0908 when her firing became irregular and intermittent. *Bismarck*'s "A" and "B" turrets must have been damaged during this period as only one salvo was observed from the forward turrets after this period. This salvo was fired at 0927. From about 0919 to 0931 only "X" turret of the *Bismarck* was in action, apparently in local control and very erratic. The last salvo was fired by *Bismarck* at 0931.'

0938 *Bismarck* passes astern and comes up on port side distance still 2 miles.

0940 Enemy on fire fore and aft.

0941 Enemy hit again forward turning towards *Rodney*.

0942 *Bismarck*'s 'B' turret on fire.

0944 Enemy passes astern of *Rodney*.
     Rodney turning to starboard engages enemy starboard side.

0946 *Bismarck* hit at least four times during this run on starboard side and has not herself fired.

0948 Old tactics. Enemy passing astern of *Rodney*.
     Two more hits seen during last two minutes.

0949 *Rodney* turning hard to port. Enemy engaged port side.

0951 Engagement continuing port side.[3]

0955 Torpedo fired port side. No results observed.

0957 Torpedo fired port side and seen to leap out of the water two-thirds of the way across.

0958 Torpedo hit *Bismarck* amidships starboard side.[4]

0959 Enemy turning to starboard.

1000 Engagement on starboard side, enemy turning away.

1002 County Class cruiser, perhaps *Norfolk* on *Rodney*'s starboard bow attacking enemy.
     Dorsetshire (?) on *Rodney*'s port bow.[5]

---

[3] The word *engagement* used in this and subsequent entries should not be taken literally. Since the *Bismarck* was not able to fire after 0931, what was going on was a one-sided cannonade.

[4] I doubt that the *Bismarck* was hit by a torpedo at 0958.

[5] The *Dorsetshire* took part in the action from 0904 to 0913, from 0920 to 0924, from 0935 to 0938, and from 0954 to 1018. Altogether, she fired 254 shells. The interruptions were caused by her difficulty in identifying and evaluating the fall of her own shot amid the storm of shells hitting around the German battleship. During these interruptions she helped the *King George V* and *Rodney* observe their fire. In his after-action report the *Dorsetshire*'s commanding officer, Captain B. C. S. Martin, did not claim any hits for his ship before 1002. It is doubtful that the *Dorsetshire*'s gunnery inflicted significant damage on the *Bismarck*.

1003   Lull in action. *Bismarck* well alight, clouds of black smoke from fire aft.

1005   *Bismarck* has been slowly turning around and is now passing down *Rodney*'s starboard side 1½ miles away smoking heavily.

1006   Enemy hit starboard amidships.
       King George V, 5 miles astern, firing as opportunity offers.

1007   *Bismarck* passes astern. *Rodney* turns hard to port engagement continuing on port side. Much black smoke from the enemy.

1011   Salvo from *Rodney* blows pieces off stern of *Bismarck* and sets up a fire with greyish white smoke.

1012   *King George V* ahead of *Bismarck*.

1013   Salvo from *Rodney* explodes amidships enemy.

1014   Big flames for three seconds from enemy 'A' turret. Flash of exploding shell on enemy spotting top.

1016   *King George V* approaching *Rodney* on port bow, turns on parallel course and fires at *Bismarck* from 'Y' turret.

1019   Enemy smoking heavily. *Rodney*'s guns will not bear.

1021   *Bismarck* dead astern of *Rodney*.

1023   Red 145 degs [port 145°]. Six aircraft.[6]
       Driving rain from port bow.
       Red 145. An unidentified ship firing at aircraft.[7]

[6] Swordfish from the *Ark Royal*, which did not carry out their intended attack.
[7] The ship was the *King George V*. According to Russell Grenfell, *The Bismarck Episode*, p. 186, the Swordfish flew towards the British flagship to request that the firing cease so that they could make their attack. The *King George V* did not heed them, however; in fact, they were taken under fire. When her commanding officer, Captain W. R. Patterson, asked the antiaircraft battery commander if he did not see the flight crews waving, he replied that he took them for Germans 'shaking their fists.'

1026 Green 130 degs [starboard 130°] County Class cruiser (*Dorsetshire*). *Bismarck* still smoking heavily passing to port well astern.

1027 Sudden red flash visible from enemy's stern.

1028 Enemy ship now about five miles astern.

1029 Enemy a smoking mass bows-on. *Dorsetshire* crossing her bows.

1038 *Bismarck* disappears in a cloud of smoke, sinking, bow or stern visible momentarily sticking out of the water.

1039 *Bismarck* sank.

APPENDIX F

A Break in the Code?

I have often been asked whether the British success in breaking the German naval code at the beginning of the Second World War had anything to do with the pursuit and destruction of the *Bismarck*. Such questions have been inspired by new publications describing this break-through, which was discreetly handled for many years after the war, in a sometimes sensational manner.[1] British experts did succeed in decoding some of the German operational radio transmissions so rapidly that the Admiralty was able to take timely countermeasures and, at times, to frustrate the intentions of the Seekriegsleitung. But in May 1941 they could not read the secret radio traffic between the *Bismarck* and headquarters ashore. It is true that in the second week of May they were able to decode the radio signals of German reconnaissance planes – which, however, because of the limited coding facilities of an aircraft, were not in the most secure code – and through them to anticipate an imminent sortie of German naval forces into the Atlantic. Likewise, during Exercise Rhine they were able to read the Luftwaffe's lightly encoded radio signals regarding preparations to provide the *Bismarck* with air cover from France on 26 May. But it was mainly by using then-conventional methods of reconnaissance that the British gained their success against Exercise Rhine.

[1] *See*, among others: F. W. Winterbotham, *The Ultra Secret* (London: Weidenfeld & Nicolson, 1974); Anthony Cave-Brown, *Bodyguard of Lies* (London: W. H. Allen, 1976); David Kahn, *The Codebreakers* (New York: Macmillan, 1967); D. McLachlan, *Room 39* (London: Weidenfeld & Nicolson, 1968); and, especially recommended, Patrick Beesly, *Very Special Intelligence* (London: Hamish Hamilton, 1977).

Annotated Bibliography

Books

Beesly, Patrick. *Very Special Intelligence*. London: Hamish Hamilton, 1977.

Bekker, Cajus. *Verdammte See*. Berlin? Ullstein, 1977.

Brennecke, Jochen. *Schlachtschiff* Bismarck. Herford: Koehlers Verlagsgesellschaft, 1st and 4th editions, 1960 and 1967. The standard German work on the battleship *Bismarck*. A painstakingly prepared study that examines the strategic, tactical, technical, and personal aspects of the ship's Atlantic operation and makes well-grounded and perceptive obervations on many problems. It is, however, not free from questionable descriptions and interpretations of events.

Busch, Fritz Otto. *Das Geheimnis der* Bismarck. Hanover: Adolf Sponholtz Verlag, 1950. To my knowledge, the first book on the *Bismarck* to be published in Germany. Written in a popular style, it was obviously intended for the general public. Many important facts about the course of events in the *Bismarck* were not known at the time this book was written.

Churchill, Winston. *The Second World War*. Vols. II and III. London: Cassell & Co., 1967–68.

Elfrath, Ulrich, and Bodo Herzog. *Schlachtschiff* Bismarck: *Ein Bericht in Bildern und Dokumenten*. Friedberg: Podzun-Verlag, 1975. A volume with an abundance of good illustrations, but whose text unfortunately, contains numerous errors.

Grenfell, Russell. *The Bismarck Episode*. London: Faber & Faber, 1948. A comprehensive and, in my opinion, the classic account of British operations against Exercise Rhine. Invaluable for any serious study of the *Bismarck*'s operation in the Atlantic.

Kennedy, Ludovic. *Pursuit*. London: Collins, 1974. A lively and absorbing book, written in narrative style. Magnificently researched. Very fair in its treatment of both sides, it emphasizes the human aspects of the events described. For the student, a good supplement to Grenfell and Schofield.

Raeder, Erich. *Mein Leben*. Vol. 2. Tübingen: Verlag Schlichtenmayer, 1957.

Roskill, S. W. *The War at Sea 1939–1945*. Vol. I. London: Her Majesty's Stationery Office, 1954. The official British naval history of the Second World War.

Schmalenback, Paul. *Die Geschichte der Deutschen Schiffsartillerie*. Herford: Koehlers Verlagsgesellschaft, 1968.

—. *Kreuzer* Prinz Eugen . . . *unter 3 Flaggen*. Herford: Koehlers Verlagsgesellschaft, 1978.

—. *Warships in Profile*. Vol. 2, 'Kriegsmarine Bismarck'. Windsor, Berkshire: Profile Publications, 1973.

Schofield, B. B. *Loss of* the Bismarck. Shepperton, Surrey: Ian Allan, 1972. A concise account, basically from a British perspective, of the operations against the *Bismarck*, which includes the latest research on tactical considerations and operational details. Important for an historical assessment of Exercise Rhine.

Periodicals and Newspapers

Bidlingmaier, Gerhard. 'Exploits and End of the Battleship *Bismarck*.' United States Naval Institute *Proceedings*, July 1958.

Schmalenbach, Paul. 'Admiral Günther Lütjens.' *Atlantische Welt*, 1967.

Schulze-Hinrichs, Alfred. 'Schlachtschiff *Bismarck* und Seemannschaft.' *Marine-Offizier-Verband Nachrichten*, Vol. 17, No. 1 (1968).

Munchener Illustrierte, 1957: Original statements of the *Bismarck*'s survivors.

Documents

A. Bundesarchiv-Militärarchiv-Freiburg:

War Diary of the Battleship *Bismarck*, original and reconstructed.

War Diary of Naval Group Command North, May 1941.

War Diary of Naval Group Command West, May 1941.

Personal Notes of the Commander-in-Chief of the Navy, Grossadmiral Erich Raeder, January through June 1941.

Naval War Staff (Seekriegsleitung), preliminary instructions and operational orders, March 1941 through May 1941.

Naval War Staff, Situation Room Reports, 1941.

Naval War Staff, File 'Rheinübung': *Bismarck* operation, after-action, and final reports.

Naval High Command (Oberkommando der Kriegsmarine), 'Die Atlantikunternehmung der Kampfgruppe *Bismarck–Prinz Eugen*, Mai 1941.' Berlin: *Marine-Dienst-Vorschrift* Nr. 601, October 1942.

Preliminary examination of Matrosengefreiter Herzog, Höntzsch, and Manthey on board the *U-74*.

Protocol of the statements by *Bismarck* survivors, recorded by Naval Group Command West, Paris, June 1941:

    Matrosengefreiter George Herzog

    Matrosengefreiter Otto Höntzsch

    Matrosengefreiter Herbert Manthey

Matrosengefreiter Otto Maus
Maschinengefreiter Walter Lorenzen
War Diary of the *U-74*, 26–29 May 1941
War Diary of the *U-556*, 24–27 May 1941
Report on the operations of the battleship *Bismarck* by
   Weather Observation Ship 7 (*Sachsenwald*), Leutnant
   zur See Wilhelm Schütte, 30 May 1941.

B. Other:
Reports of the German embassy in London, 1937–1939,
   and report of the German consulate in Glasgow, 1939.
   Archiv des Aüswärtigen Amtes, Bonn.
'Sinking of the German Battleship *Bismarck* on 27th May,
   1941.' Dispatch by Admiral Sir John Tovey, Supple-
   ment No. 3 to the *London Gazette*, 14 October 1947.
'Operations and Battle of German Battleship *Bismarck*,
   23–27 May 1941.' Narrative and enclosures (A) through
   (H), Intelligence Division, U. S. Navy Department.
Script of the BBC Television Documentary, 'Rheinü-
   bung,' March 1971.
Schneider, Dr Otto. Private memoir, 'Last Meeting'.

Correspondence

Captain Robert L. Bridges, USN (Ret.), Castle Creek,
   New York
Herr Joachim Fensch, Weingarten, Federal Republic of
   Germany
Mr Daniel Gibson Harris, Ottawa, Canada
Herr Franz Hahn, Mürwick, Federal Republic of Germany
Dr Mathias Haupt, Bundesarchiv, Koblenz, Federal Re-
   public of Germany
Herr Bodo Herzog, Oberhausen, Federal Republic of
   Germany

Herr Hans H. Hildebrand, Hamburg, Federal Republic of Germany

Konteradmiral Günther Horstmann, German Navy (Ret.), Basle, Switzerland

Imperial War Museum, London

Mr Esmond Knight, London

Dr Hansjoseph Maierhöfer, Chier Archivist, Bundesarchiv-Militärarchiv-Freiburg, Federal Republic of Germany

Mr Philip Mathias, Toronto, Canada

Mrs Mary Z. Pain, London

Fregattenkapitän Dr Werner Rahn, Mürwik, Federal Republic of Germany

Professor Dr Jürgen Rohwer, Stuttgart, Federal Republic of Germany

Dr Hans Ulrich Sareyko, Aüswärtigen Amt, Bonn, Federal Republic of Germany

Herr Rolf Schindler, Freiburg, Federal Republic of Germany

Fregattenkapitän Paul Schmalenbach, German Navy (Ret.), Altenholz, Federal Republic of Germany

Vice Admiral B. B. Schofield, Royal Navy (Ret.), Henley-on-Thames, England

Kapitän zur See Hans-Henning von Schultz, German Navy (Ret.), Ramsau, Federal Republic of Germany

Herr Torsten Spiller, *Deutsche Dienststelle (WASt)*, Berlin, Federal Republic of Germany

Mr Tom Wharam, Cardiff, Wales

Kapitänleutnant Herbert Wohlfarth, German Navy (Ret.), VS-Villingen, Federal Republic of Germany

Index